Building an RPG with Unity 5.x

Unleash the full potential of Unity to build a fully playable, high-quality multiplayer RPG

Vahé Karamian

BIRMINGHAM - MUMBAI

Building an RPG with Unity 5.x

Copyright © 2016 Packt Publishing

All rights reserved. No part of this book may be reproduced, stored in a retrieval system, or transmitted in any form or by any means, without the prior written permission of the publisher, except in the case of brief quotations embedded in critical articles or reviews.

Every effort has been made in the preparation of this book to ensure the accuracy of the information presented. However, the information contained in this book is sold without warranty, either express or implied. Neither the author, nor Packt Publishing, and its dealers and distributors will be held liable for any damages caused or alleged to be caused directly or indirectly by this book.

Packt Publishing has endeavored to provide trademark information about all of the companies and products mentioned in this book by the appropriate use of capitals. However, Packt Publishing cannot guarantee the accuracy of this information.

First published: October 2016

Production reference: 1101015

Published by Packt Publishing Ltd.
Livery Place
35 Livery Street
Birmingham
B3 2PB, UK.
ISBN 978-1-78528-500-4

www.packtpub.com

Credits

Author
Vahé Karamian

Reviewers
Spencer Grey

Commissioning Editor
Ashwin Nair

Acquisition Editor
Divya Poojari

Content Development Editor
Deepti Thore

Technical Editor
Anushree Arun Tendulkar

Copy Editor
Safis Editing

Project Coordinator
Sheejal Shah

Proofreader
Safis Editing

Indexer
Mariammal Chettiyar

Graphics
Abhinash Sahu

Production Coordinator
Nilesh Mohite

About the Author

Vahé Karamian is a software consultant and author based in Los Angeles, CA. He has been providing software development services to some of the top pharmaceutical, biotech, and medical device manufacturing companies in the world. His latest clients included Department of Planning and Evox Imaging. Providing web, mobile, and virtual reality experiences.

He came across Unity when he was searching for a game engine for his projects in 2010. The rest is history. He is the founder of the Granada Hills Unity User Group and is actively working with the user community to educate new developers.

He is the author of *Introduction to Game Programming: Using C# and Unity 3D*. The book targets individuals with no programming background. The objective of the book is to give the reader a good foundation on the fundamentals of programming concepts and the essentials for Unity. It is available in both eBook and paperback editions. Visit www.noorcon.com for more information.

Vahé holds a master's degree in computer science, and is currently lecturing the following topics: Introduction to Computer Science, Data Structures and Algorithms, Operating Systems, Game Design and Development.

In no particular order, I would like to acknowledge the following individuals who have been working on the reparation and production of this title: Spencer Grey, Divya Poojari, Sweta Basu, Divij Kotian, and Anushree Tendulkar. I am sure there are many more involved in the process. These are the folks who I have had the pleasure to meet during the process. Your comments and feedback were a valuable part of the final result of this work. Last but not least,

I would like to acknowledge my wife Armineh and our two beautiful children Maximilian and Makayla for their support through the long nights in the preparation of this book. Thank you and love you.

About the Reviewer

Spencer Grey is an award-winning designer-developer. He was creative director at Sesame Street's Interactive group then co-founded Electric FunStuff. For 15 years he was creative and technical lead working with companies such as Sony, Lego, and Scholastic. And developing products with ActionScript and C#. He was technical reviewer for David Brackeen's *Developing Games in Java*.

www.PacktPub.com

For support files and downloads related to your book, please visit www.PacktPub.com.

Did you know that Packt offers eBook versions of every book published, with PDF and ePub files available? You can upgrade to the eBook version at www.PacktPub.com and as a print book customer, you are entitled to a discount on the eBook copy. Get in touch with us at service@packtpub.com for more details.

At www.PacktPub.com, you can also read a collection of free technical articles, sign up for a range of free newsletters and receive exclusive discounts and offers on Packt books and eBooks.

https://www2.packtpub.com/books/subscription/packtlib

Do you need instant solutions to your IT questions? PacktLib is Packt's online digital book library. Here, you can search, access, and read Packt's entire library of books.

Why subscribe?

- Fully searchable across every book published by Packt
- Copy and paste, print, and bookmark content
- On demand and accessible via a web browser

Table of Contents

Preface	1
Chapter 1: In the Beginning	7
A brief history	7
Characteristics of an RPG	9
Story and setting	9
A glimpse at our cRPG story	10
Exploration and quests	10
A glimpse at our exploration and quests	11
Inventory system	12
Character development	15
Experience and levelling	17
Combat system	19
User interface and graphics	20
Existing or upcoming RPG games	23
Dark Souls 3	24
Fallout 4	25
Divinity: Original Sin	26
Patterns in RPG	28
Terminology	29
Contest Tree	31
Last Man Standing	32
Negotiated Contest	33
Summary	34
Chapter 2: Setting the Atmosphere	35
Building our RPG	36
The story of the Zazar Dynasty	36
Plot	36
Exploration and quests	36
Awakening	37
The village	37
Broken forest – the horizon	38
The kingdom	39
Asset inventory	39
Environment assets	39
Character assets	40

Level design	41
Setting the stage	42
Terrain toolkit in a nutshell	46
The awakening	47
Testing the level	58
Creating the Main Menu	58
Creating the Game Master	60
Summary	63

Chapter 3: Character Design — 65

Character definitions	65
Base character class attributes	66
Character states	68
Character model	69
Rigging your model	72
Character motion	74
Animator Controller	74
Animation states	76
Character controller	80
Modification to animations	86
Inverse Kinematics	88
Summary	93

Chapter 4: Player Character and Non-Player Character Design — 95

Customizing the Player Character	95
Customizable parts	98
User interface	98
The Code for character customization	101
Preserving our character state	113
Recap	114
Non-Player Characters	115
Non-Player Character basics	116
Setting up the Non-Player Character	116
NPC Animator Controller	122
NPC attack	124
NPC AI	127
PC and NPC interaction	136
Summary	145

Chapter 5: Game Master and Game Mechanics — 147

The Game Master	148
Managing game settings and audio	149

[ii]

Managing scenes	153
Improving Game Master	158
Level controller	158
Audio controller	161
Player data management	164
PC class enhancements	164
Character customization class update	166
Changes to UI Controller	182
Testing	183
Summary	184

Chapter 6: Inventory System   187

Inventory system	188
Weighted Inventory	188
Determining item types	189
Creating inventory item	197
Creating the Prefab	198
Adding Inventory Item Agent	199
Inventory Items Defined as Prefabs	203
Inventory Interface	204
Creating the inventory UI framework	206
Designing a Dynamic Item Viewer	209
Adding a Scroll View	209
Adding Elements to PanelItem and Scroll View	211
Adding txtItemElement Dynamically	213
Building the Final Inventory Item UI	215
Integrating the UI with the actual inventory system	217
Hooking the category buttons and displaying the data	217
Testing the Inventory System	227
Inventory items and the Player Character	230
Applying inventory items	231
How It Looks	249
Summary	252

Chapter 7: User Interface and System Feedback   255

Designing a Heads Up Display	256
Basic information for a HUD	256
Our design	257
HUD framework	258
Completing HUD design	259
Panel character Info	259

[iii]

Panel active inventory items	265
Special items panel	268
Integrating the code	270
Enemy stats in the HUD	290
NPC stats user interface	290
Creating the NPC canvas	290
NPC health	294
Enhancing the code	298
Summary	305

Chapter 8: Multiplayer Setup — 307

Challenges of a Multiplayer Game	308
Initial Multiplayer Game	309
Fundamental Networking Components	309
Networking Project	310
Adding Player Character	311
Variable Synchronization	315
Network Callbacks	315
Sending Commands	315
Client RPC Calls	316
Creating the Canon Ball for the Tank	318
Creating Tank Prefab and Configuring NetworkManager	320
Adding the Enemy Tank	324
Building and Testing	329
Network Enabling RPG Characters	331
Creating a Scene for RPG	331
Networked Player Character	331
Networked Non-Player Character	341
Synchronizing Player Customization and Items	350
Spawning NPC and Other Items	352
Testing Our Network-Enabled PC and NPC	353
What's Next	359
Summary	360

Index — 361

Preface

Everyone wants to make a game, today this is possible more than ever due to the democratization of the game industry and the tools that are used to design and develop games. This books is written with several purposes in mind. Unity has come a long way from its early and humble beginnings. As of the writing of this book, Unity stands at version 5.4. Some games that have been developed using the Unity engine are: *Republique Remastered*, *The Room Three* and *Mevius Final Fantasy*, to name a few.

This book is intended as a reference guide for individuals who want to learn Unity and apply their skills for the creation of a role-playing game.

What this book covers

Chapter 1, *In the Beginning*, provides a good background of what a role-playing game is. It covers some historical aspects and gives examples of existing role-playing games. It discuss the main aspects of a role-playing game, covers some terminology and prepares the reader for the rest of the chapters.

Chapter 2, *Setting the Atmosphere*, the chapter sets the theme and atmosphere of the game. We discuss the different types of assets and resources we would need during the creation of our game, introduce a third-person character controller and create our initial level and scripts.

Chapter 3, *Character Design*, discusses how to define your character and character data. Setup your character model for the mecanim, animator, state machines, blend trees, inverse kinematics, and custom character controller scripts.

Chapter 4, *Player Character and Non-Player Character Design*, discusses the structure of your character models, customization of your character model, defined the non-player character, looked at pathfinding, animator controller, and the initial NPC A.I. script for the NPC.

Chapter 5, *Game Master and Game Mechanics*, enhanced the Game Master script, introduced a Level Controller script, introduces an Audio Controller script, discuss the storage of character data and character customization state and the initial user interface for the main menu.

Chapter 6, *Inventory System*, covers the creation of a generic inventory system, create the necessary scripts, assets/prefabs that represent the inventory items, design of the inventory user interface and how to represent the inventory system and its items.

Preface

Chapter 7, *User Interface and System Feedback*, discusses the design and implementation of a heads up display, player character information panel, active inventory items panel, special inventory items panel are designed and implemented, non-player character health bar and UI are also designed and developed.

Chapter 8, *Multiplayer Setup*, discusses multiplayer programming using the Unity's Unet architecture. The chapter illustrates the concepts using two sample projects, the initial project is a tank game illustrating the concepts of server client and data synchronization. The second project applies what we have learned to create a scene supporting our character models.

What you need for this book

Required software: All chapters require Unity 5.4 or above. You will also need an IDE for the editing of the C# code described in this book. This can be done using any text editor, but it is recommended to use Visual Studio on the Windows platform or Mono Develop/Code on Mac OS X.

Required OS: Windows 10 64-bit or above, or Mac OS X

Required hardware: Please see required hardware for running Unity

Who this book is for

This book is written for individuals who want to learn and apply their Unity skills for the creation of an RPG. It is assumed that the reader has the basics understanding and concepts of programming and is comfortable with the basics of Unity's IDE. The books gives a strong and solid foundation of core concepts and topics that can be applied to build your own game experience.

Conventions

In this book, you will find a number of text styles that distinguish between different kinds of information. Here are some examples of these styles and an explanation of their meaning.

Code words in text, database table names, folder names, filenames, file extensions, pathnames, dummy URLs, user input, and Twitter handles are shown as follows: "Drill-down in the extracted folder to get to the Unity Package called `TerrainToolkit_1_0_2.unitypackage`."

A block of code is set as follows:

```
public void StartGame()
{
  // NOTE: You should put in the name of the Scene
  // that respresents your level 1
  SceneManager.LoadScene("CH1_Awakening");
}
```

New terms and **important words** are shown in bold. Words that you see on the screen, for example, in menus or dialog boxes, appear in the text like this: "Go ahead and select a location and a name you desire for your project and click the **Create project** button."

Warnings or important notes appear in a box like this.

Tips and tricks appear like this.

Reader feedback

Feedback from our readers is always welcome. Let us know what you think about this book-what you liked or disliked. Reader feedback is important for us as it helps us develop titles that you will really get the most out of. To send us general feedback, simply e-mail feedback@packtpub.com, and mention the book's title in the subject of your message. If there is a topic that you have expertise in and you are interested in either writing or contributing to a book, see our author guide at www.packtpub.com/authors.

Customer support

Now that you are the proud owner of a Packt book, we have a number of things to help you to get the most from your purchase.

Downloading the example code

You can download the example code files for this book from your account at http://www.packtpub.com. If you purchased this book elsewhere, you can visit http://www.packtpub.com/support and register to have the files e-mailed directly to you.

Preface

You can download the code files by following these steps:

1. Log in or register to our website using your e-mail address and password.
2. Hover the mouse pointer on the **SUPPORT** tab at the top.
3. Click on **Code Downloads & Errata**.
4. Enter the name of the book in the **Search** box.
5. Select the book for which you're looking to download the code files.
6. Choose from the drop-down menu where you purchased this book from.
7. Click on **Code Download**.

Once the file is downloaded, please make sure that you unzip or extract the folder using the latest version of:

- WinRAR / 7-Zip for Windows
- Zipeg / iZip / UnRarX for Mac
- 7-Zip / PeaZip for Linux

The code bundle for the book is also hosted on GitHub at `https://github.com/PacktPubl ishing/Building-an-RPF-with-Unity5x` We also have other code bundles from our rich catalog of books and videos available at `https://github.com/PacktPublishing/`. Check them out!

Downloading the color images of this book

We also provide you with a PDF file that has color images of the screenshots/diagrams used in this book. The color images will help you better understand the changes in the output. You can download this file from `http://www.packtpub.com/sites/default/files/downl oads/BuildinganRPGwithUnity5x_ColorImages.pdf`.

Errata

Although we have taken every care to ensure the accuracy of our content, mistakes do happen. If you find a mistake in one of our books-maybe a mistake in the text or the code-we would be grateful if you could report this to us. By doing so, you can save other readers from frustration and help us improve subsequent versions of this book. If you find any errata, please report them by visiting `http://www.packtpub.com/submit-errata`, selecting your book, clicking on the **Errata Submission Form** link, and entering the details of your errata. Once your errata are verified, your submission will be accepted and the errata will be uploaded to our website or added to any list of existing errata under the Errata section of that title.

[4]

Preface

To view the previously submitted errata, go to `https://www.packtpub.com/books/content/support` and enter the name of the book in the search field. The required information will appear under the **Errata** section.

Piracy

Piracy of copyrighted material on the Internet is an ongoing problem across all media. At Packt, we take the protection of our copyright and licenses very seriously. If you come across any illegal copies of our works in any form on the Internet, please provide us with the location address or website name immediately so that we can pursue a remedy.

Please contact us at `copyright@packtpub.com` with a link to the suspected pirated material.

We appreciate your help in protecting our authors and our ability to bring you valuable content.

Questions

If you have a problem with any aspect of this book, you can contact us at `questions@packtpub.com`, and we will do our best to address the problem.

1
In the Beginning

So you want to build a Role Playing Game, or RPG. Well, you might have just started one of the most challenging undertakings you can attempt.

- Brief history of the genre
- Characteristics of an RPG
  - Story and setting
  - Exploration and quests
  - Inventory system
  - Character development
  - Experience and levelling
  - Combat system
  - User interaction and graphics
- Existing or upcoming RPGs
- Patterns in RPGs

Before we get started, it would be best to get a brief history of the genre and understand some of the key elements you will need to consider throughout the design of your RPG.

A brief history

So what is an RPG? In short, it is a game in which players assume the roles of characters in a fictional setting. Your game design will dictate how the player character will act, advance, and so on…

In the Beginning

There are three varieties of RPGs:

- Tabletop
- Live Action
- Computer RPG (cRPG)

Tabletop and pen-and-paper (PnP) RPGs are conducted through discussion in a small social gathering. There is usually a **Game Master** (**GM**) who describes the game world and its inhabitants. The other players describe the intended actions of their characters, and the GM describes the outcomes. This is the format in which RPGs were first popularized, namely through **Dungeons & Dragons** (**D&D**).

Live Action Role Playing (**LARP**) is played more like improvisational theatre. Participants act out their character's actions instead of describing them, and the real environment is used to represent the imaginary setting of the game world. Some live action LARPs use rock-paper-scissors or comparison of attributes to resolve symbolically, while other LARPs use physical combat with simulated arms. A movie can be considered as a simple LARP, the difference would be that in a movie all actions are scripted, and the players do not have to make decisions, whereas in a LARP, the characters can change the outcome of their actions based on their decisions.

Computer RPG (**cRPGs**) are tabletop RPGs that have been translated into an electronic format. The early cRPGs influenced all electronic gaming, as well as spanning the role-playing video game genre. In short, a cRPG is a video game genre where the player controls the actions of a main character immersed in a well-defined world.

Our book is going to concentrate on the design and development of a cRPG.

Going forward, when we state RPG in the book we are referring to cRPG.

Computer role-playing games take their roots from tabletop versions of the genre. Much of the same terminology, settings, and game mechanics have carried over from the original tabletop games. Some of these similarities include story-telling and narrative elements where, throughout the story the player character will continuously develop in skills and abilities to meet the objective of the game.

Chapter 1

Characteristics of an RPG

Role-playing video games typically rely on a highly developed story and setting, which is divided into a number of quests or levels. Players typically control one or more characters by issuing commands, which are then performed by player characters based on their defined abilities and attributes. Throughout the game, these attributes increase or decrease and set the personality of the character.

An RPG usually also has more complex and dynamic interaction mechanics defined and developed between the player character and the world which they are immersed within. These include the interaction with the world environment and also other non-character players defined within the world. Due to these factors, there is usually more time allocated to design and develop the code base which deals with the behavior and artificial-intelligence (AI) handling such events throughout the game.

Key elements of an RPG:

- Story and setting
- Exploration and quests
- Items and inventory
- Character development
- Experience and levels
- Combat
- User interface and graphics

Story and setting

The premise of most role-playing games tasks the player with saving the world, or whichever level of society is threatened. There are often twists and turns as the story progresses, such as the surprise appearance of estranged relatives, or enemies who become friends or vice versa.

The game world tends to be set in a historical, fantasy, or science fiction universe, which allows the players to do things they cannot do in real life and helps players suspend their disbelief about the rapid character growth.

In the Beginning

As stated previously, RPGs are heavily invested in storytelling. This is one of the main, key entertaining factors of the genre. Due to this fact, when you are developing your RPG, you will need to pay close attention to how you develop your story, and the characters that are within your story. This in turn translates into the kind of environments and settings you will have for your game and characters within the game.

Traditionally, RPGs progress the plot based on decisions that the player character makes during gameplay. This puts a great deal of pressure on the game designer who needs to be able to integrate such forks in the gameplay with the main storyline of the game. This also raises the issue of how to program the game to take into consideration all the different paths within the story.

To make the game more interesting and attractive, the game designer can introduce special triggers within the story to make it more interesting or challenging. This is usually done by introducing new characters and/or areas to discover within the existing level.

The following is a simplified description of the storyline and the setting we are going to be building for our cRPG.

A glimpse at our cRPG story

Once upon a time there was a great kingdom, ruled by the great King Zazar. The ruler of the kingdom was a generous lord to his subjects. The kingdom under the rule of Zazar was peaceful and prosperous, however, over time internal family rivalries and struggles have caused cracks in the strong bond that keeps the kingdom intact.

Due to mysterious events, the great king has decided to move his family away from the kingdom and leave his son with one of his trusted, wise elders. The kingdom was never the same. Until now!

Exploration and quests

The whole idea behind an RPG is the ability for the player to have the freedom to explore the world which they have been immersed into. The more well defined the world is, the more interesting it will be for the player to explore, and in return retain their curiosity and engagement throughout the gameplay.

This is achieved by the narrative of the story developed for the RPG. Players will be specifically given the opportunity to walk around the world and explore their surroundings in order to meet their objectives.

In an open world RPG, the player is free to roam in the world after they have met their objective set by the storyline. In such cases, the player can still explore any area which is no longer needed for the continuation of the quest, but they can spend time exploring the area and maybe meet some other non-player characters that they had not previously met while completing their mission. But generally speaking this is not done by the player, once they meet their objective they are eager to move on to the next quest, hence the question is; how much time and effort do the game designers and developers apply to a region after the main objective is met? The answer would be not much.

Historically, the player follows a linear-sequence of quests in order to realize their goals and objectives within the game. To make the game more engaging, the developer can introduce mini-quests within the main plot of the game at that particular location to give the player the ability to explore and gain more skills and or abilities. Since these are not part of the main storyline, they can be triggered any time a player enters a specific area.

For instance, assume the player has completed the main objective of the level, and is ready to move on to the next objective. Now, imagine that we have created an open world environment where the user can revisit the world anytime they choose. If the player decides to go back and explore a certain area of the world they just completed, and they happen to trigger the event to launch this mini-quest, wouldn't that be a great surprise for the player? Keep in mind that these mini-quests should not affect the main storyline, but they can be used to enhance the player's experience. These types of decisions are important when you are developing your game. If they choose not to take on the challenge you should not penalize them, except if you want to be really mean J.

Quests may involve defeating one or many enemies, rescuing a non-player character, item fetch quests, or location puzzles such as mysteriously locked doors.

A glimpse at our exploration and quests

Our game will have a total of four quests. Each quest will have unique objectives that the player will need to complete. The design and development of each quest will be discussed throughout the book as we progress.

In the Beginning

Here is a list of the levels we will be designing:

- Awakening
- The Village
- Broken Forest – The Horizon
- The Kingdom

The game will start by immersing the player in the environment where our hero will be given the basic training he will need to complete his mission.

Inventory system

One of the main functions and features of an RPG is the inventory system. Throughout the game, the user will come across a vast number of collectable items that can be used for different purposes within the game to help them progress through the journey. Therefore, RPGs needs to provide mechanics to help the player store, retrieve, and organize the content relevant to their journey.

Chapter 1

When the player is progressing through their journey in an RPG, they interact with the world they are immersed in. The storyline of the game usually forces the player to interact with the surrounding world and other non-player characters. These interactions are usually in the form of some sort of an exchange. Whether this exchange is done through narration to provide the player with a better sense of the quest, or real exchange in terms of items is up to the game designers and developers.

The game needs a way to keep track of all the interactions between the player character and everything and everyone else. One system that is used to keep track of this interaction is the inventory system.

During the gameplay, players usually start off as a very simple character and part of the gameplay is to elevate their character by exploring the world and collecting items that will help them increase their skills and abilities.

For instance, a player can start their journey with very basic clothes. Throughout the quest, they will either interact with a non-character player, such as a merchant who will provide them with a better set of clothes, and or some sort of a weapon to get them started. These items will be stored and managed by the inventory system.

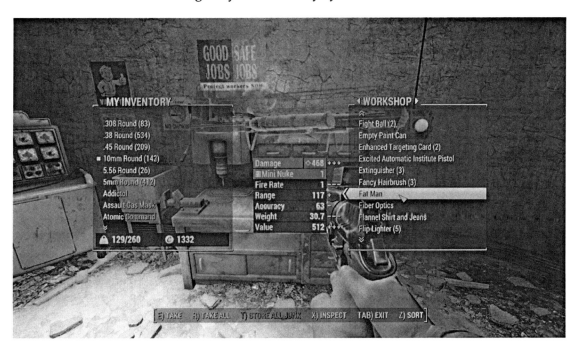

[13]

In the Beginning

The simplicity or the complexity of the inventory system will be defined by the complexity of the game and the complexity of the characters within the game. In our game we will be designing and developing a generic inventory system that can be applied to many different types of items.

Here are some items that are usually collected in a game:

- Weapons
- Armor
- Clothing
- Special Objects

Some of the items are collected or discovered by world exploration, and some of the items are specifically traded through the game. If you are setting up a trade system in a game, then you will need to provide the mechanics for the trade. A trade usually takes place while interacting with a non-player character, usually a merchant, and it will use a special window to enable the interaction of the trade to take place.

There is usually a cost associated with any trade. In general, there is a cost associated with everything the player does within the game, and the cost is usually either increasing the player-character's ability and/or experience, or decreasing it. This can get pretty complex if you dig deep into it.

The main point to keep in mind is that everything that the player will need to collect and/or manage will be done through the inventory system. Hence, this is one of the most critical features that you will need to put effort into as a game designer and developer.

One other element that can be used to enhance the gameplay for the player, and push them to strategize their quest, is to limit the number of items they can carry in their inventory.

For instance, in real life, a warrior will have limited ability to carry different types of weapons. Let's assume, that in the real world, a warrior can carry a maximum of five different types of weapon at any given time. Now, in the game world, there might be 20 different types of weapon. Do you allow the player to carry all 20 different types when they discover them? Or are you going to limit them to five?

These are small things that make the gameplay more interesting when planned out properly. There is more to an inventory system, and we will take a look at it in more detail in later chapters.

Chapter 1

Character development

As with any other part of the RPG development, character attributes and actions are highly defined by the storyline of the game. These actions in turn are performed indirectly within the game, when the player commands the character to perform a specific task.

For instance, in a given RPG there is going to be at least a couple of character classes. The following are some sample class types:

- Barbarians
- Orcs
- Magicians/Wizards
- Zombies
- Humans

Each character class might even have subclasses of their own with its own uniquely defined attributes. Again, this will be tightly coupled to your storyline for your RPG.

For instance, the player character is technically the hero of our story and of the game. The hero is usually of a certain character class, let's assume the hero is part of the Human Class.

The Human Class or Race then will have some specific characteristics that will be inherited by the player character or any other non-player character of the same type or class.

The character class and race usually determines the abilities of a character within the game, which then define the types of actions the character can perform.

The strength of a character within the game is defined by the character class it belongs to and what type of actions it can perform. The performance of a character is defined by the value of the attributes defined within the character's class and race.

In the Beginning

For instance, if we take two different character classes and compare them side-by-side such as a Human and an Orc, the Orc will have far superior strength and brute force then the human. However, the human, may have higher intelligence and problem-solving skills which will out-rate the strength of the Orc if applied properly.

This is another key area where an RPG designer will have to spend a lot of time defining and specifying the design and development of the characters within the game. The sky is the limit when it comes to designing and defining your characters, but there are some key attributes that you will need to consider for any RPG.

Most RPGs allow the player to modify their characters before the game starts or even during gameplay. By default, every character class will have some default attributes and the player is allowed to adjust the values based on some modifier. The basic fundamental features allowed for modification are the sex, class, or race of a character.

These days, character customization is one of the main features that players are looking for in a given RPG. Some games, allow you to modify every aspect of the physical appearance of the player-character, such as the skin color, the eye color, the hair style, and so forth.

It all comes down to the budget and the resources that are available to you during the production of the game. In some games, you can also introduce ethical attributes into the characteristics of the character. For instance, if you allow the ability to kill or rob innocents by standards within the game, then the player will become less liked by the friendly non-player characters and they may not be as friendly or helpful as needed to complete your quest. In other words, you will live by the consequences of your actions!

As a final takeaway, character classes define your character attributes and hence define your character's strength and weaknesses. These physical attributes can be simplified into the following: dexterity and strength, which determine the performance of a character during battle!

Experience and levelling

To engage the player and to get them hooked on the game, game designers use mechanics to enhance the performance of the player-character. The progress is what is termed Levelling or Experience in RPGs.

Levelling and experience are key elements of any role-playing game. A good levelling or experience tree will be defined for any RPG. This allows the player to develop their avatar through gameplay and become functionally more powerful by gaining more skills, points and other resources necessary to complete their quest.

In the Beginning

To acquire new weapons, armor, clothing, and/or any other gameplay items defined in the world, the player will need to meet some specific thresholds within the game. These thresholds can be a combination of the player's acquired experience points, financial gains, and or combat experience. There is no right or wrong when it comes to designing any of these hierarchies and or systems. You will need to see which one works for your specific needs and how to best apply them.

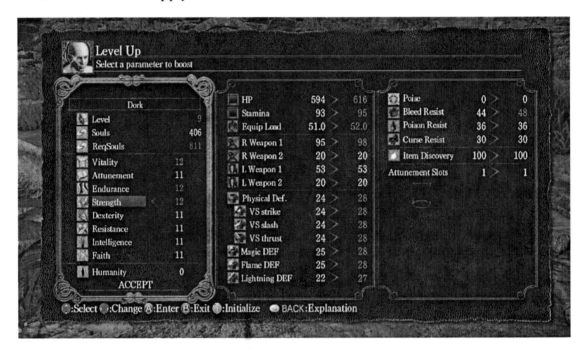

In RPGs, the progress of the character-player is measured by counting some defined attributes specified by the game designer. Usually the advancements are defined by the player completing a certain task to get experience points, and slowly the tasks and the point rewards are increased throughout the game. The player then can use the experience points to enhance his or her avatar within the game.

Again, this is highly integrated with the storyline, Character Classes and or Race the player has selected. Some common ways to acquire points are by killing enemies, combating non-player characters of no importance, and performing quests that have been defined within the game.

[18]

Just like in real-life, the more you play and apply your skills, the more experienced you become. The accumulation of your experience then will allow you to acquire better weapons and/or armor to strengthen your attack or defense for the next quest. Some games might give the player 100+ points and allow the player to distribute the points across the available character attributes for their avatar. Sometimes, the game automatically applies all of the experience to a specific area such as strength.

Gaining experience will also allow the user to unlock more features and skills to be acquired by the player in during gameplay. This is a great way to monetize your games. In reality, most free games use this principal. They provide the basics of the world and the character for free, and they monetize the game through what is called In-Game purchases to increase either resources and/or character performance.

How is this implemented? Just like the inventory system, we need a way to keep track of the progress of the player's skills. This is usually done through a Skill Tree. Learning or acquiring a particular skill in the tree will unlock more powerful skills and give the player the ability to utilize the skills in the game.

Combat system

Time for battle! This is the moment every player looks forward to during their journey; to kill the boss, the bad guy, the evil war lord! Every RPG has some type of combat or battle component built into the gameplay. This is when the player gets to use all of their acquired skills and experience to destroy the opponent, or be destroyed by the opponent J depending on how the day goes.

Traditionally there have been three basic types of RPG combat systems. What type of combat system you choose to implement for your game is going to have a big impact on the gameplay and also the implementation of the game.

The three types are:

- Traditional turn based system
- Real-time combat
- Real-time with pause

Historically, role-playing games used to implement turn-based combat systems. This type of combat system is as follows: only one character could have acted at a given time. During this time, all other characters had to remain still. In other words, they could not have taken any action. This type of combat system is designed to put more emphasis on rewarding strategic planning.

[19]

In the Beginning

The next type would be Real-time with pause combat system. This type of combat system is also strictly turn-based, but with a catch. If the player waits more than a certain period of time to make a move or issue a command, the game will automatically pass on the command to the other player. This in turn will allow the other player, such as the enemy to take a turn and attack the player.

In this book we will be using a real-time combat system. Real-time combat imports features from action games and creates a hybrid of action and RPG game genre. Action RPG combat systems combine the RPG mechanics of role-playing with the direct, reflex-oriented, arcade-style, real-time combat systems of action games, instead of the more traditional battle systems of RPGs.

In action RPGs, the player has direct control over the character's movement and actions in combat, and an attack button must be pressed to attack enemies in real-time. Action RPGs most often use arcade-style hack & slash combat systems, though many also use fighting, brawling, or shooting mechanics.

The action RPG genre was largely pioneered by Japanese developers during the early-mid 1980s. Nintendo's Shigeru Miyamoto adapted elements from several different types of action RPGs for home consoles and in 1986 created The Legend of Zelda franchise, which is responsible for popularizing the action RPG genre in the Western world since the late 1980s.

 Shigeru Miyamoto is best known as the creator of many of Nintendo's most beloved characters and franchises including Mario, Donkey Kong, The Legend of Zelda, and many others. He was also the chief designer of Nintendo's Touch! Generation console series, which includes the Nintendo DS, Wii, and 3DS.

User interface and graphics

The question arises, how do we present our game world to the player? What kind of user interface are we going to provide for our game? What kind of view are we going to allow for our game? Are we going to design our world to be viewed as a top-down camera view? Are we going to create an isometric view of the world? Or are we going to create a first-person or a third-person perspective of our world?

Answering these questions is crucial, as when you are designing your game assets you will need to understand how they will be viewed in the game world. For instance, when designing your characters and or 3D models for the game, if you know that you are going to be using isometric view, then you will approach your modeling differently to, for instance, when you are designing for a first-person or third-person camera.

In our game, we will be using third-person camera for the presentation of our world.

The next question would be how to provide critical information to the player in a simple and meaningful fashion. Role playing games require the player to manage a large amount of information, and frequently make use of windowed interfaces to arrange the data for the player. This is usually designed and implemented through a **Heads Up Display (HUD)**.

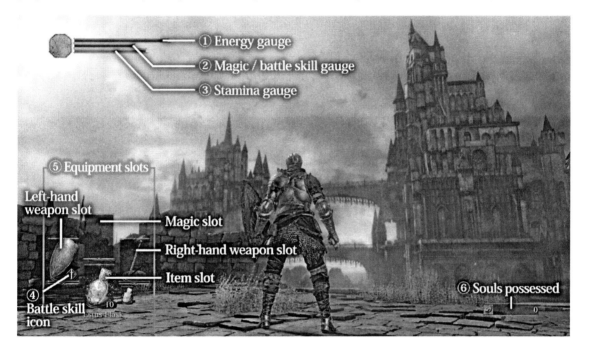

The HUD is frequently used to simultaneously display several pieces of information including the main character's health, items, and indication of game progression. You can think of the HUD as the access point for all the information the user will be required to have access to and interact with during gameplay.

The design of the HUD is crucial for RPG games. Typically, there are a few key data elements that you would like to continuously communicate with the player throughout the gameplay, these data points are:

- Health
- Energy
- Stamina

In the Beginning

- Active weapon
- Active shield
- Special items
- Number of lives
- Access to main menu
- Access to inventory
- *Access to skills*

Once again, the design of your HUD is derived from the type of the game you are designing and also the type of information that will be required to be available to the player during gameplay.

Since, most RPGs collect and store large amounts of data for the player-character, it is very important to create an easy to use yet clean HUD.

A very important thing to remember when designing a HUD is it should never overpower the screen or become a distraction. It usually takes a few stabs to come up with a great HUD design for your game. From initial artistic concepts to the actual implementation and testing by gamers to get some feedback before finalizing the design and internal workings.

At the end of the day, the HUD is supposed to simplify the gameplay for the player, and not make it more confusing. Today, many games are moving away from the traditional HUDs, and they are leaning more towards cinematic and extremely simplistic experiences during the gameplay. This enables the game designer to immerse the player into the world and not to distract them with a constant static HUD.

Creating a HUD that will fit into the gameplay and style of your game is essential. While a feature-rich HUD may be great for some games, a simplistic HUD can be just as effective or more. It all depends on the player experience you want. So when you're ready to create the HUD for your next game, make sure you're designing the HUD to enhance the player's experience and never give the player an overload of information.

Existing or upcoming RPG games

This section of the book will take a look at some of the existing or upcoming RPGs on the market. The main idea behind this section is to provide you with a point of reference on multiple RPGs and the game design implemented. It is also a good idea to research existing or upcoming games to get ideas of your own!

In the Beginning

Dark Souls 3

Dark Souls 3 is an action role-playing game developed by FromSoftware and published by Bandai Namco Entertainment for PlayStation 4, Xbox One and MS Windows. It was released in Japan in March of 2016 and worldwide in April of 2016.

The game is set in the Kingdom of Lothric, an undead warrior known as the Ashen One is tasked by a mysterious woman known as the Fire Keeper, to avert an oncoming apocalypse brought about by the ongoing conflict between Light and Dark. But the only means to avert this event is with the destruction of the Lords of Cinder, previous heroes who have linked the First Flame across eons.

The game is set in a third-person perspective. Players are equipped with a variety of weapons including bows, explosive fire bombs, great-swords, and dual-wielded swords to fight against enemies. Shields are used to deflect an enemy's attack and protect the player from suffering damage.

Throughout the game, players encounter different types of enemies, each with different behaviors. Some change their combat pattern during battles. New combat features are introduced in the game, including weapon and shield skill, which are special abilities that vary from weapon to weapon that enable unique attacks and features at the cost of focus points. The game puts more focus on role-playing, in which the character builder is expanded and weapons are improved to provide more tactical options to players.

Fallout 4

Fallout 4 is an action role-playing game developed by Bethesda Game Studios and published by Bethesda Softworks. The game was released worldwide on November 10, 2015 for Microsoft Windows, PlayStation 4, and Xbox One.

In the Beginning

The game takes place in the year 2287, ten years after the events of Fallout 3 and 210 years after a resource war over natural resources that ended in a nuclear holocaust in 2077. The setting is a post-apocalyptic retro-future, covering a region that includes Boston, Massachusetts and other parts of New England known as **The Commonwealth**.

The story begins on the day the bombs dropped: October 23, 2077. The player's character takes shelter in Vault 111, emerging exactly 210 years later, on October 23, 2287.

The game takes place in an alternate version of history that sees the 1940's and 1950's aesthetics, design and technology advance in the directions imagined at the time. The resulting universe is thus a retro-futuristic one, where the technology has evolved enough to produce laser weapons, manipulate genes and create nearly autonomous artificial intelligence, but all within the confines of 1950's solutions like the widespread use of atomic power and vacuum tubes, as well as having the integrated circuitry of the digital age.

The overall setting of the game is that of the 1950s, from the architecture, to the advertisements and general living styles and so on.

Divinity: Original Sin

Divinity: Original Sin, is a single player and cooperative multiplayer fantasy role-playing game, developed by Larian Studios. The game ships with the editor that created the game, allowing players to create their own single-player and multiplayer adventures, and publish them online.

The customizable protagonists of the game are a pair of Source Hunters, members of an organization dedicated to eradicating a dangerous magic named the Source and its adepts, the Sourcerers.

In the single-player mode, the player controls them both, while in the multiplayer mode, each player takes control over one of them. At the start of the game, the Source Hunters receive orders to investigate the murder of a town councilor by a suspected Sourcerer in Cyseal, a port town in southern Rivellon.

Upon arrival, they find Cyseal under siege by orcs and undead and soon discover that it was orchestrated by a Sourcerer conspiracy linked to the Immaculates, a cult based in the Luculla Forest further inland.

Patterns in RPG

Just like any other technical project that might have patterns defined, an RPG can also utilize similar patterns that have been documented by *Whitson John Kirk III* in his book titled, *Design Patterns for Successful Role-Playing Games*.

Whitson was inspired by the book *Design Patterns: Elements of Reusable Object-Oriented Software*. His objective was to see if there existed special patterns in existing RPGs, and he approached this by examining specific patterns in the successful games of the genre to detect and identify them.

In this section we will be looking at some of the design patterns that have been identified and that can be utilized for your own games.

Anytime you start a new project, regardless of what type of a project, you need to have some clear idea of what exactly it is that you are trying to accomplish. This is even truer for designing a game. Since designing a game has many different components to it, you will need to identify what your game is going to be about. Some questions to start the thinking process are:

1. What are you trying to accomplish?
2. What mood are you trying to evoke?
3. What do the characters do?
4. What does the player or players, in a multiplayer environment, do?
5. What kind of activities do you want to reward and what kinds of rewards do you want to provide?
6. What age group does your game target?
7. Is your game going to have cinematic sequences?
8. Will the game and the story extend with supplemental assets?

These are all important questions that will affect the design of your game. As you read this chapter and the book in general, keep a pen and paper handy so that you can write down all ideas that flash in your mind. This way you can keep track of all your thoughts and if you need to expand on them you can at a later time.

Chapter 1

Terminology

Every discipline has its own terminology; the following is a list of terminology that is used in RPG games. It is a good idea to take a moment and study them to expand your vocabulary or to refresh your memory:

- **Attribute:** A gauge that is a common characteristic, a commonality.
- **Character:** A person in a game portrayed by a player, including possibly the Game Master.
- **Characteristics:** An aspect of a character. A character's name, height, age, beauty, and strength are some possible characteristics.
- **Common Characteristics:** A characteristic common to all characters of a given type in a game. A character's name, height, age, beauty, and strength are frequently common characteristics.
- **Conflict:** Contention between characters, players, and/or game forces, especially contention that shapes the game's plot. This includes oppositions between two or more players concerning what facts should be introduced into a game world.
- **Contest:** A conflict that is resolved through mechanical means.
- **Derived Attributes:** An attribute whose value is determined by a formula. Typically, the formula uses other attribute values to generate a number.
- **Drama:** An outcome based purely on story consideration. Outcomes in a drama are exclusively determined by what would be most entertaining for the participants.
- **Flaw:** A selected characteristic that is specifically not also a gauge. A character either has a flaw or he does not. Flaws are structurally very similar to gifts. But, flaws are generally considered detrimental to a character rather than beneficial.
- **Fortune:** An outcome that is at least partly based on random factors. This may include rolling dice, drawing cards, or some other random value generator.
- **Game Master:** Traditionally, a player assigned responsibilities and who manages the game flow. With computer RPGs, the Game Master (GM) is the glue that holds everything together.
- **Gauge:** A graduated value generally associated with a name. Commonly the graduated values are numeric values.
- **Gift:** A selected characteristic that is specifically not a gauge. A character either has a gift or not. In general, gifts are considered beneficial to a character's well-being.

In the Beginning

- **Karma:** An outcome based on non-random value comparison. A karma-based contest directly compares two values to determine an outcome.
- **Non-Player Character (NPC):** Any character portrayed by the Game Master as part of the role.
- **Optional Characteristics:** A characteristic that is not common to all characters of a given type.
- **Player:** Any person participating in a role-playing game.
- **Player Character (PC):** a character portrayed by any player while not assuming the role of a Game Master.
- **Primary Attribute:** An attribute whose value is set directly by a player rather than being derived by a formula from other attributes. Commonly, primary attributes are used in formulae to determine the values of Derived Attributes but their own values are not determined by formulas. Typically, they are generated by random numbers or set by spending some resources.
- **Rank:** The specific value of a gauge skill, handicap, or ranked trait. Also used as an adjective in place of gauge when describing such skills and traits.
- **Ranked Trait:** A trait that is also a gauge.
- **Selected Characteristic:** A characteristic selected from a predefined list of choices.
- **Shared Gauge:** A gauge that is shared by many characters.
- **Skill:** a selected characteristic that is also a gauge and is generally considered beneficial to a character.
- **Trait:** A characteristic made up by a player without drawing it from a predefined list of choices.

To get a better understanding about the relationships between the attributes and characteristics, we have put together a visual diagram to make it explainable:

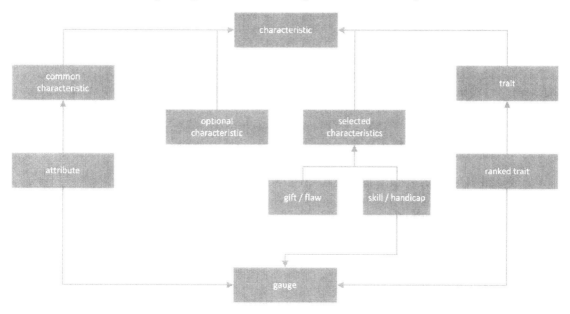

Contest Tree

The intent of a Contest Tree is to provide a mechanical means to create rising tension within a game. This is also known as **Escalating Conflict**.

Contest trees are high-level conflict resolution systems made up of many levels of contests arranged in a hierarchical fashion. The way they work, is that lower level contests feed into the higher level contests and therefore affect the outcome of the higher level contests.

In other words, the higher level contest could be to kill the big boss, but before you get to the big boss, there could be other mini battles that you will have to complete, and the outcome of the mini battles will drive the outcome of the big battle. To give a simple example would be by the amount of experience points you have gained before reaching the main boss.

In the Beginning

Since the higher level contests are somehow related to the lower level contest, players do pay attention to the outcome of the higher level contests, therefore, tensions arise concerning the eventual success or failure of a higher level contest as a lower level contest succeeds or fails.

It is best to use a Contest Tree when you want to create a sense of rising tension in your game. This can be achieved by applying different mechanics as the player progresses through the levels. Creating suspense in a cRPG is very simple as you have a lot of control in the way levels and gameplay are designed. Since we have the ability to create our 3D worlds as we like, it would be easy to incorporate suspense into the game.

A few key points for creating tension in your game:

- The hero and enemy should be evenly matched.
- The hero and enemy should both periodically fail in their attempts, providing they are worthy adversaries.
- The hero and enemy successes and failures are never so great that all hope of success of attaining the high level goals is eliminated from either side.
- A highlight concerning Contest Trees is that it can only resolve high-level conflicts dealing with the mechanical inputs by the system. That is, if damage and remaining hit points are the only gauges used as an input into a conflict resolution, then the mechanics can only resolve issues dealing with Damage and Hit Points. When designing a flexible Contest Tree you will need to consider both the inputs and also the outputs.

Last Man Standing

Last Man Standing conflict system provides a generalized Contest Tree to resolve which side attains victory in battle.

The Last Man Standing is also one of the most traditional forms of generalized Contest Trees. The basic idea behind the pattern is to identify who the winner is by the simple fact of who manages to destroy the opponent. He who does is the winner. This is also one of the simplest ways to implement a Contest Tree.

Chapter 1

It is used when there is a strong emphasis on tactical combat. Keep in mind that you are not obligated to use one pattern or the other. You can very well combine several patterns together, and you should to make it more interesting. For instance, if your game has a great emphasis on combat, but you want to also introduce some negotiation into the conflict resolution, you can certainly do so. Again, it all depends on you and your game design.

Something to keep in mind; if the only way to resolve a high-level contest is through battle, then players will focus their efforts on being the best they possibly can at winning battles. In other words, if a game only provides a single tool to resolve disputes, then you can be assured that players will become very adept and focused on using that tool.

Negotiated Contest

A Negotiated Contest provides a mechanical means to resolve disputes where the set of inputs and possible outcomes is negotiated by the player and non-player characters specifically for the conflict.

Designing and developing a Negotiated Contest mechanism is pretty complex. In order for the pattern to work properly, you will need to consider all of the inputs and outputs of the negotiations. The challenge of developing such a system is not so much the actual technical implementation, but the database that you will have to create and retain based on the available selection by the player and the outcome of each input.

The implementation of the mechanics can be as simple as a few options and outcomes, and as complex as a variety of options and their eventual outcomes down the line. The important point is that you will have introduced a negotiation mechanism after a conflict has been introduced but before any action has been taken! The outcome is obviously what a win/lose is concerned with, based on the negotiation before the conflict.

The Negotiated Contest pattern requires that players be allowed to negotiate the effects of success and failure before the conflict is mechanically resolved.

Use the Negotiates Contest pattern when your design goals include one of more of the following:

1. A desire to unambiguously decide whether the outcome of a contest means a player wins or loses his stated goals rather than whether or not his character succeeds in performing discrete actions.

In the Beginning

2. A need to scale the resolution of contests to levels of granularity different than that of individual actions.
3. A willingness to allow players a great deal of narrative freedom in describing the results of contests, both good and bad.

For computer role-playing games, the negotiated contest will have some restrictions as we cannot afford to create an AI system to be open ended. But we can design a simpler means to provide the player a sense of some control on the negotiations as part of the gameplay.

Negotiation can be a great mechanic for exchanging information with non-player characters in your role playing game. There are three parts to a Negotiation pattern:

- *Initiation* is the phase at which a character action is introduced into the game world
- *Execution* is the phase in which the success or failure of a character action is determined
- *Effect* is the phase in which the results of a character's actions are determined

Here are some questions to consider when designing a Negotiation system:

1. What does the winner get?
2. What does the loser get?
3. How do we know who's the winner and who's the loser?
4. What do we need to establish before resolution begins, and how?

Summary

In this chapter, we covered what a role-playing game is in great detail. We briefly covered some of the historical aspects of the genre and looked at the different varieties. We discussed the key elements for designing a role-playing game, and provided some examples to demonstrate.

We looked into the characteristics of an RPG and discussed how to plan for your game such as story and setting, exploration, and quests within your game, different types of inventory systems, character development, user interaction, and some combat system patterns. We also covered some basic terminology that is used in RPGs.

By the end of the chapter you should have a clear idea of what you will need to prepare for and the kind of effort it would take for making a role-playing game.

In the next chapter, we will start developing our own RPG.

Setting the Atmosphere

2

The intention of `Chapter 1`, *In the Beginning*, was to give you a good footing on the topic and spark your imagination. In this chapter, we are going to start laying the groundwork for our own RPG. We will first define the story for our game, define the plot, and define the quests that will make the game playable. We will look at the assets that will be required to create our environment and characters and finally design the first level.

The following is a breakdown of the topics we will be covering in this chapter.

- Building Our RPG
- The Story of the Zazar Dynasty
    - Plot
    - Exploration and Quests
        - Awakening
        - The Village
        - Broken Forest
        - The Kingdom

- Asset Inventory
    - Environment Assets
    - Character Assets
- Level Design
    - Setting the Stage
    - Terrain Toolkit in a Nut-Shell
- The Awakening
- Testing the Level
- Creating the Main Menu

Awaken your creativity and let your imagination go wild!

Setting the Atmosphere

Building our RPG

As discussed, building a role-playing game is no small task, but once you start down the path, you will come to realize that it is not as difficult as it seems initially. The idea is to get started and as you put your ideas down on paper and start the design process, more and more ideas will come into perspective.

As we have learned, there are some key elements that we would need to establish for our RPG. Let's recall them, and maybe even fine tune them as we go along.

Key Elements:

- Story and setting
- Exploration and quests
- Inventory system
- Character development
- Experience and levelling
- Combat system
- User interface and graphics

The story of the Zazar Dynasty

The premise of most role-playing games tasks the player with saving the world. There are often twists and turns as the story progresses, such as the surprise appearance of an estranged relative, or enemies who become friends and vice versa. We will create our story and game based on such a story.

Plot

Once upon a time there was a great kingdom. Ruled by the great King Zazar. The ruler of the kingdom was a generous lord to his subjects. The kingdom under the rule of Zazar was peaceful and prosperous, however, over time internal family rivalries and struggles caused cracks in the strong bond that kept the kingdom intact.

Due to mysterious events, the great king decided to move his family away from the kingdom and trust his son with one of his trusted, wise elders. The kingdom was never the same. Until now!

Chapter 2

Exploration and quests

Now that we have defined our plot for the game. We can start working on developing the story further and breaking it down into different levels. To keep things simple, we will concentrate on basic quests and level design, the important point is to understand the concepts and apply them to your own story.

Awakening

The game will start by immersing the player in the environment where our hero has been raised and trained by the elder who was entrusted by the great King Zazar.

The main objectives of this level will be for the player to engage with the environment and learn how to interact with his/her surroundings.

Objectives:

- Introduce the player to the user interface
- How to move the character
- How to interact with Non-Player Characters
- How to interact with the environment

Outcome:

- Player gets points for completing in-game tasks.
- Player gets his first weapon.
- Player learns how to interact with the surrounding world.

The village

Our hero will start his journey of self-fulfillment. He will be traveling in the outskirts of the Kingdom and arriving at one of the villages that has been terrorized by the thugs and mercenaries hired by the Evil Overlord Shaquil.

Our hero, himself unaware of who he is and why he is on this journey, will find out about the austerity that has been going on since the departure of his father. This will be mostly accomplished through the interaction of the village peasants.

The primary objective of this level will be for the player to learn social skills and engage with the village people and create relationships.

[37]

Setting the Atmosphere

Rumor has it, that there are spies in the village, and that everyone is suspicious of each other and the unity that once was the strength of the village is crumbling.

Objectives:

- Interact with the village peasants to acquire social skills
- Create trust between the hero and the villagers
- Seek out who the spy is among the villagers

Outcome:

- Improved social skills
- Establish relationships that can be tapped into at a later point
- Learn some basic combat skills

Broken forest – the horizon

Our hero will be travelling along his quest into the horizon. The horizon is the initial exposure to the main kingdom's borders, where the main castle and inner city is within reach.

It is basically a vast lush forest that protects the main domain of the kingdom from outside threats. It also has a few secrets and surprises for the uninitiated passer-by. The forest is where the barbarians reside and cause havoc on the surrounding areas. What is not apparent at the time, is the connection between the barbarians and the current Over Lord of the Kingdom.

As far as the hero is concerned, he or she will need to be able to safely pass through the forest.

The horizon is going to have several unexpected surprises for the hero, the outcome of the quest will heavily rely on the way the player interacts with the surrounding environment and also with the non-player characters.

Objective:

- Ability to pass through the forest without getting killed

Outcomes:

- Hero can be captured by the Barbarians.
- Hero could face other life threatening scenarios and or non-player characters.

[38]

- Hero successfully passes through the forest and is ready to take on the next challenge.
- Hero can establish new relationships to enhance their skills and abilities.

The kingdom

The hero has progressed through the previous quests and now is ready to take down the Evil Over Lord and retake what is inherently his. Our hero has progressed and acquired a vast amount of skills and abilities throughout the quests, and now he is going to undertake one of the most difficult and epic battles in the game.

Our hero is surprised by the vast army of the Over Lord. He will need to figure out a way to pass through the city and into the main castle to defeat the enemy.

Objectives:

- Kill the Overlord and retake his Kingdom.

Outcomes:

- Call to action the relationships he has established throughout game-play.
- Use his negotiation skills and wisdom to outwit more powerful enemies.
- Destroy the enemy.

Ah, the pure joy of defeating your nemesis and taking over your Kingdom!

Asset inventory

It is a good time to discuss some of the basic assets that are going to be required for the development of our RPG. Our game assets are defined by the scenes we describe for our game. For our RPG, we have described four unique scenes. Each one has been described in enough detail for us to get an idea of the types of assets we are going to require.

Environment assets

The general theme of our game is going to be medieval. There are several ways to go about this. The first and preferred way would be to either create yourself the environment models by yourself or a teammate, second to find a freely available model that has been created by a third-party, or third to purchase the 3D Models that have been created by a third party.

Setting the Atmosphere

The Asset Store is a great place for you to start hunting for great content if you do not have the ability to create your own 3D models. You can use the Asset Store to search for medieval themed environments that can be used for the game.

One of my favorites is called Medieval Environment. You might want to consider searching for a few more that are to your liking and taste.

Things to consider as part of your environment assets:

- Buildings
- Props and add-ons
    - Banners
    - Barrels
    - Windows
    - Boxes
    - Wagons
- Rocks/plants/trees
- Particle assets
    - Fire
    - Fog
    - Smoke
    - Water
- Skyboxes

The preceding list is just a starting point, but it is a starting point for your environment assets.

Character assets

RPGs are heavily based on characters. Therefore, the next important game asset is going to be the characters themselves. The models that you need to define for your game are again heavily related to your story line and setting. The Asset Store provides a wealth of character models that you can download and use as a proof of concept for your game.

For our game, here are the characters that are required: humans, these will represent the hero as well as the villagers and other non-player character types of human. We need a Barbarian class, these are some of the characters that the hero must confront during the game play. We have the Orc character class which are animals in their own right.

You can either get the free models or the paid models to represent your characters. We will get more into the character assets in future chapters.

Level design

Now that we have our game story on paper and have an idea of what we want to achieve, it is time to apply our skills to actually making it happen.

 Since this book is targeting an audience who is already familiar with the basics of Unity, we are not going to cover the fundamental aspects of the software.

To get started, we need to launch Unity. I am using the *64-bit edition* of *Unity 5.3.x Pro*. You do not need to have the Pro version of Unity for completing the project in this book.

Setting the Atmosphere

Go ahead and select a location and a name you desire for your project and select the **Create project** button. At this point Unity will create an empty project for you, and display the Unity IDE, it should look something like the following:

Your view might be a bit different, depending on how you have configured your Unity layout. If this is the first time you have launched Unity, you will need to get up to speed with the basics, since we are not going to be covering them in this book.

 If you have not used Unity before, you should get familiar with the IDE before you continue on reading.

Setting the stage

So the first things we would like to do is to create a landscape for our first level called *Awakening*.

Unity itself has some good tools for creating terrains, but truth be told, it is not a practical means of achieving nice beautiful terrains for the game. For this purpose, we are going to use another set of tools called Terrain Toolkit and it was developed by *Sander as part of the Unity Summer of Code 2009.*

Chapter 2

 The toolkit is available on Google code repository:
https://code.google.com/archive/p/unityterraintoolkit/downloads

I have also included the library as part of the download provided by this book, just in case the original link gets deprecated in the future.

Once you get the ZIP file containing the Terrain Toolkit, go ahead and unzip it to a desired location on your computer. Drill-down in the extracted folder to get to the Unity Package called `TerrainToolkit_1_0_2.unitypackage`.

At this point let's take a moment and go back into Unity and actually create a Terrain GameObject and see the built-in tool for terrain modification. To create a Terrain, you will need to select the following from the Main Menu: **GameObject|3D Object|Terrain.** This will create a default terrain in your scene which should look something like the following:

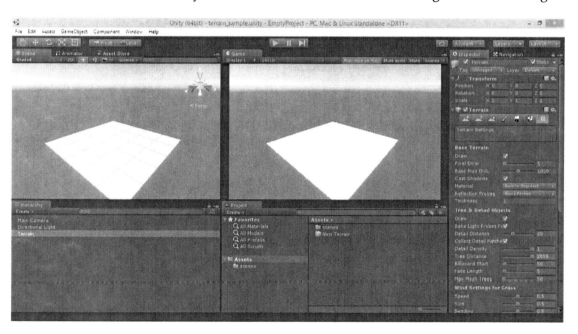

When you select the Terrain GameObject in the Hierarchy Window, you will see the Inspector Window displaying the properties and components that are accessible through the designer for the Terrain GameObject. As you can see, there are a lot of attributes that you can modify and by doing so create a nice looking terrain. When you start playing around with the terrain tool you will soon realize that it is not practical for large terrain models, or for natural looking terrains.

[43]

Setting the Atmosphere

To enhance our terrain generation, we will use the Terrain Toolkit. The first thing we need to do is to import the unity package into our project, and this is done by selecting from the main menu: **Assets** | **Import Package** | **Custom** Package which will open up your file explorer. Using the file explorer, you will need to navigate to the location where you extracted the ZIP file, and select the unity package to import.

If all goes well you will see the following screen displaying the assets that are included in the package we are trying to import. You can take a look at the content of the package before importing it. In our case, we want to import everything, so we can just click the **Import** button.

 Sometimes when you import older Unity Assets, Unity will prompt you to automatically upgrade it to the latest version. This is usually OK. So just accept it and let Unity do what it needs to do.

When Unity imports the Terrain Toolkit, you will notice a new folder under your Project Window called **TerrainToolkit**. All the code will be listed under the folder if you want to make any modifications to it. There is also a readme file which you can use to get started.

You will also notice that a new Unity Editor feature has been added under the **Component Menu** called **Terrain | Terrain Toolkit**. All you need to do to apply the Terrain Toolkit to your existing Terrain is to select that option and it will automatically attach the correct component to the Terrain GameObject for you.

You will notice a few options that are now available to you through the Terrain Toolkit for the generation of more natural and realistic terrains. You should take the time and get familiar with each attribute and play around with the values to get an idea of how they affect the terrain generation algorithm.

Setting the Atmosphere

Terrain toolkit in a nutshell

There are a number of predefined generators in the toolkit for the creation of the terrain. These are **Voronoi, Fractal, Perlin**. The following is a brief explanation of each.

- **Voronoi** generates a random height-map consisting of a series of mountain-like peaks using a Voronoi diagram and applies it to the terrain object.
- **Fractal** generates a random height-map using the *cloud* or *plasma* fractal algorithm and applies it to the terrain object.
- **Perlin** generates a random height-map using Perlin noise and applies it to the terrain object.

There are also two filter types that can be applied after the generation of the terrain. These are the **Smooth** and **Normalize** filters.

- **Smooth** is a filter which applies smoothing to the terrain object repeatedly over a number of iterations.
- **Normalize** is a filter which normalizes the terrain object by setting the highest point in the current terrain height-map to the maximum and the lowest point to the minimum. All other points are interpolated between the maximum and minimum.

The next step would be to apply some erosion to the terrain. There are three built in erosion types in the toolkit: **Thermal Erosion, Hydraulic Erosion**, and **Tidal Erosion**. You can apply these erosion types either by a brush, or by the actual erosion filters.

- **Thermal Erosion** removes material from areas with a slope greater than the minimum slope and deposits it further down the slope. This tends to smooth and flatten inclines in the terrain.
- **Hydraulic Erosion** removes material from areas with a slope less than the maximum slope and deposits it further down the slope. This tends to steepen inclines in the terrain and further smooth and flatten other areas.

Chapter 2

 There are three different Hydraulic Erosion Types.

- **Tidal Erosion** applies smoothing at the chosen sea level, except in areas where the slope exceeds a given value. This simulates the erosive action of waves around a shoreline and creates beaches.

Final step would be to apply texturing. This will give our terrain a more realistic look and feel at runtime. The toolkit provides procedural terrain texturing, which automatically textures the terrain object using the slope and altitude attributes of the terrain to determine which texture will be used.

The awakening

The setting and the atmosphere of the level is going to be in a secluded area within the jungle. We are now going to generate our terrain using the Terrain Toolkit discussed in the previous section.

Let's create a new scene and call it Awakening. By default, the scene is just going to have a camera and a directional light GameObject defined.

 You can save your scenes and assets within the Asset folder without much thought. However, it is usually a good idea to have some file structure in place to make organization of your assets easier and be able to find them faster.

A preferred folder structure would include: scenes, prefabs, textures, audio, models. Within each folder you can then create subfolders and so forth for your own organizational purposes.

Now we are ready to add a Terrain GameObject to the scene. Go ahead and select **GameObject | 3D Object | Terrain**. This will place a **Terrain GameObject** in the scene, double click on the **Terrain GameObject** in the Hierarchy Window to make it centered in the Scene View.

Setting the Atmosphere

By default, the Terrain object will be very large, let's go ahead and make some adjustments before we do anything else.

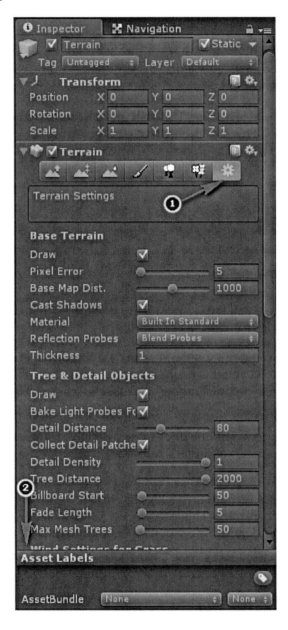

To make the adjustments to the terrain size, select the **Settings Icon** as indicated in the preceding screenshot. This will display the basic attributes of the terrain. As you can see there are a bunch of properties that can be adjusted to make it behave to your liking. We are mostly concerned with the size of the terrain and also the maximum height that the terrain can raise to. Therefore, scroll down until you get to the **Resolution** section.

Change the **Terrain Width** and **Terrain Length** to 50. Change the **Terrain Height** to 50. This will change the dimension so that we can handle our scene easier. Our original terrain size was very large and it would have taken us a long time to decorate it.

Now, we have a good size terrain. Assuming you have already imported the Terrain Toolkit, go ahead and select **Component | Terrain | Terrain Toolkit** from the main menu.

I have used the fractal terrain generator function with a **Delta** of 0.4 and **Blend** of 0.445. This will generate a nice looking terrain with a good proportion of hills and valleys. Since the terrain is randomly generated yours may not look exactly like mine, but it should look something similar to the following screenshot:

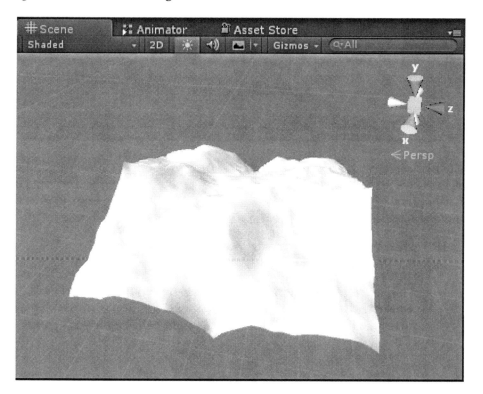

Setting the Atmosphere

I usually apply the **Smooth** filter after my terrain generation to make things look even nicer. After applying the **Smooth** filter, my terrain looks like the following:

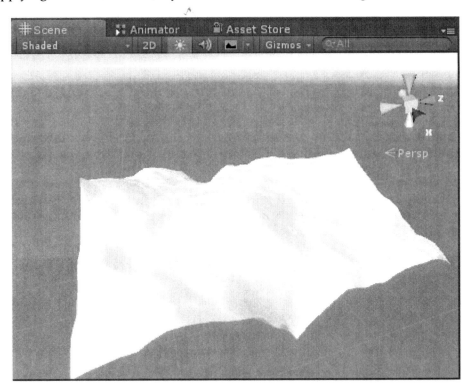

You can see the difference of the filter once it has been applied. Let's go ahead and now apply some textures to make it nice. Selecting the **Texture** tab within the **Terrain Toolkit**, you will have several options. We would like to apply at least two textures to give our terrain a more realistic look. You can apply up to four textures if you choose to!

Click the **Add Texture** button twice to create the texture placeholder.

 Textures are very important in graphics and especially games. The better and higher resolution your textures, the better your scene will look. However, this is a catch-22. Usually higher resolution textures take up more resources. So you have to find the right balance for your game.

Once the placeholders have been added, you can click on the placeholder, a window will pop-up and you will be able to select your desired texture.

Now is a good time to stop and discuss one of the main advantages of Unity, the **Asset Store**. The Asset Store is a great online community that Unity Developers can either acquire assets to be used in their games, or develop assets that will be used by other developers. You can either get free assets from the Asset Store or you can get better quality ones for a little bit of money.

For our game, I will be using some free assets and some paid assets. If you want to use the same assets that I am using in the book you will need to purchase them:

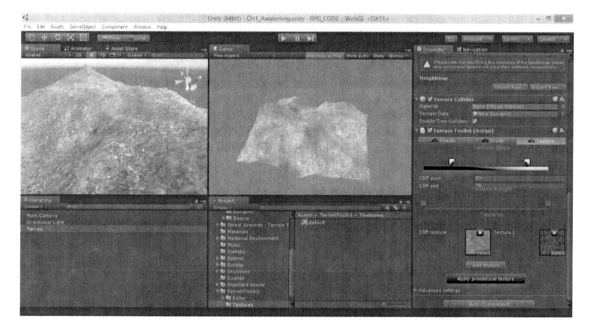

Setting the Atmosphere

The next thing I like to do is locate a position on the terrain where I will be using to create the scene objects necessary to play out the level. For this particular scene, I want to use an asset that represents an old cottage in the woods, where the hero will be awakening in the beginning of the game.

I have found this nice asset in the Asset Store that I would like to use for my starting point of the game. The model itself does not have any interior. This fits in well, because I am not planning on having any game play inside the shelter. It is just an eye catching object in the scene and a point of reference.

In order for me to place the shack in the scene, I will need to first do some more adjustments to the terrain. If you notice, our terrain does not have any level areas where we can properly place the shack. We would need to use the terrain objects terrain components to make some more changes.

Again select the Terrain GameObject in the Hierarchy View and use the Inspector Window to select the **Paint Height** tab, shown as (1) in the preceding image, to enable the feature.

This is a great feature to sample the terrain height at a particular point, and apply the same height using the brush to any other region. This will level the terrain to the same height that was sampled. It's a great way to quickly level a region and place your items, if those items need to be on a level ground, like a house or a shelter.

Chapter 2

The next step is to place some tree models on our terrain to create the jungle look and feel. To achieve this, we are going to need to select the terrain object in the scene and use the **Inspector Window** to select the **Tree Placement** feature. You will then need to select the **Edit Trees...** button to add a Tree model.

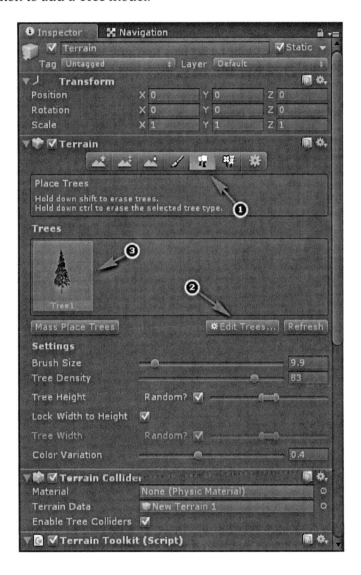

[53]

Using the Inspector Window, you will need to select the Tree Placement tab, select **Edit Tree... Add Tree** feature, locate a Tree prefab and you are done!

Take a look at the settings, and change the brush size to meet your needs. In my case, I have changed it to 9.9. I have left the rest of the attributes at the default value, you can certainly change them as needed.

Now, when you move your mouse in the Scene View, you will notice a brush-like highlight. This is where the trees will be placed during design time.

The following screenshot will display how my scene looks after I have made some of the adjustments and placements of my trees and the building.

The next step of the process would be filling the level with other environment assets such as rocks, vegetation, and other props to make the level come to life. The idea here is to make it interesting and at the same time functional. It is a good idea to have some sort of a sketch of your level design. This way you can have a good idea of how you will develop your level.

Chapter 2

Keep in mind that this can also be used as a means of communication with your team; the level designers and artists, providing them a direction. The following diagram is a top-down view of our intended level design.

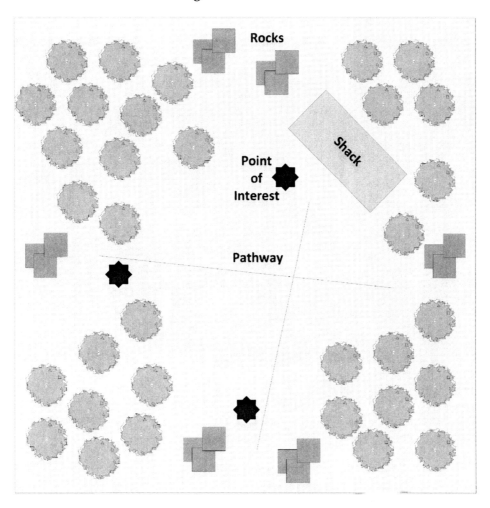

I am going to now build my level based on the layout I have. Now is the time to get creative and use your imagination to design your level. This part of the exercise is free form, you are the designer, so you will decide how to go about placing and creating your level, as long as it meets the requirements.

Setting the Atmosphere

Keep in mind the following important point, the player will be interacting with the environment or non-player characters at the designated points of interest. So make sure when you design your level, they have an easy way to access the areas where they need to get to, so that they can perform the given task.

One thing to notice is the limitation of the terrain as we have it defined here. When the player goes to the edge of the terrain they will fall through! Yes, they will freefall forever! We don't want that to happen. So we will need to also incorporate some boundaries in the level design that will prevent the player from basically going overboard.

It is very simple to create some restrictions and boundaries in such cases. We can use wooden fences, or we can use the actual environment to restrict the level of access by the player to the danger zones in the level. This method can be very time consuming if your level is large.

Another way to solve this problem is to create four planes that will be used on each side of the terrain. The plains will have a special texture giving them an atmospheric look, but they will have colliders which will stop the player from moving forward upon contact. This is an easier method and will take less time to place in the scene.

Chapter 2

Go ahead and create a plane by choosing **Game Object|3D Object|Plane**. When the plane is placed in the scene, arrange it in a way that it will be the length of the terrain. The scale of my plane is `<4,1,4>` at position `<25,20,25>`, I have also rotated the plane 90 degree on the Z axis.

You will need to also attach a collider to the plane object. The collider component will be used to detect collisions between the plane and other objects, in this case the player character, and stop the player from going through.

To attach a collider, select the Plane object and from the Inspector Window, use the **Add Component** button to select **Physics|Box Collider**. The plane now will have a box collider that will be used for collision detection by the engine.

A plane object will only render on one side. Therefore, when you apply your texture to the plane, make sure that the visible side is towards the inside of the level.

Once you are satisfied with the look and feel, you will need to duplicate it and place it on all the side edges to protect the player from falling.

Setting the Atmosphere

In the preceding screenshot, notice that the two planes on the far side are not visible. That is how the player will see the environment during gameplay. The player will collide and not be able to move forward, but they will see the skyline go far into the distance.

It is time to do a test run. We can use the 3rd person character controller provided in the Standard Assets to quickly drop our character placeholder and roam around the level to get a feel for it.

Testing the level

At some point you will want to test out the level and look at it through the eyes of the camera. We can use the built-in 3rd person character controller that comes in the Standard Assets, and do a quick walk-through of the level.

If you have not imported the Standard Assets when you created the project. You will need to import them by selecting **Assets**, and select **Import Package | Characters.**

In your *Project Window,* you will see a folder called **Standard Assets**, there is a subfolder called **Character Controllers**. You will need to select the **3rd Person Controller Prefab** and drop it somewhere on the current scene. A good location will be next to the shack. Make sure that the **3rd Person Controller (3rdPC)** is above the terrain so it does not fall through!

In the `ThirdPersonController.js` component, you might have to assign the Idle, Walk, Run and Jump animations.

You will have to attach a Rigidbody component to the 3rdPC GameObject. This is needed to make sure that our **player-character (PC)** will use the built-in physics for collisions detection.

Go ahead and run the level and walk-through the scene. Test and make sure that the PC is behaving the way it is supposed to when you are navigating through the environment. When I test run my PC, I realized I had not attached Box colliders to all of the Planes. I also realized that there was no collider defined for my Shack. Take an inventory of such errors and when you stop testing make the needed corrections.

[58]

Creating the Main Menu

Now is a good time to create the starting point for our game. Go ahead and save the current scene. We are going to make a new scene that will be used as the starting point of our game. To create the new scene, you will need to select **File | New Scene**. Go ahead and save the scene. I called my scene Main Menu.

Now we have a clear canvas that we can work with to create our Main Menu. In the *Hierarchy Window*, right-click and select **UI | Panel**. This will create a Canvas GameObject and an EventSystem GameObject and place them in your **Hierarchy** window. You will notice that the **Panel** UI object is a child of the **Canvas**. All UI elements will be a child of a **Canvas**.

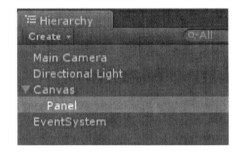

Your Hierarchy should look something like the preceding.

There are several key aspects that we want to make sure are set properly. These are namely on the **Canvas GameObject**. Select the **Canvas GameObject** and look at the **Inspector Window**.

For this particular Canvas, make sure that the **Render Mode** is set to **Screen Space – Overlay**. The next property you need to check is the **UI Scale Mode**. Change this to **Scale With Screen Size**. This will make sure that the UI will always be scaled to the screen size of the device that the game is being run in.

 For best results, you will want to create multiple menus for different device types.

So for now, let's go ahead and create a button that will basically load our level called Awakening.

Setting the Atmosphere

Right click on the **Panel Object** in the **Hierarchy Window** and select **UI | Button**. This will place a button on the Canvas as a child to the Panel object. The parent child relationships are important to consider when you are building your user interface. When you place a UI element as part of a child to another UI element, the child will be scaled and moved according to the Parent's scale and location.

You can learn more about UI development in *Chapter 5* of the book *Introduction to Game Programming: Using C# and Unity 3D.*

We will spend time fine tuning our menu in the future chapters. Change the caption of the button to `Start Game`. It is also a good idea to name your scene object appropriately just to keep things nice and organized. I have changed the name of the button to `butStartGame`. This can be done by selecting the Button object in the **Hierarchy Window** and changing the name in the **Inspector Window**.

Creating the Game Master

As discussed in `Chapter 1`, *In the Beginning,* we are going to need a way to manage our game. We are going to create a script that will be called `GameMaster`. This is going to be the core of the game that glues everything together. As we progress with the book you will see how we are going to modify the core to meet our needs.

For now, we are just going to create a simple C# script and name it `GameMaster.cs`. We will then create the code that will be used to handle some of the basic events we want to perform at this point namely navigating from scene to scene.

From your **Project Window**, under your `scripts` folder, right-click and select **Create | C# Script**. Name it `GameMaster.cs`. Double-click your script to start your code editor and place the following code in there:

```
using UnityEngine;
using UnityEngine.SceneManagement;
using System.Collections;

public class GameMaster : MonoBehaviour {

    // Use this for initialization
    void Start () {
    }
    // Update is called once per frame
    void Update () {
    }
```

[60]

```
    public void StartGame()
    {
        // NOTE: You should put in the name of the Scene
        // that represents your level 1
        SceneManager.LoadScene("CH1_Awakening");
    }
}
```

In the **Hierarchy** window, you will need to create an *Empty GameObject*. The best way to do this, is by right-clicking and selecting **Create Empty**. An empty GameObject will be created. Select it and change the name to *_GameMaster*.

We need to attach our script to the _GameMaster GameObject in our scene. Select the GameMaster.cs script and drag and drop it on the _GameMaster. This will attach the script to the _GameMaster object and make it available in the scene.

The next step is creating the event call from the button. This can easily be achieved by selecting the butStartGame button element and from the **Inspector** window adding a new event call on the OnClick() component. Click the **(+)** button to create a new event.

Setting the Atmosphere

We need to call the function we created in the `GameMaster.cs` script. To do so, we would need to somehow refer to it. This is done really easily. We can drag and drop the `_GameMaster GameObject` into the slot as indicated in the screenshot by number **2**.

Once you place your `_GameMaster` GameObject in the slot, you will need to select the script from the drop-down menu as indicated in the screenshot by number **3**.

That's all there is to it! We have now connected our button click event to the code that will be responsible to load our first level.

Now is a good time to save your scene and test your application. When you run the application for the first time, you will get an error. Don't be surprised, we have not done anything wrong. But there is one more step that we need to do before we can actually run our game successfully.

In order to be able to load scenes in the game, you will need to make sure they are listed in the Build Settings. To do so, select **File** | **Build Settings...** and add the current scene to the list by selecting **Add Open Scenes**. Your Build Setting should look like the following:

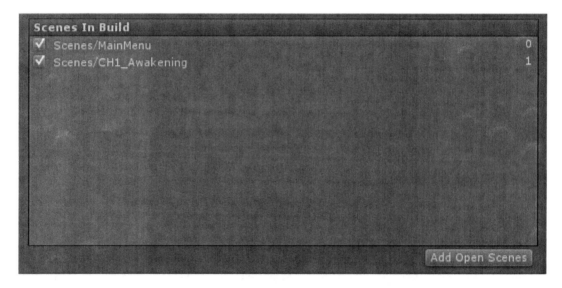

Load the MainMenu scene once more, and run the application. Nice! It is working as expected. The only other item I would like to add to this chapter before we move on, is the following code in the GameMaster.cs script.

```
using UnityEngine;
using UnityEngine.SceneManagement;
using System.Collections;
```

```
public class GameMaster : MonoBehaviour {

    // Use this for initialization
    void Start () {
        DontDestroyOnLoad(this);
    }
    // Update is called once per frame
    void Update () {

    }

    public void StartGame()
    {
        // NOTE: You should put in the name of the Scene
        // that respresents your level 1
        SceneManager.LoadScene("CH1_Awakening");
    }
}
```

The single line of code in the `Start()` function will make sure that the `_GameMaster` `GameObject` does not get destroyed when we move from one scene to the next. This is important, because we will be storing all of our game configuration and stats and so on. in this particular GameObject. When you run the game now from the `MainMenu` scene, you will notice that when you load level 1, the `_GameMaster` GameObject comes over automatically from the `MainMenu`. This is cool!

Summary

In this chapter, we established the atmosphere and the environment that is going to be representing our RPG. We have defined our levels, the setting of each level, the objective of each level and the outcome for each level.

We took the first level called Awakening and created the environment. We looked at how to use our assets and the Asset Store to incorporate 3D models in our scene. We also looked at how to plan the layout of the level. We introduced a third-person character controller into the scene to help us visualize how the level looks from the player's perspective and help us fine tune it as needed.

By the end of the chapter we also developed our `MainMenu` scene and our initial `GameMaster` script that will be used to glue the core of the game together.

In the next chapter we will start creating our player character and enhancing our `GameMaster` and `MainMenu` system.

3
Character Design

We are now at an interesting point in our development. In this chapter, we are going to discuss the design of our RPG characters and look at some of the attributes and characteristics that we need to design and implement.

Character definitions

To have a meaningful and interesting RPG, the game should usually have more than one character class. In `Chapter 1`, *In the Beginning*, we had defined the following class types:

- Barbarians
- Orcs
- Magician/Wizards
- Zombies
- Humans

We won't be able to implement all of the character types due to time. The demonstration of the implementation of one or two character types should give you a good ground to develop your own character classes. After all, that is the overall objective of this book.

One of the main characters is of course the PC. Let's go ahead and concentrate on the implementation of the PC and then we can start defining and designing the Barbarian class, the Human class, and perhaps the Orc class.

My character models are going to be from the Asset Store. You may either download the same characters or design your own. You can also use different type of character models. The point is to implement the character based on the specifications which will be defined in this chapter and beyond.

Let's take a look at some of the attributes that our player will have in general.

Base character class attributes

Let's start laying down the foundation we are going to need for the implementation of our character classes. The following is a list of attributes that are going to be part of the Base character class:

- Character class name
- Character class description
- List of attributes
    - Strength
    - Dexterity
    - Endurance
    - Intelligence
    - Social standing
    - Agility
    - Alertness
    - Vitality
    - Willpower

The attributes you define for your characters depend on the character type, but there are going to be some similarities between all character attributes, we would like to implement these similarities in a base class that will be shared with all character classes.

The list provided is just a sample, and you can add or subtract as you see fit.

Let's keep things simple, we will use only the four primary statistics for now:

- **Strength:** This is a measure of how physically strong a character is. Strength controls the maximum weight the character can carry, melee attack and/or damage, and sometimes hit points. Armor and weapons might also have a Strength requirement.
- **Defense:** This is a measure of how resilient a character is. Defense usually decreases taken damage by either a percentage or a fixed amount per hit.

Chapter 3

- **Dexterity:** This is a measure of how agile a character is. Dexterity controls attack and movement speed and accuracy, as well as evading an opponent's attack.
- **Intelligence:** This is a measure of a character's problem-solving ability. Intelligence often controls a character's ability to comprehend foreign languages and their skill in magic. In some cases, intelligence controls how many skill points the character gets at "level up". In some games, it controls the rate at which experience points are earned, or the amount needed to level up. This is sometimes combined with wisdom and/or willpower.
- **Health:** This determines if the character is alive or dead.

The attributes listed will be inherited by all character classes. Now let's put this into code. Create a new C# script and name it `BaseCharacter.cs`. Open the script and place the following code in file:

```
using UnityEngine;
using System.Collections;

public class BaseCharacter
{
    private string name;
    private string description;

    private float strength;
    private float defense;
    private float dexterity;
    private float intelligence;
    private float health;

    public string NAME
    {
        get { return this.name; }
        set { this.name = value; }
    }

    public string DESCRIPTION
    {
        get { return this.description; }
        set { this.description = value; }
    }

    public float STRENGTH
    {
        get { return this.strength; }
        set { this.strength = value; }
    }
```

[67]

Character Design

```csharp
    public float DEFENSE
    {
       get { return this.defense; }
       set { this.defense = value; }
    }

    public float DEXTERITY
    {
       get { return this.dexterity; }
       set { this.dexterity = value; }
    }

    public float INTELLIGENCE
    {
       get { return this.intelligence; }
       set { this.intelligence = value; }
    }

    public float HEALTH
    {
       get { return this.health; }
       set { this.health = value; }
    }
}
```

Character states

States are an important part of the character design. They will also drive the kind of actions and movement you will need to create for each state. For instance, at a minimum our character will need to have the following states implemented:

- Idle
- Walking
- Running
- Jumping
- Attacking
- Die

You character may have more states defined, this is something that you as the designer of the game will need to identify and eventually implement. Each one of the states identified will need to be implemented as an animation. The person creating the character models will usually also develop the animations for the character.

[68]

With the latest release of Unity 5, the **Mecanim Animation System** was introduced which is used to create easy workflow and setup of animations on humanoid characters, retargeting of animation from one character to the next, previewing of the animation clips, managing complex interactions between animations with a visual tool and animating different body parts with different logic.

> You can download *RawMocap Data* for Mecanim 1.1 from the asset store. The package contains several raw motion capture data files for your use. Beware, that you might have to do some adjustments on your own.

When creating your character models, it is a good idea to follow the proper bone structure setup for your characters. This will help make it easier controlling the states and the animations of your character as well as re-using your Animation Controller on multiple characters. This is also true if you are going to use a character from the Asset Store.

Character model

We should now consider how our player character is going to look. There are several approaches that can be taken. An easy way would be to have a predefined hero where the player does not have many options and choices when it comes to customization of the character. The other way would be to provide the player the ability to change and modify their character to an extent or fully. This all really depends on your budget!

We are going to do something in-between, to get the benefit of both worlds.

> You may use the Asset Store to download predefined characters that can be used as placeholders for your game while you create your own. You can even use some of the characters that are freely available through the Asset Store and modify them for your needs.

Once you have determined your character model, the next step is configuring it and customizing it for your game. The character model I have, can be visually modified to represent several unique characters.

You will need to study your character model carefully and understand how it is built so that you can modify it during design time and also during runtime if necessary.

[69]

Character Design

For instance, this is how my character model looks like in its raw format:

This particular model has several visual elements attached for weapons, clothing and so on... Your model may have been configured differently, if so, you will need to create your own attachment points and instantiate the weapons and or other character related assets accordingly:

Chapter 3

Select your model and investigate the structure of your model. You will notice that there is a certain pattern and naming convention to the model hierarchy as show in the preceding screenshot. Some models might have animations attached, to check them you will need to select the model from the project window and select the **Animation** tab in the **Inspector** window to get a list of the embedded animations for the model.

Character Design

In the **Inspector** Window select the Animations tab shown in the preceding screenshot, and notice the **Clips** section for all animations developed for your character model, as indicated in the following screenshot:

Notice that the animation clips have a start time and an end time. The actual character model is visually displayed at the bottom of the **Inspector** Window.

Rigging your model

There might be times that you will need to Rig your model to make it suitable for your game. This can be achieved by selecting your model source, and from the **Inspector** Window selecting the **Rig** tab as shown in the following screenshot:

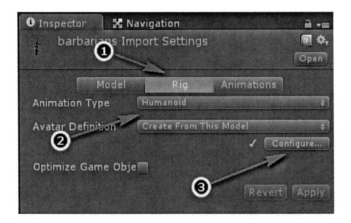

In the **Rig** tab, there are several options that you can apply to your model. Assuming that your character is of **Humanoid** type, you will need to select the **Humanoid Animation Type** if not already selected. The **Avatar Definition** can also be either created from the model or assigned if you have an avatar defined. Finally, you can click on the **Configure...** button to see the configuration of the rigged model.

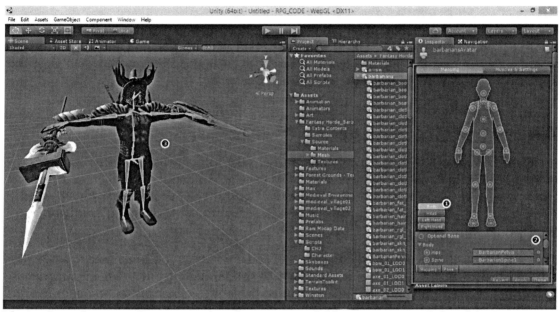

Notice from the preceding screenshot that your model has a mapping defined for its skeleton. If your model is of Humanoid type and if your model structure has been named properly, the system will automatically assign the correct bones and joints. If your naming is not per Unity specification, you can navigate your model structure and manually assign each point in the **Body**, **Head**, **Left Hand**, and **Right Hand**.

The **Muscles & Settings** tab will enable you to define and restrict the movement of the joints for your model. These can be very useful and practical for creating more realistic movements for your characters. You can study these topics further on your own as they will require a whole chapter or two to cover them.

Character Design

Character motion

Traditionally, the motion and movement of the characters were done separately through code. With the introduction of *Mecanim*, you are now able to apply what is called **Root motion**. This in return modifies the character's in-game transform based on the data in the root motion.

We are going to use root motion for our characters. Root motion works with the Animator Controller and the Animation State Machine. The Body Transform and Orientation are stored in the Animation Clip. This makes it easier for creating a state machine that plays the appropriate animation clip through the *Animator Controller*.

Animator Controller

In this section we will use the new Animator Controller to create our character states and determine the criteria for a change of states. To create an Animator Controller, in the project window right-click and select **Create | Animator Controller**. Give it a name. I have called mine CH3_Animator_Controller. Double-click the controller to open the Animator window.

The Animator Controller is a very complex tool and it will take you some time to study the different aspects and features that are available to you through it. The following diagram is a snapshot of an empty controller. I have marked the main sections of the Animator Window. There are two visible tabs, the **Layers** tab and the **Parameters** tab. In the **Layers** tab you will be able to create different layers that hold your animation states and the relevant *Transitions* from one state to the next. The **Parameters** tab is where you define your parameters that will be accessed and modified by the *Animator Controller* as well as through your code.

Chapter 3

There are a wide range of topics that you will need to know to fully appreciate the Mecanim system. We won't be going through all of the aspects in this book, but we will touch on some of the key aspects that are needed for our game.

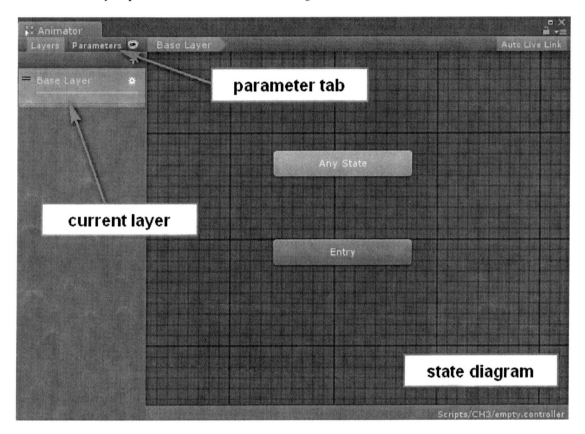

Animation states

To create a new state, you can simply drag and drop an animation from your project window. This will name and assign the relevant animation to the state in the layer. You can also create an empty state by right-clicking in the layer and selecting **Create State** | **Empty**. When a state is created, you can click on the state and observe its properties in the **Inspector** window:

 Your model may or may not have animations attached to it. The whole idea of the Mecanim system is to enable character modelers to work on their models while animators can use the skeleton of a humanoid Avatar to animate the character. This in turn makes it easier and better to have a set of animations applied to different types of character models!

To identify the state, it is best to provide it with a unique name that can be easily recognized in the state diagram. You will need to assign a Motion to it, this is the animation clip that will be playing when the state is active. The next important property would be the Transitions property. A transition will determine the condition of which state will be moving to another state, if there is such a requirement.

For instance, when the character is in an idle state, what the condition is for the character to change its state to a walking state, to a running state and so forth.

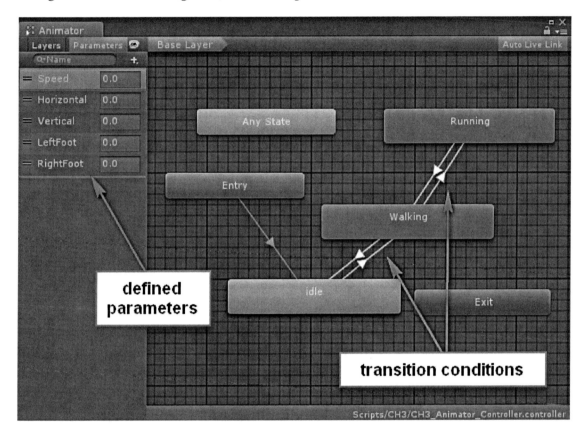

In the preceding screenshot, you will see I have defined three different states: idle, Walking, and Running. You also notice in the **Parameters** tab, I have defined some parameters. These parameters are used to determine when to move from idle to walking to running and back. The parameters are there to help you create the conditions for your state machine.

To create a Transition from one state to the next, right-click your state, and select **Make Transition**, then select the state it will transition to. This will create the visual arrow from the start state to the end state. Select the **Transition** arrow to get its properties and set the conditions in the **Inspector** window.

Character Design

The Walking and Running states are actually **Blend Tree** in this instance. A Blend Tree is used to make the transition from one animation state to the next more natural. In order for the blended motion to make sense, the motions that are blended must be of a similar nature and timing.

 Blend Trees are used for allowing multiple animations to be blended smoothly by incorporating parts of them all to varying degrees. The amount that each of the motions contribute to the final effect is controlled using a blending parameter, which is just one of the numeric animation parameters associated with the Animator Controller.

For instance, the walking state could look something like the following screenshot:

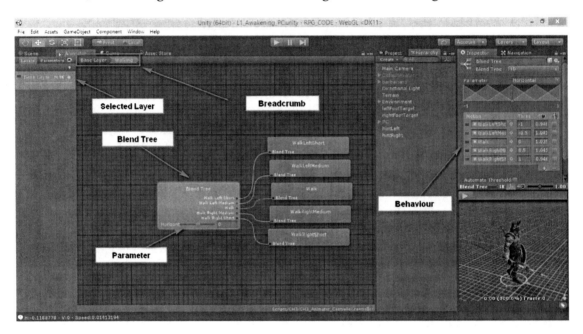

In our first Blend Tree node, we have five outputs: WalkLeftMedium, WalkLeftShort, Walk, WalkRightMedium, WalkRightShort. These are the animation clips that will be playing based on the value of the parameter called **Horizontal**. In the behavior region, you will notice a few thresholds that have been set up for the parameter, these thresholds are what determine which animation is to be played. The value of the **Horizontal** parameter is set through our C# code by passing in the value of the **Horizontal Axis** which is defined in the **Input Manager**.

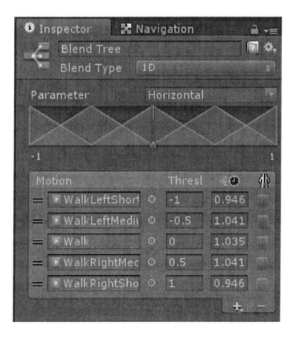

When you select a Blend Tree node, your **Inspector** window will give you the ability to add or remove the different animation states and also the parameter and the threshold of the parameter that will determine which animation will be rendered.

 The key to have a smooth looking blending in your animation, you will need to pay attention to your animation data.

Let's take a look at our final state diagram:

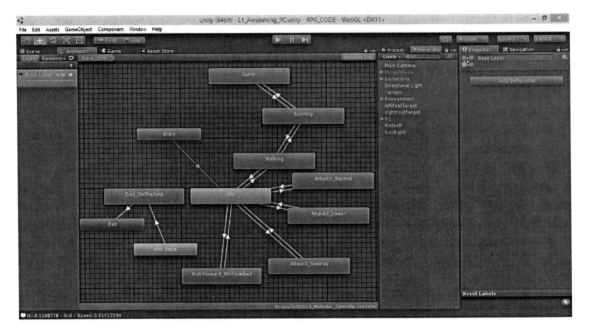

At this stage, I have gone ahead and implemented the state diagram for **idle**, **Walking**, **Running**, **Jump**, **Attack**, and **Walking** backwards. There is also a state for when the character dies.

The parameter that defines the transition from the Idle state to the Walking and Running States is the Speed parameter. If the speed value is greater than 0.1 it will transition from Idle to Walking, if it is greater than 0.6 it will transition from Walking to Running. The opposite is true for going from Running to Walking, and from Walking to Running.

Notice however, that the character can only enter the Jump state from the Running state. The parameter that controls this transition is the Jump parameter that is a Boolean value set by pressing the spacebar button on the keyboard.

There are also three unique attack states that can be entered from the Idle state. And a Die state that can be entered from any state. Well, because your character can die at any given time if you are not careful!

Let's take a look at how we can control these parameters.

Chapter 3

Character controller

It is time to enable our character to move around the scene. This is generally handled by the character controller. The character controller will be used to handle most of the interaction the player will have with the character in the game.

Create a new C# script and call it `CharacterController.cs`. Enter the following code in the `CharacterController` class. At the moment the code is very basic. Let's get a listing of the code and we can start discussing the different parts of the code after the listing:

```
using UnityEngine;
using System.Collections;

public class CharacterController : MonoBehaviour
{

    public Animator animator;
    public float directionDampTime;

    public float speed = 6.0f;
    public float h = 0.0f;
    public float v = 0.0f;

    public bool attack1 = false;
    public bool attack2 = false;
    public bool attack3 = false;

    public bool jump - false;

    public bool die = false;

    // Use this for initialization
    void Start()
    {
        this.animator = GetComponent<Animator>() as Animator;
    }

    // Update is called once per frame
    private Vector3 moveDirection = Vector3.zero;

    void Update()
    {

        if (Input.GetKeyDown(KeyCode.C))
        {
            this.attack1 = true;
            this.GetComponent<IKHandle>().enabled = false;
```

[81]

Character Design

```
   }
   if (Input.GetKeyUp(KeyCode.C))
   {
      this.attack1 = false;
      this.GetComponent<IKHandle>().enabled = true;
   }
   animator.SetBool("Attack1", attack1);

   if (Input.GetKeyDown(KeyCode.Z))
   {
      this.attack2 = true;
      this.GetComponent<IKHandle>().enabled = false;
   }
   if (Input.GetKeyUp(KeyCode.Z))
   {
      this.attack2 = false;
      this.GetComponent<IKHandle>().enabled = true;
   }
   animator.SetBool("Attack2", attack2);

   if (Input.GetKeyDown(KeyCode.X))
   {
      this.attack3 = true;
      this.GetComponent<IKHandle>().enabled = false;
   }
   if (Input.GetKeyUp(KeyCode.X))
   {
      this.attack3 = false;
      this.GetComponent<IKHandle>().enabled = true;
   }
   animator.SetBool("Attack3", attack3);

   if (Input.GetKeyDown(KeyCode.Space))
   {
      this.jump = true;
      this.GetComponent<IKHandle>().enabled = false;
   }
   if (Input.GetKeyUp(KeyCode.Space))
   {
      this.jump = false;
      this.GetComponent<IKHandle>().enabled = true;
   }
   animator.SetBool("Jump", jump);

   if (Input.GetKeyDown(KeyCode.I))
   {
      this.die = true;
      SendMessage("Died");
```

```
    }

    animator.SetBool("Die", die);
}

void FixedUpdate()
{

    // The Inputs are defined in the Input Manager
    // get value for horizontal axis
    h = Input.GetAxis("Horizontal");
    // get value for vertical axis
    v = Input.GetAxis("Vertical");

    speed = new Vector2(h, v).sqrMagnitude;

    // Used to get values on console
    Debug.Log(string.Format("H:{0} - V:{1} - Speed:{2}", h, v, speed));

    animator.SetFloat("Speed", speed);
    animator.SetFloat("Horizontal", h);
    animator.SetFloat("Vertical", v);
}
}
```

In the `Start()` function we are going to get a reference to the Animator Controller. We will be using the `FixedUpdate()` function to perform our updates for the character movement.

What is the difference between the `Update()` function and the `FixedUpdate()`? The `Update()` function is called every frame and is used regularly to update the moving of non-physics object, simple timers, and input processing. The update interval time varies for the *Update()* function. `FixedUpdate()` is called every physics step. The interval is consistent and used for adjusting physics on Rigidbody.

In the `FixedUpdate()` function, we get the inputs for our Horizontal and Vertical axis, we calculate the `speed` value, and set the parameters defined in the Animator Controller using the `animator.SetFloat()` function. These parameters are then used by the animator controller to decide which state the character is at.

Character Design

For instance, to go from an idle state to the walking state, the `speed` parameter needs to be greater than 0.1, and from walking to running, the `speed` parameter will need to be greater than 0.6. The opposite is true when you want to go back from the running state to the walking state and from the walking state to the idle state. The Horizontal and Vertical parameters control the movement for turning left or turning right. All these three parameters combined control what state and what animation the character is rendering.

The next step is for us to enable the Jump, Die and Attack states. The Jump state can be only entered while the character is running and the `Jump` Boolean variable is set to true. The jump condition is set in the `Update()` function when the spacebar is pressed by the player. This sets the variable to `true` and passes the variable to the animator controller.

The same mechanism is used for the three attack states: `Attack1_Normal`, `Attack2_Lower`, and `Attack3_Destroy`. These are mapped to the following keys on the keyboard: *C, Z, and X* respectively. Each one will set its Boolean value to true and pass it into the animator controller. However, the player can only enter these three states from the idle state. We will leave it as is for now.

Finally, the Die state is implemented and for now we are using the keyboard input I to test it out. The main difference between the die state and the other states so far is that the die state can be entered from any state.

We are not using Blend Trees for these states as there is only one type of animation for the state. You will also notice that the states can only be transitioned to from the idle state. This is due to how the animations and model was set up initially. Yours could be different.

Chapter 3

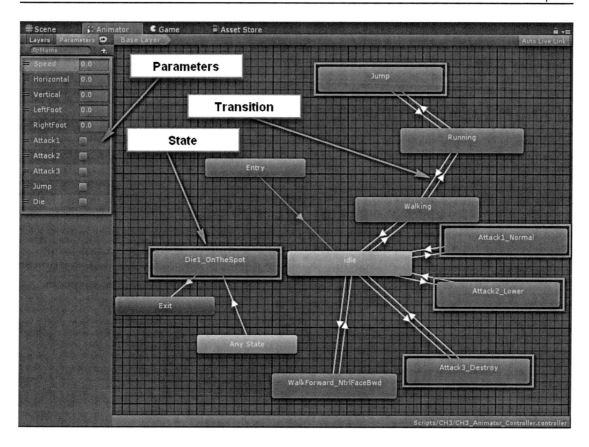

The character can get into a die state from any state. That is, your character player can die at any time in the game during whatever state he or she is at. However, for the attack and jump states, we need to be at the idle state for us to be able to transition smoothly into the proper state. You can improve these transitions and state based on the level of your animation complexity, but for now, this should do.

Character Design

These states are controlled through Boolean parameters defined in the animator. At this stage, you should be able to use your model to test the scene and also your character animations and states.

Modification to animations

There might be times that you will need to make some changes and or modifications to the existing modification that will make it work properly with your game and the state machine.

The attack animations prepared for my character model need to be adjusted to make them loop while the character is still in that particular state. For instance, if I use the existing animation and the character state goes into attack mode, the animation will play only once. This is not what I intend to do, I am building the attack input to perform the attack while the attack key is pressed down. Changing the animation loop setting is easy, to do so, select the animation from your project window and select the **Edit...** button from the **Inspector** window as shown in the screenshot:

You will now be in the **Edit** mode of the animation as displayed in the next screenshot. I have placed the **Inspector** window side by side to illustrate the **Animation** tab, selecting each animation we want to modify, one at a time, and setting the **Loop Time** property to true (checked).

Chapter 3

In this particular screenshot you will also notice several other important properties for the animation such as: **Root Transform Rotation**, **Mirror**, **Curves**, **Events**, **Mask**, and **Motion**. We are going to use the Curves property when we set out Inverse Kinematics for some of our animations regarding our character. This basically sets the values of predefined parameters that can be used to set or get them through Mecanim:

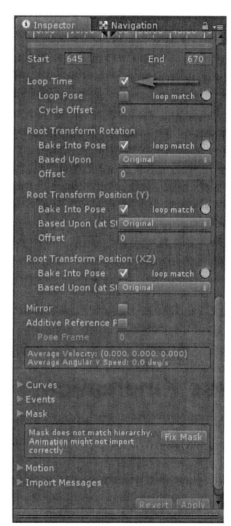

Character Design

If your animations are attached to your model and your animations and models are older, you will most likely need to make some modifications to them. For instance, one of the main properties that you might have to set for a particular animation clip would be the **Loop Time** property as shown in the preceding screenshot. This will make sure that the animation will loop as long as you are in the state which is running the animation. If looping is not enabled, the animation will run once and stop, even if you are still in the state representing the animation.

So make sure the **Loop Time** property is set for the idle, walking, running, and attacking animations. At the same time, not all animation clips need to be looped, for instance, the jump and die animations just need to be played once. So you will need to be diligent and check all of these properties.

Other animation will need to be modified to enable baking the transform into the model. For instance, the die and jump animations have the following properties checked: **Root Transform Rotation** and **Root Transform Position (Y)**, make sure that the **Bake Into Pose** property is checked. This is important to make sure the animation and the skeletal movement of the character are harmonized at the root transform position.

Your animation might seem funky if these properties are not set properly. So if there is something weird going on, make sure to double check these properties.

If you have not done so by now, you should attach your `CharacterController.cs` script to your player character.

Inverse Kinematics

Inverse Kinematics (IK) are important in game programming. It is typically used to make the character's movement more realistic in the world. One of the main uses of IK is the calculation of the player's feet and how they relate to the ground they are standing on.

In short, IK, is used to determine the position and rotation of the joints in a character based on a given position in space. For instance, to make sure the foot of a player is landing properly on the terrain it is walking on.

Unity has a built in IK system that can be used to do some basic calculation in this regard. Let's go ahead and implement the foot IK for our character. There are a few things that you will need to set up before we can enable IK for our humanoid character. The first thing to do is check your layer in the Animator Controller and use the *engine icon* to enter the settings window. Make sure that **IK Pass** is checked as shown in the following screenshot. You will also need to provide a **Mask** if you have not done so already. The mask is used to dictate which parts of the skeleton are affected by the IK.

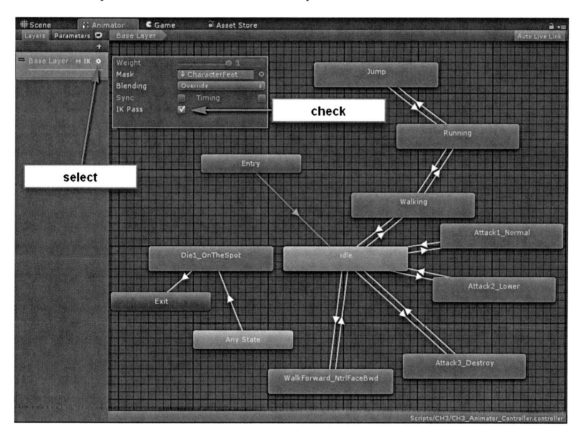

Once you have set up this, the fun begins. We need to create a C# script that will handle our IK. Create a C# script and call it `IKHandle.cs`. Type the following code into the script:

```
using UnityEngine;
using System.Collections;

public class IKHandle : MonoBehaviour
{
    Animator anim;
```

Character Design

```csharp
    public Transform leftIKTarget;
    public Transform rightIKTarget;

    public Transform hintLeft;
    public Transform hintRight;

    public float ikWeight = 1f;

    // to make it dynamic
    Vector3 leftFootPosition;
    Vector3 rightFootPosition;

    Quaternion leftFootRotation;
    Quaternion rightFootRotation;

    float leftFootWeight;
    float rightFootWeight;

    Transform leftFoot;
    Transform rightFoot;

    public float offsetY;

    // Use this for initialization
    void Start()
    {
        anim = GetComponent<Animator>();

        leftFoot = anim.GetBoneTransform(HumanBodyBones.LeftFoot);
        rightFoot = anim.GetBoneTransform(HumanBodyBones.RightFoot);

        leftFootRotation = leftFoot.rotation;
        rightFootRotation = rightFoot.rotation;

    }

    // Update is called once per frame
    void Update()
    {
        RaycastHit leftHit;
        RaycastHit rightHit;

        Vector3 lpos = leftFoot.TransformPoint(Vector3.zero);
        Vector3 rpos = rightFoot.TransformPoint(Vector3.zero);

        if (Physics.Raycast(lpos, -Vector3.up, out leftHit, 1))
        {
            leftFootPosition = leftHit.point;
```

Chapter 3

```
        leftFootRotation = Quaternion.FromToRotation(transform.up,
        leftHit.normal) * transform.rotation;
    }

    if (Physics.Raycast(rpos, -Vector3.up, out rightHit, 1))
    {
        rightFootPosition = rightHit.point;
        rightFootRotation = Quaternion.FromToRotation(transform.up,
        rightHit.normal) * transform.rotation;
    }
}

public bool Die = false;
public void Died()
{

    Debug.Log("I AM DEAD!");
    this.Die = true;
}

void OnAnimatorIK()
{
    leftFootWeight = anim.GetFloat("LeftFoot");
    rightFootWeight = anim.GetFloat("RightFoot");

    anim.SetIKPositionWeight(AvatarIKGoal.LeftFoot, leftFootWeight);
    anim.SetIKPositionWeight(AvatarIKGoal.RightFoot, rightFootWeight);
    anim.SetIKPosition(AvatarIKGoal.LeftFoot, leftFootPosition +
    new Vector3(0f, offsetY, 0f));
    anim.SetIKPosition(AvatarIKGoal.RightFoot, rightFootPosition +
    new Vector3(0f, offsetY, 0f));

    anim.SetIKRotationWeight(AvatarIKGoal.LeftFoot, leftFootWeight);
    anim.SetIKRotationWeight(AvatarIKGoal.RightFoot, rightFootWeight);
    anim.SetIKRotation(AvatarIKGoal.LeftFoot, leftFootRotation);
    anim.SetIKRotation(AvatarIKGoal.RightFoot, rightFootRotation);

    }
}
```

This script is a bit involved. In order for the IK to work properly, we need important points in space. One of these points is the position of the target in space that we want our foot to move to, and the second point in space is the hint. These two points in space are used to control the movement and translations of the skeleton for a particular joint to be made in order to successfully complete the IK for the target position.

Character Design

The variables `leftFootPosition` and `rightFootPosition` are used to represent the target position for the left and right foot during runtime. `leftFootRotation` and `rightFootRotation` is used to store the rotation of the left and right foot.

We also need two variables to actually reference our left and right foot in the model. These are done by the `leftFoot` and `rightFoot` variables.

Some of these variables are initialized in the `Start()` function. Specifically speaking, we get a reference to the left and right foot from the Animator Controller bone structure defined for humanoids.

In the `Update()` function, we use `Physics.Raycast()` to perform some raycasting to determine the position of our left and right foot. This data is then used and stored in the variables `leftFootPosition` and `rightFootPosition` variables with their equivalent rotation data in the `leftFootRotation` and right `FootRotation` variables:

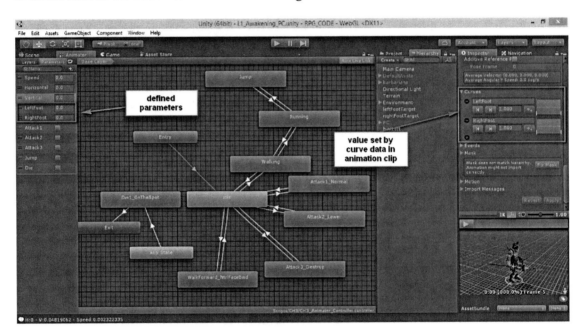

The actual IK Animation is applied in the `OnAnimatorIK()` function. The `leftFootWight` and `rightFootWeight` variables are used to get the parameter values set for the `LeftFoot` and `RightFoot` in the Animator Controller through the animation clip Curve function.

> The key here is to properly define the curve of the animation clip that will be used to drive the weight of the IK. The preceding screenshot only shows the curve of the idle state, both feet are on the ground, therefore the value is set to 1. For your walking and running clips, your curve will be different.

Finally, the SetIKPositionWeight() and SetIKPosition() functions are used to properly adjust the position and rotation of the feet relative to the ground! Notice that this is performed for each foot separately.

Attach the IKHandle.cs script to your character and do a test run. Notice the difference of your character and the way it is interacting with the floor or the terrain you have set up.

Summary

We covered a lot of topics in this chapter. We discussed the different character definitions we are going to be using for our game, looked at the base character class attributes that will be shared by all of our characters, created the BaseCharacter class to be used later in the game, discussed the primary states our character will have in the game and how to implement them using the Animator Controller.

We looked at how to rig our character model to be prepared for the Mecanim system and how to use the Mecanim system to create animation and state diagrams that will determine how the character is behaving during game play. Then we implemented our initial character controller script that handles the state of our character. This gave us the opportunity to look at the Blend Trees and transition from one state to the next using parameters. Looked at how to modify animation clips if there is a need for it.

Finally looked at Inverse Kinematics that will help our character behave more realistically in the game environment.

By the end of the chapter you should have a good grasp of all of the different components that are working together to make your character look, behave, and move in the game environment.

In the next chapter we will be introducing non-character behaviors.

4

Player Character and Non-Player Character Design

In Chapter 3, *Character Design*, we covered a wide range of topics to prepare your character model for the game. We looked at how to import and set up our character model, created the BaseCharacter class, used the Animator Controller to set up the state diagram and created the initial character controller to handle the motion and behavior of our character model and finally looked at some basic inverse kinematics for the foot.

In this chapter we will expand on the character player and also the non-character player.

- Customizing the Player Character
    - Customizable parts (Model)
    - C# Code for customization
    - Preserving character state
    - Recap
- Non-Player Characters (NPCs)
    - Non-Player character basics
    - Setting up the Non-Player Character
    - Navmesh setup
    - NPC Animator Controller
    - NPC attack
    - NPC AI
- PC and NPC Interaction

Customizing the Player Character

One of the key features of an RPG is to be able to customize your character player. In this section we will take a look at how we can provide a means to achieve this.

Once again, the approach and concept are universal, but the actual implementation might be a little different based on your model structure.

Create a new scene and name it `CharacterCustomization`. Create a `Cube` prefab and set it to the origin. Change the `Scale` of the cube to <5, 0.1, 5>, you can also change the name of the GameObject to `Base`. This will be the platform that our character model stands on while the player customizes his/her character before game play.

Drag and drop the `fbx` file representing your character model into the `Scene View`. The next few steps will entirely depend on your model hierarchy and structure as designed by the modeler.

To illustrate the point, I have placed the same model in the scene twice. The one on the left is the model that has been configured to display only the basics, the model on the right is the model in its original state as shown in the following screenshot:

Chapter 4

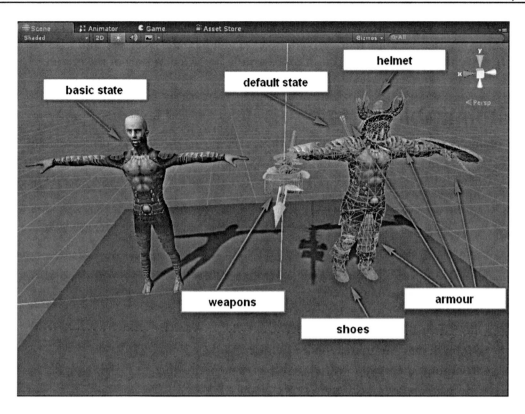

Notice that this particular model I am using has everything attached. These include the different types of weapons, shoes, helmets, and armour. The instantiated prefab on the left hand side has turned off all of the extras from the GameObject's hierarchy. Here is how the hierarchy looks in the `Hierarchy View`:

[97]

The model has a very extensive hierarchy in its structure, the preceding screenshot is a small snippet to demonstrate that you will need to navigate the structure and manually identify and enable or disable the mesh representing a particular part of the model.

Customizable parts

Based on my model, I can customize a few things on my 3D model. I can customize the shoulder pads, I can customize the body type, I can customize the weapons and armor it has, I can customize the helmet and shoes, and finally I can also customize the skin texture to give it different looks.

Let's get a listing of all the different customizable items we have for our character:

- **Shoulder Shields:** there are four types
- **Body Type:** there are three body types; skinny, buff, and chubby
- **Armor:** knee pad, leg plate
- **Shields:** there are two types of shields
- **Boots:** there are two types of boots
- **Helmet:** there are four types of helmets
- **Weapons:** there are 13 different types of weapons
- **Skins:** there are 13 different types of skins

User interface

Now that we know what our options are for customizing our player character, we can start thinking about the User Interface (UI) that will be used to enable the customization of the character.

To design our UI, we will need to create a `Canvas` GameObject, this is done by right-clicking in the **Hierarchy View** and selecting **Create | UI | Canvas**. This will place a `Canvas` GameObject and an `EventSystem` GameObject in the `Hierarchy View`.

It is assumed that you already know how to create a UI in Unity. If you do not, please refer to *Chapter 5, Introduction to Game Programming: Using C# and Unity 3D*.

Chapter 4

I am going to use a Panel to group the customizable items. For the moment I will be using checkboxes for some items and scroll bars for the weapons and skin texture. The following screenshot will illustrate how my UI for customization looks:

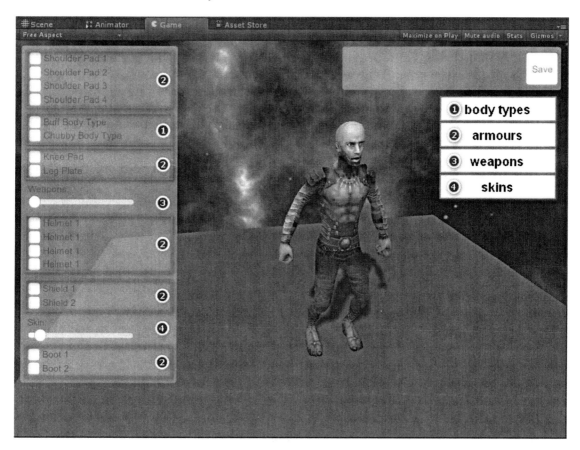

These UI elements will need to be integrated with Event Handlers that will perform the necessary actions for enabling or disabling certain parts of the character model.

For instance, using the UI I can select Shoulder Pad 4, Buff Body Type, move the scroll bar until the Hammer weapon shows up, selecting the second Helmet checkbox, selecting Shield 1 and Boot 2, my character will look like the following screenshot:

We need a way to refer to each one of the meshes representing the different types of customizable objects on the model. This will be done through a C# script. The script will need to keep track of all the parts we are going to be managing for customization.

Some models will not have the extra meshes attached. You can always create empty GameObjects at a particular location on the model, and you can dynamically instantiate the prefab representing your custom object at the given point. This can also be done for our current model, for instance, if we have a special space weapon that somehow gets dropped by the aliens in the game world, we can attach the weapon to our model through C# code. The important thing is to understand the concept, and the rest is up to you!

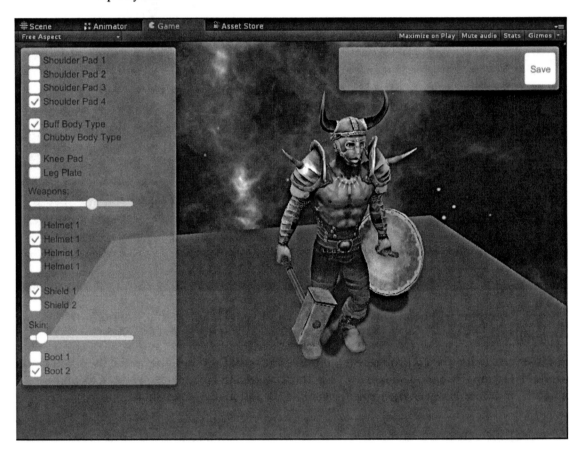

Chapter 4

The Code for character customization

Things don't happen automatically. So we need to create some C# code that will handle the customization of our character model. The script we create here will handle the UI events that will drive the enabling and disabling of different parts of the model mesh.

Create a new C# script and call it `CharacterCustomization.cs`. This script will be attached to the `Base` GameObject in the scene. Here is a listing of the script:

```
using UnityEngine;
using UnityEngine.UI;
using System.Collections;
using UnityEngine.SceneManagement;

public class CharacterCustomization : MonoBehaviour
{

    public GameObject PLAYER_CHARACTER;

    public Material[] PLAYER_SKIN;

    public GameObject CLOTH_01LOD0;
    public GameObject CLOTH_01LOD0_SKIN;
    public GameObject CLOTH_02LOD0;
    public GameObject CLOTH_02LOD0_SKIN;
    public GameObject CLOTH_03LOD0;
    public GameObject CLOTH_03LOD0_SKIN;
    public GameObject CLOTH_03LOD0_FAT;

    public GameObject BELT_LOD0;

    public GameObject SKN_LOD0;
    public GameObject FAT_LOD0;
    public GameObject RGL_LOD0;

    public GameObject HAIR_LOD0;

    public GameObject BOW_LOD0;

    // Head Equipment
    public GameObject GLADIATOR_01LOD0;
    public GameObject HELMET_01LOD0;
    public GameObject HELMET_02LOD0;
    public GameObject HELMET_03LOD0;
    public GameObject HELMET_04LOD0;

    // Shoulder Pad - Right Arm / Left Arm
```

[101]

Player Character and Non-Player Character Design

```
public GameObject SHOULDER_PAD_R_01LOD0;
public GameObject SHOULDER_PAD_R_02LOD0;
public GameObject SHOULDER_PAD_R_03LOD0;
public GameObject SHOULDER_PAD_R_04LOD0;

public GameObject SHOULDER_PAD_L_01LOD0;
public GameObject SHOULDER_PAD_L_02LOD0;
public GameObject SHOULDER_PAD_L_03LOD0;
public GameObject SHOULDER_PAD_L_04LOD0;

// Fore Arm - Right / Left Plates
public GameObject ARM_PLATE_R_1LOD0;
public GameObject ARM_PLATE_R_2LOD0;

public GameObject ARM_PLATE_L_1LOD0;
public GameObject ARM_PLATE_L_2LOD0;

// Player Character Weapons
public GameObject AXE_01LOD0;
public GameObject AXE_02LOD0;
public GameObject CLUB_01LOD0;
public GameObject CLUB_02LOD0;
public GameObject FALCHION_LOD0;
public GameObject GLADIUS_LOD0;
public GameObject MACE_LOD0;
public GameObject MAUL_LOD0;
public GameObject SCIMITAR_LOD0;
public GameObject SPEAR_LOD0;
public GameObject SWORD_BASTARD_LOD0;
public GameObject SWORD_BOARD_01LOD0;
public GameObject SWORD_SHORT_LOD0;

// Player Character Defense Weapons
public GameObject SHIELD_01LOD0;
public GameObject SHIELD_02LOD0;

public GameObject QUIVER_LOD0;
public GameObject BOW_01_LOD0;

// Player Character Calf - Right / Left
public GameObject KNEE_PAD_R_LOD0;
public GameObject LEG_PLATE_R_LOD0;

public GameObject KNEE_PAD_L_LOD0;
public GameObject LEG_PLATE_L_LOD0;

public GameObject BOOT_01LOD0;
public GameObject BOOT_02LOD0;
```

```csharp
    // Use this for initialization
    void Start()
    {

    }

    public bool ROTATE_MODEL = false;
    // Update is called once per frame
    void Update()
    {
        if (Input.GetKeyUp(KeyCode.R))
        {
            this.ROTATE_MODEL = !this.ROTATE_MODEL;
        }

        if (this.ROTATE_MODEL)
        {
            this.PLAYER_CHARACTER.transform.Rotate(new Vector3(0, 1, 0), 33.0f
* Time.deltaTime);
        }

        if (Input.GetKeyUp(KeyCode.L))
        {

            Debug.Log(PlayerPrefs.GetString("NAME"));
        }

    }


    public void SetShoulderPad(Toggle id)
    {
        switch (id.name)
        {
            case "SP-01":
                {
                    this.SHOULDER_PAD_R_01LOD0.SetActive(id.isOn);
                    this.SHOULDER_PAD_R_02LOD0.SetActive(false);
                    this.SHOULDER_PAD_R_03LOD0.SetActive(false);
                    this.SHOULDER_PAD_R_04LOD0.SetActive(false);

                    this.SHOULDER_PAD_L_01LOD0.SetActive(id.isOn);
                    this.SHOULDER_PAD_L_02LOD0.SetActive(false);
                    this.SHOULDER_PAD_L_03LOD0.SetActive(false);
                    this.SHOULDER_PAD_L_04LOD0.SetActive(false);

                    PlayerPrefs.SetInt("SP-01", 1);
                    PlayerPrefs.SetInt("SP-02", 0);
```

Player Character and Non-Player Character Design

```
        PlayerPrefs.SetInt("SP-03", 0);
        PlayerPrefs.SetInt("SP-04", 0);
        break;
    }
case "SP-02":
    {
        this.SHOULDER_PAD_R_01LOD0.SetActive(false);
        this.SHOULDER_PAD_R_02LOD0.SetActive(id.isOn);
        this.SHOULDER_PAD_R_03LOD0.SetActive(false);
        this.SHOULDER_PAD_R_04LOD0.SetActive(false);

        this.SHOULDER_PAD_L_01LOD0.SetActive(false);
        this.SHOULDER_PAD_L_02LOD0.SetActive(id.isOn);
        this.SHOULDER_PAD_L_03LOD0.SetActive(false);
        this.SHOULDER_PAD_L_04LOD0.SetActive(false);

        PlayerPrefs.SetInt("SP-01", 0);
        PlayerPrefs.SetInt("SP-02", 1);
        PlayerPrefs.SetInt("SP-03", 0);
        PlayerPrefs.SetInt("SP-04", 0);
        break;
    }
case "SP-03":
    {
        this.SHOULDER_PAD_R_01LOD0.SetActive(false);
        this.SHOULDER_PAD_R_02LOD0.SetActive(false);
        this.SHOULDER_PAD_R_03LOD0.SetActive(id.isOn);
        this.SHOULDER_PAD_R_04LOD0.SetActive(false);

        this.SHOULDER_PAD_L_01LOD0.SetActive(false);
        this.SHOULDER_PAD_L_02LOD0.SetActive(false);
        this.SHOULDER_PAD_L_03LOD0.SetActive(id.isOn);
        this.SHOULDER_PAD_L_04LOD0.SetActive(false);

        PlayerPrefs.SetInt("SP-01", 0);
        PlayerPrefs.SetInt("SP-02", 0);
        PlayerPrefs.SetInt("SP-03", 1);
        PlayerPrefs.SetInt("SP-04", 0);
        break;
    }
case "SP-04":
    {
        this.SHOULDER_PAD_R_01LOD0.SetActive(false);
        this.SHOULDER_PAD_R_02LOD0.SetActive(false);
        this.SHOULDER_PAD_R_03LOD0.SetActive(false);
        this.SHOULDER_PAD_R_04LOD0.SetActive(id.isOn);

        this.SHOULDER_PAD_L_01LOD0.SetActive(false);
```

```csharp
                this.SHOULDER_PAD_L_02LOD0.SetActive(false);
                this.SHOULDER_PAD_L_03LOD0.SetActive(false);
                this.SHOULDER_PAD_L_04LOD0.SetActive(id.isOn);

                PlayerPrefs.SetInt("SP-01", 0);
                PlayerPrefs.SetInt("SP-02", 0);
                PlayerPrefs.SetInt("SP-03", 0);
                PlayerPrefs.SetInt("SP-04", 1);

                break;
            }
        }
    }
}

public void SetBodyType(Toggle id)
{
    switch (id.name)
    {
        case "BT-01":
            {
                this.RGL_LOD0.SetActive(id.isOn);
                this.FAT_LOD0.SetActive(false);
                break;
            }
        case "BT-02":
            {
                this.RGL_LOD0.SetActive(false);
                this.FAT_LOD0.SetActive(id.isOn);
                break;
            }
    }
}

public void SetKneePad(Toggle id)
{
    this.KNEE_PAD_R_LOD0.SetActive(id.isOn);
    this.KNEE_PAD_L_LOD0.SetActive(id.isOn);
}

public void SetLegPlate(Toggle id)
{
    this.LEG_PLATE_R_LOD0.SetActive(id.isOn);
    this.LEG_PLATE_L_LOD0.SetActive(id.isOn);
}

public void SetWeaponType(Slider id)
{
    switch (System.Convert.ToInt32(id.value))
```

Player Character and Non-Player Character Design

```
{
    case 0:
        {
            this.AXE_01LOD0.SetActive(false);
            this.AXE_02LOD0.SetActive(false);
            this.CLUB_01LOD0.SetActive(false);
            this.CLUB_02LOD0.SetActive(false);
            this.FALCHION_LOD0.SetActive(false);
            this.GLADIUS_LOD0.SetActive(false);
            this.MACE_LOD0.SetActive(false);
            this.MAUL_LOD0.SetActive(false);
            this.SCIMITAR_LOD0.SetActive(false);
            this.SPEAR_LOD0.SetActive(false);
            this.SWORD_BASTARD_LOD0.SetActive(false);
            this.SWORD_BOARD_01LOD0.SetActive(false);
            this.SWORD_SHORT_LOD0.SetActive(false);
            break;
        }
    case 1:
        {
            this.AXE_01LOD0.SetActive(true);
            this.AXE_02LOD0.SetActive(false);
            this.CLUB_01LOD0.SetActive(false);
            this.CLUB_02LOD0.SetActive(false);
            this.FALCHION_LOD0.SetActive(false);
            this.GLADIUS_LOD0.SetActive(false);
            this.MACE_LOD0.SetActive(false);
            this.MAUL_LOD0.SetActive(false);
            this.SCIMITAR_LOD0.SetActive(false);
            this.SPEAR_LOD0.SetActive(false);
            this.SWORD_BASTARD_LOD0.SetActive(false);
            this.SWORD_BOARD_01LOD0.SetActive(false);
            this.SWORD_SHORT_LOD0.SetActive(false);
            break;
        }
    case 2:
        {
            this.AXE_01LOD0.SetActive(false);
            this.AXE_02LOD0.SetActive(true);
            this.CLUB_01LOD0.SetActive(false);
            this.CLUB_02LOD0.SetActive(false);
            this.FALCHION_LOD0.SetActive(false);
            this.GLADIUS_LOD0.SetActive(false);
            this.MACE_LOD0.SetActive(false);
            this.MAUL_LOD0.SetActive(false);
            this.SCIMITAR_LOD0.SetActive(false);
            this.SPEAR_LOD0.SetActive(false);
            this.SWORD_BASTARD_LOD0.SetActive(false);
```

```
            this.SWORD_BOARD_01LOD0.SetActive(false);
            this.SWORD_SHORT_LOD0.SetActive(false);
            break;
        }
    case 3:
        {
            this.AXE_01LOD0.SetActive(false);
            this.AXE_02LOD0.SetActive(false);
            this.CLUB_01LOD0.SetActive(true);
            this.CLUB_02LOD0.SetActive(false);
            this.FALCHION_LOD0.SetActive(false);
            this.GLADIUS_LOD0.SetActive(false);
            this.MACE_LOD0.SetActive(false);
            this.MAUL_LOD0.SetActive(false);
            this.SCIMITAR_LOD0.SetActive(false);
            this.SPEAR_LOD0.SetActive(false);
            this.SWORD_BASTARD_LOD0.SetActive(false);
            this.SWORD_BOARD_01LOD0.SetActive(false);
            this.SWORD_SHORT_LOD0.SetActive(false);
            break;
        }
    case 4:
        {
            this.AXE_01LOD0.SetActive(false);
            this.AXE_02LOD0.SetActive(false);
            this.CLUB_01LOD0.SetActive(false);
            this.CLUB_02LOD0.SetActive(true);
            this.FALCHION_LOD0.SetActive(false);
            this.GLADIUS_LOD0.SetActive(false);
            this.MACE_LOD0.SetActive(false);
            this.MAUL_LOD0.SetActive(false);
            this.SCIMITAR_LOD0.SetActive(false);
            this.SPEAR_LOD0.SetActive(false);
            this.SWORD_BASTARD_LOD0.SetActive(false);
            this.SWORD_BOARD_01LOD0.SetActive(false);
            this.SWORD_SHORT_LOD0.SetActive(false);
            break;
        }
    case 5:
        {
            this.AXE_01LOD0.SetActive(false);
            this.AXE_02LOD0.SetActive(false);
            this.CLUB_01LOD0.SetActive(false);
            this.CLUB_02LOD0.SetActive(false);
            this.FALCHION_LOD0.SetActive(true);
            this.GLADIUS_LOD0.SetActive(false);
            this.MACE_LOD0.SetActive(false);
            this.MAUL_LOD0.SetActive(false);
```

Player Character and Non-Player Character Design

```
            this.SCIMITAR_LOD0.SetActive(false);
            this.SPEAR_LOD0.SetActive(false);
            this.SWORD_BASTARD_LOD0.SetActive(false);
            this.SWORD_BOARD_01LOD0.SetActive(false);
            this.SWORD_SHORT_LOD0.SetActive(false);
            break;
        }
    case 6:
        {
            this.AXE_01LOD0.SetActive(false);
            this.AXE_02LOD0.SetActive(false);
            this.CLUB_01LOD0.SetActive(false);
            this.CLUB_02LOD0.SetActive(false);
            this.FALCHION_LOD0.SetActive(false);
            this.GLADIUS_LOD0.SetActive(true);
            this.MACE_LOD0.SetActive(false);
            this.MAUL_LOD0.SetActive(false);
            this.SCIMITAR_LOD0.SetActive(false);
            this.SPEAR_LOD0.SetActive(false);
            this.SWORD_BASTARD_LOD0.SetActive(false);
            this.SWORD_BOARD_01LOD0.SetActive(false);
            this.SWORD_SHORT_LOD0.SetActive(false);
            break;
        }
    case 7:
        {
            this.AXE_01LOD0.SetActive(false);
            this.AXE_02LOD0.SetActive(false);
            this.CLUB_01LOD0.SetActive(false);
            this.CLUB_02LOD0.SetActive(false);
            this.FALCHION_LOD0.SetActive(false);
            this.GLADIUS_LOD0.SetActive(false);
            this.MACE_LOD0.SetActive(true);
            this.MAUL_LOD0.SetActive(false);
            this.SCIMITAR_LOD0.SetActive(false);
            this.SPEAR_LOD0.SetActive(false);
            this.SWORD_BASTARD_LOD0.SetActive(false);
            this.SWORD_BOARD_01LOD0.SetActive(false);
            this.SWORD_SHORT_LOD0.SetActive(false);
            break;
        }
    case 8:
        {
            this.AXE_01LOD0.SetActive(false);
            this.AXE_02LOD0.SetActive(false);
            this.CLUB_01LOD0.SetActive(false);
            this.CLUB_02LOD0.SetActive(false);
            this.FALCHION_LOD0.SetActive(false);
```

```
                this.GLADIUS_LOD0.SetActive(false);
                this.MACE_LOD0.SetActive(false);
                this.MAUL_LOD0.SetActive(true);
                this.SCIMITAR_LOD0.SetActive(false);
                this.SPEAR_LOD0.SetActive(false);
                this.SWORD_BASTARD_LOD0.SetActive(false);
                this.SWORD_BOARD_01LOD0.SetActive(false);
                this.SWORD_SHORT_LOD0.SetActive(false);
                break;
        }
        case 9:
        {
                this.AXE_01LOD0.SetActive(false);
                this.AXE_02LOD0.SetActive(false);
                this.CLUB_01LOD0.SetActive(false);
                this.CLUB_02LOD0.SetActive(false);
                this.FALCHION_LOD0.SetActive(false);
                this.GLADIUS_LOD0.SetActive(false);
                this.MACE_LOD0.SetActive(false);
                this.MAUL_LOD0.SetActive(false);
                this.SCIMITAR_LOD0.SetActive(true);
                this.SPEAR_LOD0.SetActive(false);
                this.SWORD_BASTARD_LOD0.SetActive(false);
                this.SWORD_BOARD_01LOD0.SetActive(false);
                this.SWORD_SHORT_LOD0.SetActive(false);
                break;
        }
        case 10:
        {
                this.AXE_01LOD0.SetActive(false);
                this.AXE_02LOD0.SetActive(false);
                this.CLUB_01LOD0.SetActive(false);
                this.CLUB_02LOD0.SetActive(false);
                this.FALCHION_LOD0.SetActive(false);
                this.GLADIUS_LOD0.SetActive(false);
                this.MACE_LOD0.SetActive(false);
                this.MAUL_LOD0.SetActive(false);
                this.SCIMITAR_LOD0.SetActive(false);
                this.SPEAR_LOD0.SetActive(true);
                this.SWORD_BASTARD_LOD0.SetActive(false);
                this.SWORD_BOARD_01LOD0.SetActive(false);
                this.SWORD_SHORT_LOD0.SetActive(false);
                break;
        }
        case 11:
        {
                this.AXE_01LOD0.SetActive(false);
                this.AXE_02LOD0.SetActive(false);
```

Player Character and Non-Player Character Design

```
            this.CLUB_01LOD0.SetActive(false);
            this.CLUB_02LOD0.SetActive(false);
            this.FALCHION_LOD0.SetActive(false);
            this.GLADIUS_LOD0.SetActive(false);
            this.MACE_LOD0.SetActive(false);
            this.MAUL_LOD0.SetActive(false);
            this.SCIMITAR_LOD0.SetActive(false);
            this.SPEAR_LOD0.SetActive(false);
            this.SWORD_BASTARD_LOD0.SetActive(true);
            this.SWORD_BOARD_01LOD0.SetActive(false);
            this.SWORD_SHORT_LOD0.SetActive(false);
            break;
        }
    case 12:
        {
            this.AXE_01LOD0.SetActive(false);
            this.AXE_02LOD0.SetActive(false);
            this.CLUB_01LOD0.SetActive(false);
            this.CLUB_02LOD0.SetActive(false);
            this.FALCHION_LOD0.SetActive(false);
            this.GLADIUS_LOD0.SetActive(false);
            this.MACE_LOD0.SetActive(false);
            this.MAUL_LOD0.SetActive(false);
            this.SCIMITAR_LOD0.SetActive(false);
            this.SPEAR_LOD0.SetActive(false);
            this.SWORD_BASTARD_LOD0.SetActive(false);
            this.SWORD_BOARD_01LOD0.SetActive(true);
            this.SWORD_SHORT_LOD0.SetActive(false);
            break;
        }
    case 13:
        {
            this.AXE_01LOD0.SetActive(false);
            this.AXE_02LOD0.SetActive(false);
            this.CLUB_01LOD0.SetActive(false);
            this.CLUB_02LOD0.SetActive(false);
            this.FALCHION_LOD0.SetActive(false);
            this.GLADIUS_LOD0.SetActive(false);
            this.MACE_LOD0.SetActive(false);
            this.MAUL_LOD0.SetActive(false);
            this.SCIMITAR_LOD0.SetActive(false);
            this.SPEAR_LOD0.SetActive(false);
            this.SWORD_BASTARD_LOD0.SetActive(false);
            this.SWORD_BOARD_01LOD0.SetActive(false);
            this.SWORD_SHORT_LOD0.SetActive(true);
            break;
        }
```

```
        }
    }

    public void SetHelmetType(Toggle id)
    {
        switch (id.name)
        {
            case "HL-01":
                {
                    this.HELMET_01LOD0.SetActive(id.isOn);
                    this.HELMET_02LOD0.SetActive(false);
                    this.HELMET_03LOD0.SetActive(false);
                    this.HELMET_04LOD0.SetActive(false);
                    break;
                }
            case "HL-02":
                {
                    this.HELMET_01LOD0.SetActive(false);
                    this.HELMET_02LOD0.SetActive(id.isOn);
                    this.HELMET_03LOD0.SetActive(false);
                    this.HELMET_04LOD0.SetActive(false);
                    break;
                }
            case "HL-03":
                {
                    this.HELMET_01LOD0.SetActive(false);
                    this.HELMET_02LOD0.SetActive(false);
                    this.HELMET_03LOD0.SetActive(id.isOn);
                    this.HELMET_04LOD0.SetActive(false);
                    break;
                }
            case "HL-04":
                {
                    this.HELMET_01LOD0.SetActive(false);
                    this.HELMET_02LOD0.SetActive(false);
                    this.HELMET_03LOD0.SetActive(false);
                    this.HELMET_04LOD0.SetActive(id.isOn);
                    break;
                }
        }
    }

    public void SetShieldType(Toggle id)
    {
        switch (id.name)
        {
            case "SL-01":
                {
```

Player Character and Non-Player Character Design

```
                    this.SHIELD_01LOD0.SetActive(id.isOn);
                    this.SHIELD_02LOD0.SetActive(false);
                    break;
                }
            case "SL-02":
                {
                    this.SHIELD_01LOD0.SetActive(false);
                    this.SHIELD_02LOD0.SetActive(id.isOn);
                    break;
                }
        }
    }


    public void SetSkinType(Slider id)
    {
        this.SKN_LOD0.GetComponent<Renderer>().material =
this.PLAYER_SKIN[System.Convert.ToInt32(id.value)];
        this.FAT_LOD0.GetComponent<Renderer>().material =
this.PLAYER_SKIN[System.Convert.ToInt32(id.value)];
        this.RGL_LOD0.GetComponent<Renderer>().material =
this.PLAYER_SKIN[System.Convert.ToInt32(id.value)];
    }

    public void SetBootType(Toggle id)
    {
        switch (id.name)
        {
            case "BT-01":
                {
                    this.BOOT_01LOD0.SetActive(id.isOn);
                    this.BOOT_02LOD0.SetActive(false);
                    break;
                }
            case "BT-02":
                {
                    this.BOOT_01LOD0.SetActive(false);
                    this.BOOT_02LOD0.SetActive(id.isOn);
                    break;
                }
        }
    }
}
```

Chapter 4

This is a long script but it is straightforward. At the top of the script we have defined all of the variables that will be referencing the different meshes in our model character. All variables are of type GameObject with the exception of the PLAYER_SKIN variable which is an array of `Material` data type. The array is used to store the different types of texture created for the character model.

There are a few functions defined that are called by the UI event handler. These functions are: `SetShoulderPad(Toggle id); SetBodyType(Toggle id); SetKneePad(Toggle id); SetLegPlate(Toggle id); SetWeaponType(Slider id); SetHelmetType(Toggle id); SetShieldType(Toggle id); SetSkinType(Slider id);`

All of the functions take a parameter that identifies which specific type is should enable or disable.

A BIG NOTE HERE!

You can also use the system we just built to create all of the different variations of your Non-Character Player models and store them as prefabs! Wow! This will save you so much time and effort in creating your characters representing different barbarians!!!

Preserving our character state

Now that we have spent the time to customize our character, we need to preserve our character and use it in our game. In Unity, there is a function called `DontDestroyOnLoad()`. This is a great function that can be utilized at this time. What does it do? It keeps the specified GameObject in memory going from one scene to the next. We can use these mechanisms for now, eventually though, you will want to create a system that can save and load your user data.

Go ahead and create a new C# script and call it `DoNotDestroy.cs`. This script is going to be very simple. Here is the listing:

```
using UnityEngine;
using System.Collections;

public class DoNotDestroy : MonoBehaviour
{

    // Use this for initialization
    void Start()
    {
        DontDestroyOnLoad(this);
    }
```

[113]

```
    // Update is called once per frame
    void Update()
    {

    }
}
```

After you create the script go ahead and attach it to your character model prefab in the scene. Not bad, let's do a quick recap of what we have done so far.

Recap

By now you should have three scenes that are functional. We have our scene that represents the main menu, we have our scene that represents our initial level, and we just created a scene that is used for character customization. Here is the flow of our game thus far:

We start the game, see the main menu, select the **Start Game** button to enter the character customization scene, do our customization, and when we click the **Save** button we load **level 1**.

For this to work, we have created the following C# scripts:

- **GameMaster.cs:** used as the main script to keep track of our game state
- **CharacterCustomization.cs:** used exclusively for customizing our character
- **DoNotDestroy.cs:** used to save the state of a given object
- **CharacterController.cs:** used to control the motion of our character
- **IKHandle.cs:** used to implement inverse kinematics for the foot

When you combine all of this together you now have a good framework and flow that can be extended and improved as we go along.

Non-Player Characters

So far we have concentrated on the player character, in this section we will start thinking about our non-player characters. Let's start with our Barbarians. We can use our Character Customization scene to quickly create a few prefabs that will represent our unique Barbarians.

Using the tools we have just developed, you can make your adjustments, and when satisfied with your model, drag and drop the GameObject representing your character-player into the `Prefabs` folder. This will create a copy of the instance of the GameObject as you see it and save it into a prefab. The following screenshot will demonstrate the two characters I have created and stored as a prefab:

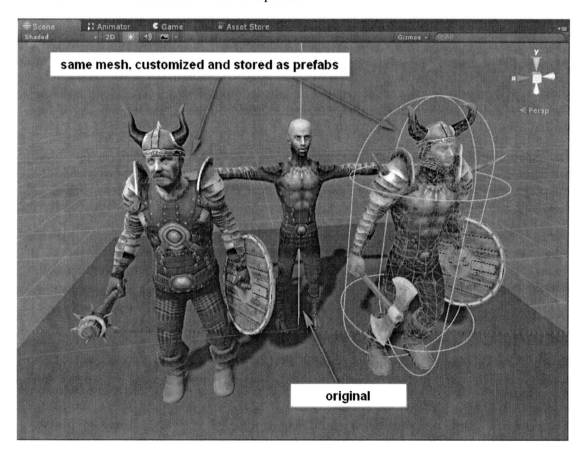

Player Character and Non-Player Character Design

What I have shown you, if done properly, could save you hours of tedious work of manually going down the model structure and individually enabling and disabling the different meshes. In other words, we not only create a scene that allows us to customize our in-game player character, we have also created a tool that can help us customize our own character models quickly for use in the game!

Another point to emphasize here is the power of prefabs. Think of a prefab as a storage object that can be used to save the state of a given GameObject and used over and over again within your game environment. When you update your prefab, all instances of the prefab will automatically get updated!!! This is great, but at the same time you have to be careful not to break anything for the same reason. When you update code logic on a script that is attached to a prefab, all instances of the prefab will use the updated script, so a bit of planning on your part can save a lot of time and headache in the long run.

Non-Player Character basics

We are going to be using the newly created prefabs to implement our non-player characters. Since there are some similarities in the character models, we can re-use some of the assets we have created so far.

For instance, all characters will be inheriting the `BaseCharacter` class defined in Chapter 3, *Character Design*. They will also incorporate the same states we have already created for the player character and extend a few more states specifically for the NPC, for instance searching and seeking.

We have used our character customization tool to create and save our non-player character, hence we are OK with the modelling part. What we need to concentrate on is the motion of our non-player characters! We would need to create a new Animator Controller that will handle the states of our NPCs.

Setting up the Non-Player Character

One of the main difficulties for implementing a NPC is the ability to give it realistic intelligence. This can be achieved easily by identifying and implementing several key areas for our NPCs.

There are a few new components we would need to attach to our NPCs. Using the prefab we have saved, we will need to add the following components:

- New `Sphere Collider`, this will be used to implement the range of sight for our NPC.

- We already have an `Animator` component attached, but we will need to create a new `Animator Controller` to capture new states for the NPC.
- We would also need to add a `Nav Mesh Agent` component. We are going to use the built-in navigation and pathfinding system for our NPC.

To add the `Sphere Collider`, you will need to select the prefab defined for the NCP, and in the **Inspector Window**, select **Add Component | Physics | Sphere Collider**. This will attach a `Sphere Collider` to our prefab.

Next we need to add the **Nav Mesh Agent**, again from the **Inspector Window**, select **Add Component | Navigation | Nav Mesh Agent**. Ok so now we have set up our main built-in components that are going to be used for the NPC.

Since, our prefab is an instance of our player character, we will need to remove some of the script components that have been carried over. If your NPC prefab contains any scripts attached to it, go ahead and remove them now.

> Make sure you also change the `Tag` property to `Untagged`, if you have not done so already.

The following screenshot will illustrate the components that we have so far on the NPC. This will include both the existing components, including the scripts we have brought over from the player character, and the newly added components that will be used for the NPC.

Player Character and Non-Player Character Design

The next step is to set up our Navmesh. To create a Navmesh, we need to get into the **Navigation Window**, to do so, select **Window | Navigation**.

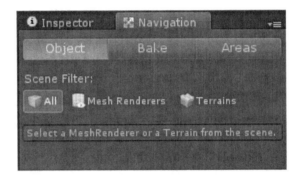

In order for the navmesh to work properly, we will need to mark all GameObjects in the scene as **Navigation Static**. This will create a navmesh based on the static objects in the scene, that is, GameObjects that are not going to be moving throughout the lifespan of the scene.

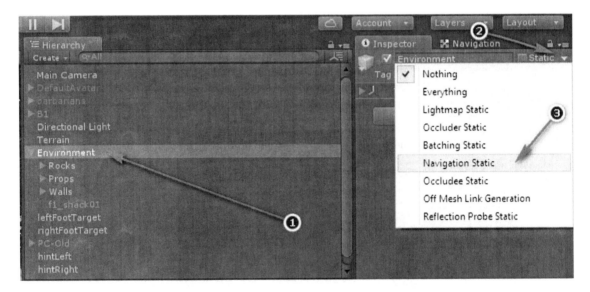

In your active scene, select the GameObjects that are going to be set as **Navigation Static** as shown in the preceding screenshot (1) and use the Static drop-down menu as shown in (2) and select the **Navigation Static** option as in (3). If your GameObject is a parent GameObject with children, Unity will ask if you want to apply the property change to all children.

Notice that I have placed all of my environment GameObjects under a GameObject called `Environment`. This way if I have many static objects, I can apply the property change to the parent and the children will automatically inherit the change as well. But make sure, everything in the group will be static!

Once this is complete, we need to go back to the Navigation Window and make some adjustments. In the **Navigation** tab, select **Terrains** and make sure it is set to **Navigation Static**, and the **Navigation Area** is set to **Walkable**.

In the **Bake** tab, change the **Agent Radius** to **0.3** and **Agent Height** to **1**. This will give the NPC more freedom to pass through tight corners.

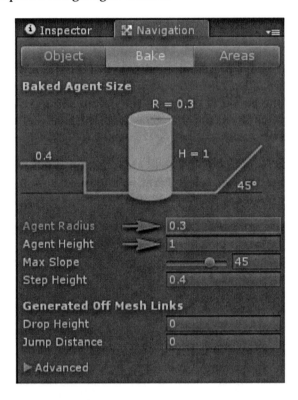

When you are ready, you can select the **Bake** button at the bottom of the **Navigation**Window.

Unity will take some time to generate the Navmesh for your scene. This will depend on the complexity of your level. If all is done correctly, you will see something similar to the following screenshot displaying your Navmesh:

Chapter 4

The blue areas you see are all the regions that the NPC can actually navigate to.

[121]

NPC Animator Controller

We now need to create the Animator Controller (AC) for our NPC. The Animator Controller will use input from the MeshAgent to control and change the state of our NPC. We also need to define a few parameters for our NPC AC. These are going to be:

- AngularSpeed: will be used for directional movement
- Speed: will be used to determine how fast the NPC will be moving
- Attack: will be used to determine if it needs to attack
- AttackWeight: used to determine damage of the attack
- PlayerInSight: will be used to determine if the PC is in sight

Go ahead and create a new `Animator Controller` in your project and name it `NPC_Animator_Controller`. Open the **Animator**Window. Create a new Blend Tree by right-clicking in the **Animator** Window and selecting **Create State | From New Blend Tree**. Change the name to **NPC_Locomotion**. Double-click it so that you can edit the blend tree. Change the node name to **NPC_Locomotion** as well. From the Inspector Window, change the **Blend Type** to **2D Freeform Cartesian**.

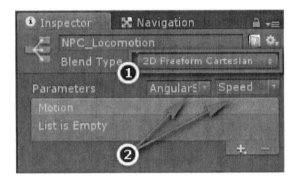

The x-axis will be represented by the **AngularSpeed**, and the y-axis will be represented by the **Speed** parameters.

The Blend Tree is going to hold all of the different locomotion animation states. These are going to be the idle, walking and running states.

I have set up 11 different animation states for the locomotion of my NPC. The following screenshot will give you an overview of the Blend Tree.

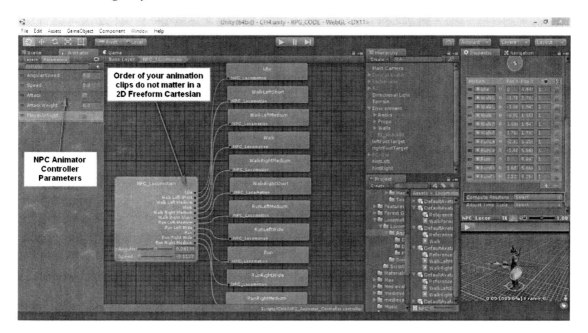

Once you include all of the animations states in the Blend Tree, you will need to compute the positions of your animations, an easy way to do this, is to select the **Compute Positions** drop-down menu and select the **AngularSpeed** and **Speed**. This will place the animation position based on the root motion as illustrated in the following screenshot

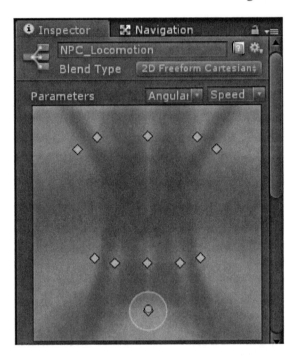

 You can use your mouse to drag the red point on the diagram to preview your animation states in action.

NPC attack

In order to implement our attack mode, we will need to create a new layer in the Animator Controller. Go ahead and create a new layer and call it **NPC_Attack**. This layer will be responsible for animating our character when we enter attack mode.

Chapter 4

We need to create a new Mask for the layer. The mask will be used to determine which parts of the humanoid body will be affected by the layer animation. To create a **Mask**, right-click in your **Project** Window and select **Create | Avatar Mask**. Name the new mask, **NPC_Attack**. Use the Inspector Window to disable the body parts that we don't want to be affected by the layer animation. See following screenshot:

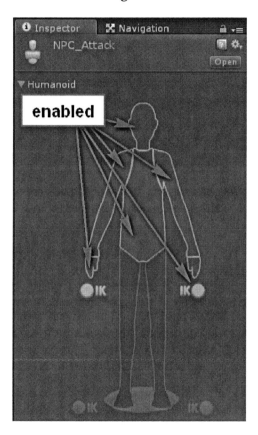

Player Character and Non-Player Character Design

Your layer setup should look like the following screenshot:

Make sure you change the **Weight** property to 1, the **Mask** property assigned to the Avatar Mask we created, and also that the **IK** property is checked. Now we are ready to create our attack state machine.

Right-click in the **Animator Window** and select **Create State | Empty**. Drag and drop your attack animation(s). The empty state is used to have a nice transition between the main layer and back.

After you have dropped your attack animation(s) into the Animator, you will need to connect them using the transition conditions. I have added three more parameters to the parameter list named: **Attack1, Attack2** and **Attack3.** These parameters in connection with the **Attack** parameter will determine which attack state our NPC will transition to.

The following screenshot shows the **NPC_Attack** layer as configured up-to this point.

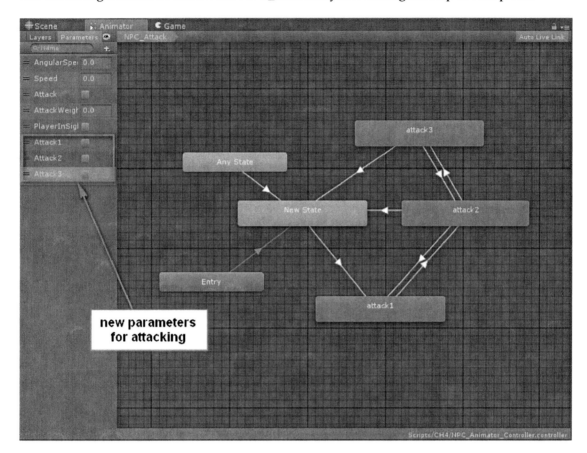

Finally, you want to assign the new NPC_Animator_Controller to the NPC prefab(s).

NPC AI

Now it is time to give some intelligence to our NPCs. One of the scripts we will need to create is the ability for the NPC to detect the player. This script will be called `NPC_Sight.cs`. The script will be used to detect if the player is in sight, calculate the field of view for the NPC, and calculate the path from the NPC to the player character.

Here is a listing of the source code:

```
using UnityEngine;
using System.Collections;
```

Player Character and Non-Player Character Design

```csharp
public class NPC_Movement : MonoBehaviour
{
    // reference to the animator
    public Animator animator;

    // these variables are used for the speed
    // horizontal and vertical movement of the NPC
    public float speed = 0.0f;
    public float h = 0.0f;
    public float v = 0.0f;

    public bool attack1 = false;   // used for attack mode 1
    public bool attack2 = false;   // used for attack mode 2
    public bool attack3 = false;   // used for attack mode 3

    public bool jump = false;      // used for jumping
    public bool die = false;       // are we alive?

    // used for debugging
    public bool DEBUG = false;
    public bool DEBUG_DRAW = false;

    // Reference to the NavMeshAgent component.
    private NavMeshAgent nav;
    // Reference to the sphere collider trigger component.
    private SphereCollider col;

    // where is the player character in relation to NPC
    public Vector3 direction;
    // how far away is the player character from NPC
    public float distance = 0.0f;
    // what is the angle between the PC and NPC
    public float angle = 0.0f;
    // a reference to the player character
    public GameObject player;
    // is the PC in sight?
    public bool playerInSight;

    // what is the field of view for our NPC?
    // currently set to 110 degrees
    public float fieldOfViewAngle = 110.0f;

    // calculate the angle between PC and NPC
    public float calculatedAngle;

    void Awake()
    {
        // get reference to the animator component
```

[128]

```csharp
        this.animator = GetComponent<Animator>() as Animator;

        // get reference to nav mesh agent
        this.nav = GetComponent<NavMeshAgent>() as NavMeshAgent;

        // get reference to the sphere collider
        this.col = GetComponent<SphereCollider>() as SphereCollider;

        // get reference to the player
        player = GameObject.FindGameObjectWithTag("Player") as GameObject;

        // we don't see the player by default
        this.playerInSight = false;
    }

    // Use this for initialization
    void Start()
    {
    }

    void Update()
    {
        // if player is in sight let's lerp towards the player
        if (playerInSight)
        {
            this.transform.rotation =
                Quaternion.Slerp(this.transform.rotation,
                Quaternion.LookRotation(direction), 0.1f);
        }
    }

    // let's update our scene using fixed update
    void FixedUpdate()
    {
        h = angle;          // assign horizontal axis
        v = distance;       // assign vertical axis

        // calculate speed based on distance and delta time
        speed = distance / Time.deltaTime;

        if (DEBUG)
            Debug.Log(string.Format("H:{0} - V:{1} - Speed:{2}", h, v,
speed));

        // set the parameters defined in the animator controller
        animator.SetFloat("Speed", speed);
        animator.SetFloat("AngularSpeed", v);
        animator.SetBool("Attack", attack1);
```

```
            animator.SetBool("Attack1", attack1);
    }

    // if the PC is in our collider, we want to examine the location of the
player
    // calculate the direction based on our position and the player's
position
    // use the DOT product to get the angle between the two vectors
    // calculate the angle between the NPC forward vector and the PC
    // if it falls within the field of view, we have the player in in sight
    // if the player is in sight, we will set the nav agent desitation
    // if we are within a certain distance from the PC, the NPC has the
ability to attack
    void OnTriggerStay(Collider other)
    {
        if (other.transform.tag.Equals("Player"))
        {
            // Create a vector from the enemy to the player and store the
angle between it and forward.
            direction = other.transform.position - transform.position;

            distance = Vector3.Distance(other.transform.position,
transform.position) - 1.0f;

            float DotResult = Vector3.Dot(transform.forward,
player.transform.position);
            angle = DotResult;

            if (DEBUG_DRAW)
            {
                Debug.DrawLine(transform.position + Vector3.up, direction *
50, Color.gray);
                Debug.DrawLine(other.transform.position,
transform.position, Color.cyan);
            }

            this.playerInSight = false;

            this.calculatedAngle = Vector3.Angle(direction,
transform.forward);

            if (calculatedAngle < fieldOfViewAngle * 0.5f)
            {
                RaycastHit hit;

                if (DEBUG_DRAW)
                    Debug.DrawRay(transform.position + transform.up,
direction.normalized, Color.magenta);
```

```csharp
                        // ... and if a raycast towards the player hits
something...
                        if (Physics.Raycast(transform.position + transform.up,
direction.normalized, out hit, col.radius))
                        {
                            // ... and if the raycast hits the player...
                            if (hit.collider.gameObject == player)
                            {
                                // ... the player is in sight.
                                this.playerInSight = true;

                                if (DEBUG)
                                    Debug.Log("PlayerInSight: " + playerInSight);
                            }
                        }
                    }

                    if (this.playerInSight)
                    {
                        this.nav.SetDestination(other.transform.position);
                        this.CalculatePathLength(other.transform.position);

                        if (distance < 1.1f)
                        {
                            this.attack1 = true;
                        }
                        else
                        {
                            this.attack1 = false;
                        }
                    }
                }
            }

    void OnTriggerExit(Collider other)
    {
        if (other.transform.tag.Equals("Player"))
        {
            distance = 0.0f;
            angle = 0.0f;
            this.attack1 = false;
            this.playerInSight = false;
        }
    }

    // this is a helper function at this point
    // in the future we will use it to calculate distance around the
corners
```

Player Character and Non-Player Character Design

```
    // it currently is also used to draw the path of the nav mesh agent in
the
    // editor
    float CalculatePathLength(Vector3 targetPosition)
    {
        // Create a path and set it based on a target position.
        NavMeshPath path = new NavMeshPath();
        if (nav.enabled)
            nav.CalculatePath(targetPosition, path);

        // Create an array of points which is the length of the number of
corners in the path + 2.
        Vector3[] allWayPoints = new Vector3[path.corners.Length + 2];

        // The first point is the enemy's position.
        allWayPoints[0] = transform.position;

        // The last point is the target position.
        allWayPoints[allWayPoints.Length - 1] = targetPosition;

        // The points in between are the corners of the path.
        for (int i = 0; i < path.corners.Length; i++)
        {
            allWayPoints[i + 1] = path.corners[i];
        }

        // Create a float to store the path length that is by default 0.
        float pathLength = 0;

        // Increment the path length by an amount equal to the distance
between each waypoint and the next.
        for (int i = 0; i < allWayPoints.Length - 1; i++)
        {
            pathLength += Vector3.Distance(allWayPoints[i], allWayPoints[i
+ 1]);

            if (DEBUG_DRAW)
                Debug.DrawLine(allWayPoints[i], allWayPoints[i + 1],
Color.red);
        }

        return pathLength;
    }
}
```

Chapter 4

Ok, so let's actually take a look and see what this code is trying to do. In the `Awake()` function we are initializing our variables that will be used in the script. We have a reference to the `NavMeshAgent`, the `SphereCollider` and the `Animator` components attached to the NPC, these are stored in the `nav`, `col` and `anim` variables respectively.

We also need to get a reference to the player and the player animator component. This is done through the `player` variable. We are also setting the `playerInSight` variable to false by default.

The `Update()` function is not performing anything major at this point, it is just checking to see if the player character is in sight, and if so, it makes sure that the NPC is orienting itself to look at the player.

Most of the meat of our code is in the `OnTriggerStay()` function. The first thing we need to do is make sure the object that has entered our collider is the player object. This is done by checking the `tag` attribute on the other collider.

If the player is within our collider, then we go ahead and calculate the direction, the distance and the angle of the player relative to the NPC. This is done with the following lines:

```
direction = other.transform.position - transform.position;

distance = Vector3.Distance(other.transform.position, transform.position) -
1.0f;

float DotResult = Vector3.Dot(transform.forward,player.transform.position);

angle = DotResult;
```

[133]

Then, if the angle is smaller than the `fieldOfViewAngle` variable we can use ray casting to determine if we can hit the player. If that is the case, the player is in NPC's sight.

There is one more critical calculation the NPC needs to perform. That is how to get to the player once it is in range! Once we have established that the player is in range and that we are facing the player, we need to make the NPC find its way to the player. This is where the `NavMesh` and the `NavMeshAgent` come into play.

The `CalculatePathLength()` is a function that takes the position of the player and using the mesh data, calculates the best path to navigate from the NPC's location to the player's location.

Chapter 4

However, there's one more additional calculation we are performing, and that is, we are calculating the length of the path between the two points. This length calculation will be used in the future to perform the following:

If the length of the path is larger than a threshold we have set, then we won't make the NPC attack, if it is, then we can make the NPC move towards the player to engage in battle.

In the last function `OnTriggerExit()`, we set the `playerInSight` variable to false. This will stop the NPC from pursuing the player.

The preceding screenshot illustrates the path between the NPC and the Player based on real-time calculation.

Player Character and Non-Player Character Design

Go ahead and attach the script to the NPC prefab if you have not done so already, and run the application to test it out. If all things are good, then you will be able to move the player character around the level, and once the player character enters the NPC's field of view, the NPC will start moving toward the player, and when close enough it will attack.

At this point your NPC should have the following components attached to its prefab:

- Animator
- Rigidbody
- Capsule and Sphere Colliders
- Nav Mesh Agent
- NPC_Movement script

We have covered a lot of information. I would encourage you to take the time to read through it one more time and understand the concepts before moving forward.

PC and NPC interaction

Thus far we have created the basic movement for both our PC and NPC. The next item I would like to complete is the attack mechanism for the PC and the NPC characters. Let's start by implementing the hit for the NPC.

Our NPC detects the player character based on the code we just created in the previous section. When the player character is in sight, the NPC will find the shortest path to the player character, and at a given range, it will attack the player character. So we have the movement and animation mechanics completed. The next objective is to keep track of the hit points when the NPC is attacking.

There are a few adjustments we need to make in the **NPC_Animator_Controller**. Open, the **Animator**Window, and select the **NPC_Attack** layer.

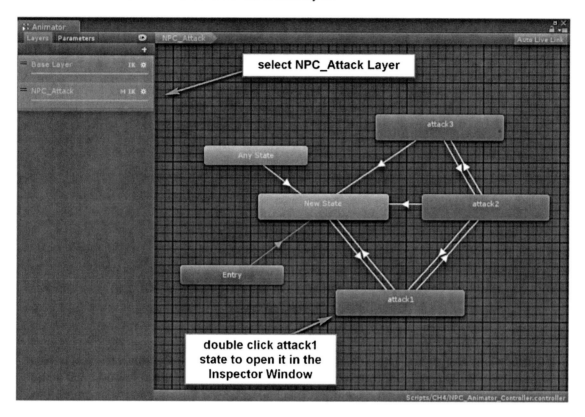

Double-click on the **attack1** state, or the attack state you have defined in your state machine. This will open the related animation in the **Inspector Window**.

In the **Inspector Window**, scroll down to the **Curves** section. We are going to create a new curve by selecting the *(+)* sign under the **Curves** section. We are also going to create a new parameter called **Attack1C** to represent the value of the curve, this parameter should be of type `float`.

Player Character and Non-Player Character Design

The curve displayed in the preceding screenshot, will be based on your animation.

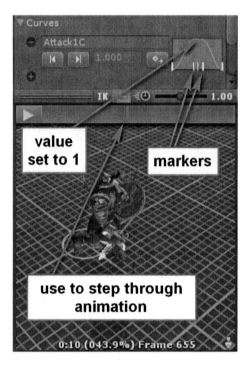

In the preceding screenshot, I have marked the important parts of the interface you will need to work with to configure the curve of an animation. The first step would be to actual preview your animation and get a feeling for it. The next step for my particular animation sequence, was determining when the right arm of the model starts moving along and I set a marker in the curve. I make another marker a bit more into the animation where the right arm has crossed a good deal from the right side to the left side. These markers will indicate a hit point during the animation when the NPC is in attack mode.

Chapter 4

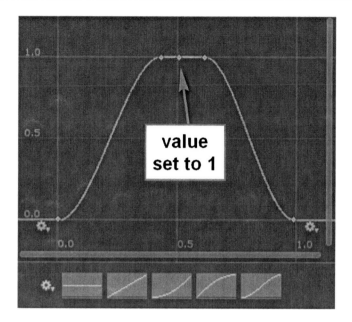

Ok, so why do we do this? Simple. This will help us only generate a hit based on the curve of the animation. This way we don't hit the player and reduce the health of the player while the weapon is away from the player's body.

Next, we need to update out `NPC_Movement.cs` code to program the NPC attack.

 I have only listed the portions that have been updated.

Here is an updated listing of the code:

```
using UnityEngine;
using System.Collections;

public class NPC_Movement : MonoBehaviour
{
...
    void Update()
    {
        // if player is in sight let's slerp towards the player
        if (playerInSight)
        {
            this.transform.rotation =
                Quaternion.Slerp(this.transform.rotation,
```

[139]

Player Character and Non-Player Character Design

```
                    Quaternion.LookRotation(direction), 0.1f);
        }

        if(this.player.transform.GetComponent<CharacterController>().die)
        {
            animator.SetBool("Attack", false);
            animator.SetFloat("Speed", 0.0f);
            animator.SetFloat("AngularSpeed", 0.0f);
        }
    }

    // let's update our scene using fixed update
    void FixedUpdate()
    {
        h = angle;          // assign horizontal axis
        v = distance;       // assign vertical axis

        // calculate speed based on distance and delta time
        speed = distance / Time.deltaTime;

        if (DEBUG)
            Debug.Log(string.Format("H:{0} - V:{1} - Speed:{2}", h, v,
speed));

        // set the parameters defined in the animator controller
        animator.SetFloat("Speed", speed);
        animator.SetFloat("AngularSpeed", v);
        animator.SetBool("Attack", attack1);
        animator.SetBool("Attack1", attack1);

        if(playerInSight)
        {
            if (animator.GetFloat("Attack1C") == 1.0f)
            {
this.player.GetComponent<PlayerAgent>().playerCharacterData.HEALTH -= 1.0f;
            }
        }
    }
...
}
```

The new addition to the code checks to see if the player is in sight, and if that is the case, we check to see if we are in range to be able to attack, if that is the case we enter the attack mode, if we are in the attack mode, the attack animation is played. In the code we check to get the value of the newly created parameter called **Attack1C**, and if it happens to be of value 1.0f, then we go ahead and reduce the health of the player character.

Chapter 4

If the player dies while the NPC is attacking it will stop attacking and go back into the idle state.

Ok, you might be wondering how we get the ability to get the information from the player character. This is because we need to make some more additional C# scripts. Let's go ahead and do so now. Create the following C# scripts:

- `PC.cs`, this is going to be our player character class which inherits from the BaseCharacter class we have defined previously
- `PlayerAgent.cs`, this is going to be used to store the PC data and also inherit MonoBehaviour
- `NPC.cs`, this is going to be our non-player character class which inherits from the BaseCharacter class as well
- `NPC_Agent.cs`, is going to be used to store the NPC data and also inherit MonoBehaviour

I have made some modifications to the `BaseCharacter.cs` script to make it more accessible through the editor. Here is the new listing:

```
using UnityEngine;
using System;
using System.Collections;

[Serializable]
public class BaseCharacter
{
    [SerializeField]
    private string name;
    [SerializeField]
    private string description;

    [SerializeField]
    private float strength;
    [SerializeField]
    private float defense;
    [SerializeField]
    private float dexterity;
    [SerializeField]
    private float intelligence;
    [SerializeField]
    private float health;


    public string NAME
```

[141]

Player Character and Non-Player Character Design

```csharp
    {
        get { return this.name; }
        set { this.name = value; }
    }

    public string DESCRIPTION
    {
        get { return this.description; }
        set { this.description = value; }
    }

    public float STRENGTH
    {
        get { return this.strength; }
        set { this.strength = value; }
    }

    public float DEFENSE
    {
        get { return this.defense; }
        set { this.defense = value; }
    }

    public float DEXTERITY
    {
        get { return this.dexterity; }
        set { this.dexterity = value; }
    }

    public float INTELLIGENCE
    {
        get { return this.intelligence; }
        set { this.intelligence = value; }
    }

    public float HEALTH
    {
        get { return this.health; }
        set { this.health = value; }
    }
}
```

I have gone ahead and made the class and the fields serializable.

Let's take a look at the listing for `PC.cs`:

```csharp
using UnityEngine;
using System;
```

[**142**]

Chapter 4

```
using System.Collections;

[Serializable]
public class PC : BaseCharacter {

}
```

Nothing much going on there at this point. Now let's take a look at the `PlayerAgent.cs`:

```
using UnityEngine;
using System;
using System.Collections;

[Serializable]
public class PlayerAgent : MonoBehaviour {

    //[SerializeField]
    public PC playerCharacterData;

    void Awake()
    {
        PC tmp = new PC();
        tmp.NAME = "Maximilian";
        tmp.HEALTH = 100.0f;
        tmp.DEFENSE = 50.0f;
        tmp.DESCRIPTION = "Our Hero";
        tmp.DEXTERITY = 33.0f;
        tmp.INTELLIGENCE = 80.0f;
        tmp.STRENGTH = 60.0f;

        this.playerCharacterData = tmp;
    }

      // Use this for initialization
      void Start () {
      }
      // Update is called once per frame
      void Update () {
         if(this.playerCharacterData.HEALTH<0.0f)
       {
          this.playerCharacterData.HEALTH = 0.0f;

          this.transform.GetComponent<CharacterController>().die = true;
       }
      }
}
```

[143]

Player Character and Non-Player Character Design

In the player agent code, we are initializing some default values for our PC data in the `Awake()` function. Since the class has been serialized, we can actually see the data during runtime for debugging purposes!

In the `Update()` function, we check to see if the health of our PC is less than 0.0f, and if it is, then this indicates the player has died. Which we then use the `CharacterController` component we have created to set the *die* property to true. The `CharacterController` then will use the new value and communicate with the animator controller for the player character to get into the die state.

Notice that our `NPC_Movement.cs` script is accessing the exact same PC data through the reference we have created in the script.

You will need to attach the `PlayerAgent.cs` script to your player character in the scene.

[144]

In the preceding screenshot you can see the additions we have done to the scripts and how they look during runtime. We will have a listing for the `NPC.cs` and `NPC_Agent.cs` in future chapters. At this point, they are not used.

Summary

Chapter 4 was very involved. We covered some very important topics and concepts in the chapter that can be used and enhanced for your games. We started the chapter by looking into how to customize your player character. The concepts you take away from the section can be applied to a wide variety of scenarios.

We look at how to understand the structure of your character model so that you can better determine the customization methods. These are the different types of weapons, clothing, armour, shields and so on…

We then looked at how to create a user interface to help enable us with the customization of our player character during gameplay. We also learned that the tool we developed can be used to quickly create several different character models (customized) and store them as Prefabs for later use! Great time saver!!! We also learned how to preserve the state of our player character after customization for gameplay.

We looked at the Non-Player Characters next. We went through the basics of setting up the NPC with the different necessary components. We then looked at how to create a Navmesh and how to work with Navmesh Agent and Pathfinding using the Navmesh.

We created a new Animator Controller for the NPC. We created a 2D Freeform Cartesian blend tree that was used for the animation of the NPC. We saw how to create multiple layers in the animation controller and enabling IK for difference regions of the humanoid skeleton. We created the initial NPC AI script to detect and determine if the player is close enough for it to make a move and/or attack. Finally, we created new scripts to make interaction between the NPC and the player character possible.

By the end of the chapter you should have a good grasp of how everything is inter-related and have an idea of how to approach your project.

In the next chapter we will create a better way to manage our game state.

5

Game Master and Game Mechanics

In chapters 1 to 4, you learned how to make some of the necessary components needed for the design and implementation of our RPG. For instance, you should have a good understanding of how to organize and arrange your player character and non-player character assets and components.

Here is a breakdown of the chapter:

- The Game Master
  - Managing game settings and scenes
  - Managing scenes
- Improving Game Master
  - Level controller
  - Audio controller
- Player Data Management
  - PC class enhancements
  - Character customization class update
- Changes to UI Controller
- Testing

In this chapter, we are going to make more adjustments and updates to everything we have done so far.

The Game Master

Even though we created a *GameMaster.cs* scripts, we have not really utilized it to manage our game. We created bits and pieces of our game assets and used them to perform quick testing. In this chapter, we will start looking at how to create a better game manager for our RPG.

There are a few things that I want the GameMaster.cs to perform. These are as follows:

- Having a reference to the UI Controller for each particular scene
- Having a reference to the Player Character in the scene
- Having a reference to the Non-Player Character(s) in the scene
- Having a reference to the Audio Source for control
- There should always be one instance of the GameMaster class available

As we create our GameMaster, we will add or subtract some of the elements as we see fit. Let's start by integrating the User Interface with the GameMaster.

Open up your Main Menu scene. It should look something like the following figure:

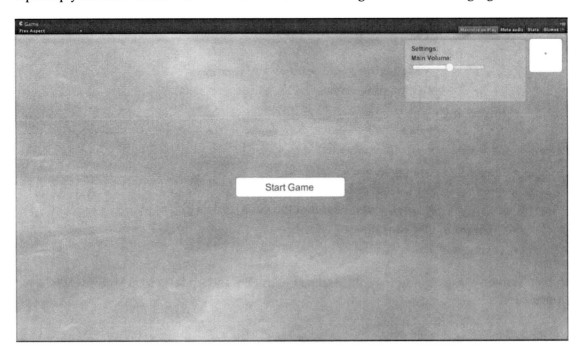

In the preceding figure, I added a few UI elements. There is a button that is a place holder for game settings indicated by the (*). When the button is pressed, you will get a panel that will give you the ability to control the master volume of the game.

Here is a screenshot of the Hierarchy Window for the main menu scene:

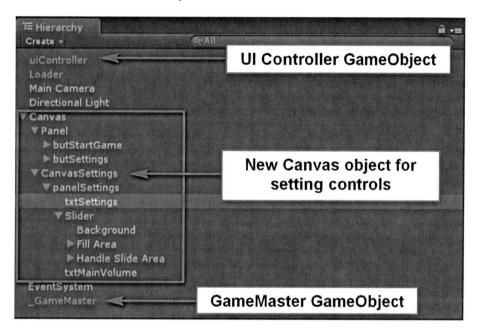

Managing game settings and audio

Create an Empty Game Object and name it *uiController*. We now need to create a UI Controller script that will handle the user interaction. Create a new C# script and name it *UIController.cs*.

> Note that the scripts in this chapter will be updated and modified as we progress.

Here is a listing of the UI Controller:

```
using UnityEngine;
using UnityEngine.UI;
using System.Collections;
```

[149]

Game Master and Game Mechanics

```
public class UIController : MonoBehaviour
{
  public Canvas SettingsCanvas;
  public Slider ControlMainVolume;

  public void Update()
  {
  }

  public void DisplaySettings()
  {
    GameMaster.instance.DISPLAY_SETTINGS =
!GameMaster.instance.DISPLAY_SETTINGS;
this.SettingsCanvas.gameObject.SetActive(GameMaster.instance.DISPLAY_SETTIN
GS);
  }

  public void MainVolume()
  {
    GameMaster.instance.MasterVolume(ControlMainVolume.value);
  }

}
```

Currently, we have just a few functions defined: `DisplaySettings()` and `MainVolume()`. The functions are really simple, they are referencing the UI components needed to display the settings panel, and also to retrieve the value of the volume control slider. The information is then passed to the `GameMaster.cs` script for further processing.

We need to make several changes to the `GameMaster.cs` script. Here is a listing of the code:

```
using UnityEngine;
using UnityEngine.UI;
using UnityEngine.SceneManagement;

using System.Collections;

public class GameMaster : MonoBehaviour
{

  public static GameMaster instance;

  // let's have a reference to the player character
  // and start position of player character
  public GameObject PC;
  public GameObject START_POSITION;
```

[150]

```
    public GameObject CHARACTER_CUSTOMIZATION;

    // let's have a reference to the current scene/level
    public Scene CURRENT_SCENE;

    // Ref to UI Elements ...
    public bool DISPLAY_SETTINGS = false;
    public UIController UI;

    public int LEVEL = 0;

    // initial audio levels for background and
    // sound FX
    public float AUDIO_LEVEL = 0.33f;
    public float FX_LEVEL = 0.33f;

    void Awake()
    {
      // simple singleton
      if (instance == null)
      {
        instance = this;
      }
      else if (instance != this)
      {
        Destroy(this);
      }

      // keep the game object when moving from
      // one scene to the next scene
      DontDestroyOnLoad(this);

    }

    // Use this for initialization
    void Start()
    {
      // let's find a reference to the UI controller of the loaded scene
      if (GameObject.FindGameObjectWithTag("UI") != null)
      {
        GameMaster.instance.UI =
GameObject.FindGameObjectWithTag("UI").GetComponent<UIController>();
      }

GameMaster.instance.UI.SettingsCanvas.gameObject.SetActive(GameMaster.insta
nce.DISPLAY_SETTINGS);
    }
```

Game Master and Game Mechanics

```
// Update is called once per frame
void Update()
{

}

public void MasterVolume(float volume)
{
   GameMaster.instance.AUDIO_LEVEL = volume;
   GameMaster.instance.GetComponent<AudioSource>().volume =
GameMaster.instance.AUDIO_LEVEL;
}

public void StartGame()
{
   // NOTE: Start the game, load the scene that allows the player
   // to customize their character
   SceneManager.LoadScene(SceneName.CharacterCustomization);
}

}
```

This code needs a bit of explanation. The first and most important concept to take away is the concept of a Singleton. This is done by first defining a static variable, which will be used to hold our GameMaster instance:

```
public static GameMaster instance;
Then in our Awake() function, we need the following code:
void Awake()
{
// simple singleton
if (instance == null)
{
instance = this;
}
else if (instance != this)
{
Destroy(this);
}
// keep the game object when moving from
// one scene to the next scene
DontDestroyOnLoad(this);
}
```

[152]

Chapter 5

In the *Awake()* function, we are checking to see if the instance variable has been initialized. It sets the instance variable once. The next check ensures that we are always having one instance; in other words, if the GameMaster object gets instantiated a second time by mistake, it will destroy it. The last line of code *DotDestroyOnLoad()* will ensure that the GameObject does not get destroyed when we move from one scene to the next.

In the *Start()* function, we are checking to see if there is a uiController present, and if one exists, we are getting a reference to it. Once we have a reference to the uiController, we make sure that the *Settings Panel* by default is disabled, hidden.

The *MasterVolume()* function gets called from the UIController.cs script, which then passes the actual value from the slider defined to control the volume of the background music.

Managing scenes

The next item I want to make is to have the GameMaster control loading the different scenes for the game. Let's look at how the *GameMaster.cs* will look like with the new addition of scene management.

```
using UnityEngine;
using UnityEngine.UI;
using UnityEngine.SceneManagement;

using System.Collections;

/// <summary>
/// This class is used to make referencing easier in the code
/// </summary>
public static class SceneName
{
  public const string MainMenu = "MainMenu";
  public const string CharacterCustomization = "CH4_CC";
  public const string Level_1 = "CH5";
}

public class GameMaster : MonoBehaviour
{

  public static GameMaster instance;

  // let's have a reference to the player character
  // and start position of player character
  public GameObject PC;
  public GameObject START_POSITION;
  public GameObject CHARACTER_CUSTOMIZATION;
```

[153]

```csharp
// let's have a reference to the current scene/level
public Scene CURRENT_SCENE;

// Ref to UI Elements ...
public bool DISPLAY_SETTINGS = false;
public UIController UI;

public int LEVEL = 0;

// initial audio levels for background and
// sound FX
public float AUDIO_LEVEL = 0.33f;
public float FX_LEVEL = 0.33f;

void Awake()
{
  // simple singleton
  if (instance == null)
  {
    instance = this;
  }
  else if (instance != this)
  {
    Destroy(this);
  }

  // keep the game object when moving from
  // one scene to the next scene
  DontDestroyOnLoad(this);
}

// for each level/scene that has been loaded
// do some of the preparation work
void OnLevelWasLoaded()
{
  GameMaster.instance.CURRENT_SCENE = SceneManager.GetActiveScene();

  if
(GameMaster.instance.CURRENT_SCENE.name.Equals(SceneName.CharacterCustomiza
tion))
    {
      if (GameObject.FindGameObjectWithTag("BASE") != null)
      {
        GameMaster.instance.CHARACTER_CUSTOMIZATION =
GameObject.FindGameObjectWithTag("BASE") as GameObject;
      }
    }
```

```
    // If we are at any other scene except character customization
    // let's go ahead and get reference to player and player
    // stat position
    if (!this.CURRENT_SCENE.name.Equals(SceneName.CharacterCustomization))
    {
      // let's get a reference to our player character
      if (GameMaster.instance.PC == null)
      {
        if (GameObject.FindGameObjectWithTag("Player") != null)
        {
          GameMaster.instance.PC =
GameObject.FindGameObjectWithTag("Player") as GameObject;
        }
      }

      if (GameObject.FindGameObjectWithTag("START_POSITION") != null)
      {
        GameMaster.instance.START_POSITION =
GameObject.FindGameObjectWithTag("START_POSITION") as GameObject;
      }

      if (GameMaster.instance.START_POSITION != null &&
GameMaster.instance.PC != null)
      {
        GameMaster.instance.PC.transform.position =
GameMaster.instance.START_POSITION.transform.position;
        GameMaster.instance.PC.transform.rotation =
GameMaster.instance.START_POSITION.transform.rotation;
      }
    }

    DetermineLevel();

  }

  private void DetermineLevel()
  {
    switch(GameMaster.instance.CURRENT_SCENE.name)
    {
      case SceneName.MainMenu:
      case SceneName.CharacterCustomization:
        {
          GameMaster.instance.LEVEL = 0;
          break;
        }

      case SceneName.Level_1:
        {
```

Game Master and Game Mechanics

```csharp
                GameMaster.instance.LEVEL = 1;
                GameMaster.instance.PC.GetComponent<IKHandle>().enabled = true;
                break;
            }
        default:
            {
                GameMaster.instance.LEVEL = 0;
                break;
            }
        }
    }

    // Use this for initialization
    void Start()
    {
        // let's find a reference to the UI controller of the loaded scene
        if (GameObject.FindGameObjectWithTag("UI") != null)
        {
            GameMaster.instance.UI =
GameObject.FindGameObjectWithTag("UI").GetComponent<UIController>();
        }

GameMaster.instance.UI.SettingsCanvas.gameObject.SetActive(GameMaster.insta
nce.DISPLAY_SETTINGS);
    }

    // Update is called once per frame
    void Update()
    {

    }

    public void MasterVolume(float volume)
    {
        GameMaster.instance.AUDIO_LEVEL = volume;
        GameMaster.instance.GetComponent<AudioSource>().volume =
GameMaster.instance.AUDIO_LEVEL;
    }

    public void StartGame()
    {
        // NOTE: Start the game, load the scene that allows the player
        // to customize their character
        SceneManager.LoadScene(SceneName.CharacterCustomization);
    }

    public void LoadLevel()
    {
```

[156]

Chapter 5

```
    switch(GameMaster.instance.LEVEL)
    {
      // load level 1
      case 1:
        {
          GameMaster.instance.PC =
GameObject.FindGameObjectWithTag("Player") as GameObject;
          SceneManager.LoadScene(SceneName.Level_1);
          break;
        }
    }
  }
}
```

We have already discussed what the *Awake()* function is doing; let's take a look at the next important function, *OnLevelWasLoaded()*.

The *OnLevelWasLoaded()* function is called by Unity after the scene had been loaded. We are using this function in the GameMaster script to perform a few tasks. The first thing we do is get the current scene we are in. This information will be used later to determine what the GameMaster will do.

We check to see if we are in the character customization scene. This is where the player can customize the PC before they start playing the game. If we are in the character customization scene, we want to get a reference to the *Base* GameObject in the scene. If you recall, the *Base* GameObject has the *CharacterCutomization.cs* script attached to it, which is used to well customize the character.

If we are in any other scene, then we want to get a reference to the Player Character, and also the starting position of the player character at the beginning of the scene, if there is one.

We then use the *DetermineLevel()* function to determine the level we are currently on to make some more configuration.

The two function currently implemented for starting the game and loading the levels are handled by the *StartGame()* function and the *LoadLevel()* function.

```
/// <summary>
/// This class is used to make referencing easier in the code
/// </summary>
public static class SceneName
{
public const string MainMenu = "MainMenu";
public const string CharacterCustomization = "CH4_CC";
public const string Level_1 = "CH5";
}
```

[157]

Game Master and Game Mechanics

The *SceneName* class is designed to make it easier to refer to the scene names in the C# code. This makes it easier to chance the actual scene name within the project, but have a consistent call name in the code.

This is all good so far, but we can try to make it better.

Improving Game Master

The code we have so far works, but it is not very clean. Let's go ahead and structure the code a little better. Let's go ahead and create a new script called `LevelController.cs`. This new script will be handling the logic for our level management.

Level controller

Here is a listing of `LevelController.cs`:

```
using UnityEngine;
using UnityEngine.SceneManagement;
using System.Collections;

/// <summary>
/// This class is used to make referencing easier in the code
/// </summary>
public static class SceneName
{
  public const string MainMenu = "MainMenu";
  public const string CharacterCustomization = "CH4_CC";
  public const string Level_1 = "CH5";
}

public class LevelController
{
  // let's have a reference to the current scene/level
  public Scene CURRENT_SCENE
  {
    get { return SceneManager.GetActiveScene(); }
  }

  // keep the numerical level value
  public int LEVEL = 0;

  public void OnLevelWasLoaded()
  {
```

[158]

```
    // if we are in the character customization scene,
    // let's get a reference to the base game object for future use.
    if (this.CURRENT_SCENE.Equals(SceneName.CharacterCustomization))
    {
      if (GameObject.FindGameObjectWithTag("BASE") != null)
      {
        GameMaster.instance.CHARACTER_CUSTOMIZATION =
GameObject.FindGameObjectWithTag("BASE") as GameObject;
      }
    }

    // If we are at any other scene except character customization
    // let's go ahead and get reference to player and player
    // stat position
    if (this.CURRENT_SCENE.name.Equals(SceneName.CharacterCustomization))
    {
      // let's get a reference to our player character
      if (GameMaster.instance.PC == null)
      {
        if (GameObject.FindGameObjectWithTag("Player") != null)
        {
          GameMaster.instance.PC =
GameObject.FindGameObjectWithTag("Player") as GameObject;
        }
      }

      if (GameObject.FindGameObjectWithTag("START_POSITION") != null)
      {
        GameMaster.instance.START_POSITION =
GameObject.FindGameObjectWithTag("START_POSITION") as GameObject;
      }

      if (GameMaster.instance.START_POSITION != null &&
GameMaster.instance.PC != null)
      {
        GameMaster.instance.PC.transform.position =
GameMaster.instance.START_POSITION.transform.position;
        GameMaster.instance.PC.transform.rotation =
GameMaster.instance.START_POSITION.transform.rotation;
      }
    }

    // determine what level we are on
    this.DetermineLevel();
  }

  // this function will set a numerical value for our levels
  private void DetermineLevel()
```

```
        {
          switch (this.CURRENT_SCENE.name)
          {
            case SceneName.MainMenu:
            case SceneName.CharacterCustomization:
              {
                this.LEVEL = 0;
                break;
              }

            case SceneName.Level_1:
              {
                this.LEVEL = 1;
                GameMaster.instance.PC.GetComponent<IKHandle>().enabled = true;
                break;
              }
            default:
              {
                this.LEVEL = 0;
                break;
              }
          }
        }

        // this function will be used to load our scenes
        public void LoadLevel()
        {
          switch (GameMaster.instance.LEVEL_CONTROLLER.LEVEL)
          {
            case 0:
              {
                SceneManager.LoadScene(SceneName.CharacterCustomization);
                break;
              }

            // load level 1
            case 1:
              {
                GameMaster.instance.PC =
        GameObject.FindGameObjectWithTag("Player") as GameObject;
                SceneManager.LoadScene(SceneName.Level_1);
                break;
              }
          }
        }
      }
```

Chapter 5

So, what I have done is basically move all of the code that deals with level management into `LevelController.cs`. Our GameMaster drives the LevelController class. We will see this a bit later.

Audio controller

The next code clean up I want to do is for the audio. Let's create a new script called `AudioController.cs`. Here is the code for the new script:

```
using UnityEngine;
using System.Collections;

public class AudioController
{
  // initial audio levels for background and
  // sound FX
  public float AUDIO_LEVEL = 0.33f;
  public float FX_LEVEL = 0.33f;

  public AudioSource AUDIO_SOURCE;

  public void SetDefaultVolume()
  {
    this.AUDIO_SOURCE.volume = AUDIO_LEVEL;
  }

  public void MasterVolume(float volume)
  {
    this.AUDIO_LEVEL = volume;
    this.AUDIO_SOURCE.volume = AUDIO_LEVEL;
  }
}
```

The code is pretty straight forward. Now, let's take a look at what our `GameMaster.cs` looks like.

```
using UnityEngine;
using UnityEngine.UI;
using UnityEngine.SceneManagement;

using System.Collections;

public class GameMaster : MonoBehaviour
{
  public static GameMaster instance;
```

[161]

Game Master and Game Mechanics

```
// let's have a reference to the player character
// and start position of player character
public GameObject PC;
public GameObject START_POSITION;

public GameObject CHARACTER_CUSTOMIZATION;

public LevelController LEVEL_CONTROLLER;
public AudioController AUDIO_CONTROLLER;

// Ref to UI Elements ...
public bool DISPLAY_SETTINGS = false;
public UIController UI;

void Awake()
{
  // simple singleton
  if (instance == null)
  {
    instance = this;

    // initialize Level Controller
    instance.LEVEL_CONTROLLER = new LevelController();

    // initialize Audio Controller
    instance.AUDIO_CONTROLLER = new AudioController();
    instance.AUDIO_CONTROLLER.AUDIO_SOURCE =
GameMaster.instance.GetComponent<AudioSource>();
    instance.AUDIO_CONTROLLER.SetDefaultVolume();
  }
  else if (instance != this)
  {
    Destroy(this);
  }

  // keep the game object when moving from
  // one scene to the next scene
  DontDestroyOnLoad(this);
}

// for each level/scene that has been loaded
// do some of the preparation work
void OnLevelWasLoaded()
{
  GameMaster.instance.LEVEL_CONTROLLER.OnLevelWasLoaded();
}

// Use this for initialization
```

[162]

```
  void Start()
  {
    // let's find a reference to the UI controller of the loaded scene
    if (GameObject.FindGameObjectWithTag("UI") != null)
    {
      GameMaster.instance.UI =
GameObject.FindGameObjectWithTag("UI").GetComponent<UIController>();
    }

GameMaster.instance.UI.SettingsCanvas.gameObject.SetActive(GameMaster.insta
nce.DISPLAY_SETTINGS);
  }

  // Update is called once per frame
  void Update()
  {

  }

  public void MasterVolume(float volume)
  {
    GameMaster.instance.AUDIO_CONTROLLER.MasterVolume(volume);
  }

  public void StartGame()
  {
    GameMaster.instance.LoadLevel();
  }

  public void LoadLevel()
  {
    GameMaster.instance.LEVEL_CONTROLLER.LoadLevel();
  }
}
```

As you can see, the code is easier to read and also it is better structured. The `GameMaster` is using the controllers for performing each specific task. This also makes it easier to maintain code for different tasks within our game. For instance, all of the audio-related code can be now implemented in the controller and so on.

Game Master and Game Mechanics

Player data management

We have not saved the actual data representing the customization of our player. The next step is to enhance our `PC.cs` and `CharacterCustomization.cs` scripts to actually save the selected data in our PC object.

PC class enhancements

To do this, we need to modify our PC.cs code; here is the new code listing:

```
using System;

[Serializable]
public class PC : BaseCharacter
{

  public enum SHOULDER_PAD
  {
    none = 0,
    SP01 = 1,
    SP02 = 2,
    SP03 = 3,
    SP04 = 4
  };

  public enum BODY_TYPE { normal = 1, BT01 = 2, BT02 = 3 };

  // Shoulder Pad
  public SHOULDER_PAD selectedShoulderPad = SHOULDER_PAD.none;
  public BODY_TYPE selectedBodyType = BODY_TYPE.normal;

  public bool kneePad = false;
  public bool legPlate = false;

  public enum WEAPON_TYPE
  {
    none = 0,
    axe1 = 1,
    axe2 = 2,
    club1 = 3,
    club2 = 4,
    falchion = 5,
    gladius = 6,
    mace = 7,
    maul = 8,
```

[164]

```
        scimitar = 9,
        spear = 10,
        sword1 = 11,
        sword2 = 12,
        sword3 = 13
    };

    public WEAPON_TYPE selectedWeapon = WEAPON_TYPE.none;

    public enum HELMET_TYPE { none = 0, HL01 = 1, HL02 = 2, HL03 = 3, HL04 =
4 };

    public HELMET_TYPE selectedHelmet = HELMET_TYPE.none;

    public enum SHIELD_TYPE { none = 0, SL01 = 1, SL02 = 2 };

    public SHIELD_TYPE selectedShield = SHIELD_TYPE.none;

    public int SKIN_ID = 1;

    public enum BOOT_TYPE { none = 0, BT01 = 1, BT02 = 2 };
    public BOOT_TYPE selectedBoot = BOOT_TYPE.none;
}
```

We defined several enumeration types that describe the different parts of the player character's customization. There are several advantages in using enumeration in our code, a few of them being named constants, the name describes what they are for, type safety and easier to change the value of the enumeration without having to check a hundred different places within your code.

As stated in the previous chapters, the character customization code is heavily related to your character model and how you have rigged up your character model to be used in the game.

Game Master and Game Mechanics

 Note that you will need to modify the name of your UI elements to match the new code.

There are a few things you will need to configure to make sure the code works properly. First, you will need to name your UI elements properly to match the enumeration. The preceding figure illustrates for one of the UI elements representing a shoulder pad.

Character customization class update

The events that drive the character customization are attached to the Base prefab, which has the `CharacterCustomization.cs` script as a component. The `CharacterCustomization.cs` script is listed here:

```
using UnityEngine;
using UnityEngine.UI;
using System.Collections;
```

```csharp
using UnityEngine.SceneManagement;
using System;

public class CharacterCustomization : MonoBehaviour
{
  // reference to PC Game Object
  public GameObject PLAYER_CHARACTER;

  // variable used to hold the PC Customization
  public PC PC_CC;

  public Material[] PLAYER_SKIN;

  public GameObject CLOTH_01LOD0;
  public GameObject CLOTH_01LOD0_SKIN;
  public GameObject CLOTH_02LOD0;
  public GameObject CLOTH_02LOD0_SKIN;
  public GameObject CLOTH_03LOD0;
  public GameObject CLOTH_03LOD0_SKIN;
  public GameObject CLOTH_03LOD0_FAT;

  public GameObject BELT_LOD0;

  public GameObject SKN_LOD0;
  public GameObject FAT_LOD0;
  public GameObject RGL_LOD0;

  public GameObject HAIR_LOD0;

  public GameObject BOW_LOD0;

  // Head Equipment
  public GameObject GLADIATOR_01LOD0;
  public GameObject HELMET_01LOD0;
  public GameObject HELMET_02LOD0;
  public GameObject HELMET_03LOD0;
  public GameObject HELMET_04LOD0;

  // Shoulder Pad - Right Arm / Left Arm
  public GameObject SHOULDER_PAD_R_01LOD0;
  public GameObject SHOULDER_PAD_R_02LOD0;
  public GameObject SHOULDER_PAD_R_03LOD0;
  public GameObject SHOULDER_PAD_R_04LOD0;

  public GameObject SHOULDER_PAD_L_01LOD0;
  public GameObject SHOULDER_PAD_L_02LOD0;
  public GameObject SHOULDER_PAD_L_03LOD0;
  public GameObject SHOULDER_PAD_L_04LOD0;
```

Game Master and Game Mechanics

```
// Fore Arm - Right / Left Plates
public GameObject ARM_PLATE_R_1LOD0;
public GameObject ARM_PLATE_R_2LOD0;

public GameObject ARM_PLATE_L_1LOD0;
public GameObject ARM_PLATE_L_2LOD0;

// Player Character Weapons
public GameObject AXE_01LOD0;
public GameObject AXE_02LOD0;
public GameObject CLUB_01LOD0;
public GameObject CLUB_02LOD0;
public GameObject FALCHION_LOD0;
public GameObject GLADIUS_LOD0;
public GameObject MACE_LOD0;
public GameObject MAUL_LOD0;
public GameObject SCIMITAR_LOD0;
public GameObject SPEAR_LOD0;
public GameObject SWORD_BASTARD_LOD0;
public GameObject SWORD_BOARD_01LOD0;
public GameObject SWORD_SHORT_LOD0;

// Player Character Defense Weapons
public GameObject SHIELD_01LOD0;
public GameObject SHIELD_02LOD0;

public GameObject QUIVER_LOD0;
public GameObject BOW_01_LOD0;

// Player Character Calf - Right / Left
public GameObject KNEE_PAD_R_LOD0;
public GameObject LEG_PLATE_R_LOD0;

public GameObject KNEE_PAD_L_LOD0;
public GameObject LEG_PLATE_L_LOD0;

public GameObject BOOT_01LOD0;
public GameObject BOOT_02LOD0;

// Use this for initialization
void Start()
{
  this.PC_CC =
this.PLAYER_CHARACTER.GetComponent<PlayerAgent>().playerCharacterData;
}

public bool ROTATE_MODEL = false;
// Update is called once per frame
```

[168]

```csharp
  void Update()
  {
    if (Input.GetKeyUp(KeyCode.R))
    {
      this.ROTATE_MODEL = !this.ROTATE_MODEL;
    }

    if (this.ROTATE_MODEL)
    {
      this.PLAYER_CHARACTER.transform.Rotate(new Vector3(0, 1, 0), 33.0f *
Time.deltaTime);
    }

    if (Input.GetKeyUp(KeyCode.L))
    {

      Debug.Log(PlayerPrefs.GetString("NAME"));
    }

  }

  public void SetShoulderPad(Toggle id)
  {

    try
    {
      PC.SHOULDER_PAD name =
(PC.SHOULDER_PAD)Enum.Parse(typeof(PC.SHOULDER_PAD), id.name, true);
      if(id.isOn)
      {
        this.PC CC.selectedShoulderPad = name;
        Debug.Log(string.Format("{0} was turned on", name));
      }
      else
      {
        this.PC_CC.selectedShoulderPad = PC.SHOULDER_PAD.none;
        Debug.Log(string.Format("{0} was turned off", name));
      }
    }
    catch
    {
      // if the value passed is not in the enumeration set it to none
      this.PC_CC.selectedShoulderPad = PC.SHOULDER_PAD.none;
      Debug.Log("Shoulder Pad Enumeration Not Found!");
    }

    switch (id.name)
    {
```

```
case "SP01":
  {
    this.SHOULDER_PAD_R_01LOD0.SetActive(id.isOn);
    this.SHOULDER_PAD_R_02LOD0.SetActive(false);
    this.SHOULDER_PAD_R_03LOD0.SetActive(false);
    this.SHOULDER_PAD_R_04LOD0.SetActive(false);

    this.SHOULDER_PAD_L_01LOD0.SetActive(id.isOn);
    this.SHOULDER_PAD_L_02LOD0.SetActive(false);
    this.SHOULDER_PAD_L_03LOD0.SetActive(false);
    this.SHOULDER_PAD_L_04LOD0.SetActive(false);
    break;
  }
case "SP02":
  {
    this.SHOULDER_PAD_R_01LOD0.SetActive(false);
    this.SHOULDER_PAD_R_02LOD0.SetActive(id.isOn);
    this.SHOULDER_PAD_R_03LOD0.SetActive(false);
    this.SHOULDER_PAD_R_04LOD0.SetActive(false);

    this.SHOULDER_PAD_L_01LOD0.SetActive(false);
    this.SHOULDER_PAD_L_02LOD0.SetActive(id.isOn);
    this.SHOULDER_PAD_L_03LOD0.SetActive(false);
    this.SHOULDER_PAD_L_04LOD0.SetActive(false);
    break;
  }
case "SP03":
  {
    this.SHOULDER_PAD_R_01LOD0.SetActive(false);
    this.SHOULDER_PAD_R_02LOD0.SetActive(false);
    this.SHOULDER_PAD_R_03LOD0.SetActive(id.isOn);
    this.SHOULDER_PAD_R_04LOD0.SetActive(false);

    this.SHOULDER_PAD_L_01LOD0.SetActive(false);
    this.SHOULDER_PAD_L_02LOD0.SetActive(false);
    this.SHOULDER_PAD_L_03LOD0.SetActive(id.isOn);
    this.SHOULDER_PAD_L_04LOD0.SetActive(false);
    break;
  }
case "SP04":
  {
    this.SHOULDER_PAD_R_01LOD0.SetActive(false);
    this.SHOULDER_PAD_R_02LOD0.SetActive(false);
    this.SHOULDER_PAD_R_03LOD0.SetActive(false);
    this.SHOULDER_PAD_R_04LOD0.SetActive(id.isOn);

    this.SHOULDER_PAD_L_01LOD0.SetActive(false);
    this.SHOULDER_PAD_L_02LOD0.SetActive(false);
```

```csharp
          this.SHOULDER_PAD_L_03LOD0.SetActive(false);
          this.SHOULDER_PAD_L_04LOD0.SetActive(id.isOn);
          break;
        }
    default:
      {
        this.SHOULDER_PAD_R_01LOD0.SetActive(false);
        this.SHOULDER_PAD_R_02LOD0.SetActive(false);
        this.SHOULDER_PAD_R_03LOD0.SetActive(false);
        this.SHOULDER_PAD_R_04LOD0.SetActive(false);

        this.SHOULDER_PAD_L_01LOD0.SetActive(false);
        this.SHOULDER_PAD_L_02LOD0.SetActive(false);
        this.SHOULDER_PAD_L_03LOD0.SetActive(false);
        this.SHOULDER_PAD_L_04LOD0.SetActive(false);
        break;
      }
    }
  }
}

public void SetBodyType(Toggle id)
{
  try
  {
    PC.BODY_TYPE name = (PC.BODY_TYPE)Enum.Parse(typeof(PC.BODY_TYPE),
id.name, true);
    if(id.isOn)
    {
      this.PC_CC.selectedBodyType = name;
      Debug.Log(string.Format("{0} was turned on", name));
    }
    else
    {
      this.PC_CC.selectedBodyType = PC.BODY_TYPE.normal;
      Debug.Log(string.Format("{0} was turned off", name));
    }
  }
  catch
  {
    // if the value passed is not in the enumeration set it to none
    this.PC_CC.selectedBodyType= PC.BODY_TYPE.normal;
    Debug.Log("Body Type Enumeration Not Found!");
  }

  switch (id.name)
  {
    case "BT01":
      {
```

Game Master and Game Mechanics

```
                this.RGL_LOD0.SetActive(id.isOn);
                this.FAT_LOD0.SetActive(false);
                break;
            }
        case "BT02":
            {
                this.RGL_LOD0.SetActive(false);
                this.FAT_LOD0.SetActive(id.isOn);
                break;
            }
        default:
            {
                this.RGL_LOD0.SetActive(false);
                this.FAT_LOD0.SetActive(false);
                break;
            }
        }
    }

    public void SetKneePad(Toggle id)
    {
        this.KNEE_PAD_R_LOD0.SetActive(id.isOn);
        this.KNEE_PAD_L_LOD0.SetActive(id.isOn);
    }

    public void SetLegPlate(Toggle id)
    {
        this.LEG_PLATE_R_LOD0.SetActive(id.isOn);
        this.LEG_PLATE_L_LOD0.SetActive(id.isOn);
    }

    public void SetWeaponType(Slider id)
    {
        try
        {
            PC.WEAPON_TYPE weapon =
(PC.WEAPON_TYPE)System.Convert.ToInt32(id.value);
            this.PC_CC.selectedWeapon = weapon;
            Debug.Log(string.Format("Weapon selected: {0}", weapon.ToString()));
        }
        catch
        {
            this.PC_CC.selectedWeapon = PC.WEAPON_TYPE.none;
        }

        switch (System.Convert.ToInt32(id.value))
        {
            case 0:
```

```
        {
          this.AXE_01LOD0.SetActive(false);
          this.AXE_02LOD0.SetActive(false);
          this.CLUB_01LOD0.SetActive(false);
          this.CLUB_02LOD0.SetActive(false);
          this.FALCHION_LOD0.SetActive(false);
          this.GLADIUS_LOD0.SetActive(false);
          this.MACE_LOD0.SetActive(false);
          this.MAUL_LOD0.SetActive(false);
          this.SCIMITAR_LOD0.SetActive(false);
          this.SPEAR_LOD0.SetActive(false);
          this.SWORD_BASTARD_LOD0.SetActive(false);
          this.SWORD_BOARD_01LOD0.SetActive(false);
          this.SWORD_SHORT_LOD0.SetActive(false);
          break;
        }
    case 1:
        {
          this.AXE_01LOD0.SetActive(true);
          this.AXE_02LOD0.SetActive(false);
          this.CLUB_01LOD0.SetActive(false);
          this.CLUB_02LOD0.SetActive(false);
          this.FALCHION_LOD0.SetActive(false);
          this.GLADIUS_LOD0.SetActive(false);
          this.MACE_LOD0.SetActive(false);
          this.MAUL_LOD0.SetActive(false);
          this.SCIMITAR_LOD0.SetActive(false);
          this.SPEAR_LOD0.SetActive(false);
          this.SWORD_BASTARD_LOD0.SetActive(false);
          this.SWORD_BOARD_01LOD0.SetActive(false);
          this.SWORD_SHORT_LOD0.SetActive(false);
          break;
        }
    case 2:
        {
          this.AXE_01LOD0.SetActive(false);
          this.AXE_02LOD0.SetActive(true);
          this.CLUB_01LOD0.SetActive(false);
          this.CLUB_02LOD0.SetActive(false);
          this.FALCHION_LOD0.SetActive(false);
          this.GLADIUS_LOD0.SetActive(false);
          this.MACE_LOD0.SetActive(false);
          this.MAUL_LOD0.SetActive(false);
          this.SCIMITAR_LOD0.SetActive(false);
          this.SPEAR_LOD0.SetActive(false);
          this.SWORD_BASTARD_LOD0.SetActive(false);
          this.SWORD_BOARD_01LOD0.SetActive(false);
          this.SWORD_SHORT_LOD0.SetActive(false);
```

```
        break;
    }
case 3:
    {
        this.AXE_01LOD0.SetActive(false);
        this.AXE_02LOD0.SetActive(false);
        this.CLUB_01LOD0.SetActive(true);
        this.CLUB_02LOD0.SetActive(false);
        this.FALCHION_LOD0.SetActive(false);
        this.GLADIUS_LOD0.SetActive(false);
        this.MACE_LOD0.SetActive(false);
        this.MAUL_LOD0.SetActive(false);
        this.SCIMITAR_LOD0.SetActive(false);
        this.SPEAR_LOD0.SetActive(false);
        this.SWORD_BASTARD_LOD0.SetActive(false);
        this.SWORD_BOARD_01LOD0.SetActive(false);
        this.SWORD_SHORT_LOD0.SetActive(false);
        break;
    }
case 4:
    {
        this.AXE_01LOD0.SetActive(false);
        this.AXE_02LOD0.SetActive(false);
        this.CLUB_01LOD0.SetActive(false);
        this.CLUB_02LOD0.SetActive(true);
        this.FALCHION_LOD0.SetActive(false);
        this.GLADIUS_LOD0.SetActive(false);
        this.MACE_LOD0.SetActive(false);
        this.MAUL_LOD0.SetActive(false);
        this.SCIMITAR_LOD0.SetActive(false);
        this.SPEAR_LOD0.SetActive(false);
        this.SWORD_BASTARD_LOD0.SetActive(false);
        this.SWORD_BOARD_01LOD0.SetActive(false);
        this.SWORD_SHORT_LOD0.SetActive(false);
        break;
    }
case 5:
    {
        this.AXE_01LOD0.SetActive(false);
        this.AXE_02LOD0.SetActive(false);
        this.CLUB_01LOD0.SetActive(false);
        this.CLUB_02LOD0.SetActive(false);
        this.FALCHION_LOD0.SetActive(true);
        this.GLADIUS_LOD0.SetActive(false);
        this.MACE_LOD0.SetActive(false);
        this.MAUL_LOD0.SetActive(false);
        this.SCIMITAR_LOD0.SetActive(false);
        this.SPEAR_LOD0.SetActive(false);
```

```
      this.SWORD_BASTARD_LOD0.SetActive(false);
      this.SWORD_BOARD_01LOD0.SetActive(false);
      this.SWORD_SHORT_LOD0.SetActive(false);
      break;
   }
case 6:
   {
      this.AXE_01LOD0.SetActive(false);
      this.AXE_02LOD0.SetActive(false);
      this.CLUB_01LOD0.SetActive(false);
      this.CLUB_02LOD0.SetActive(false);
      this.FALCHION_LOD0.SetActive(false);
      this.GLADIUS_LOD0.SetActive(true);
      this.MACE_LOD0.SetActive(false);
      this.MAUL_LOD0.SetActive(false);
      this.SCIMITAR_LOD0.SetActive(false);
      this.SPEAR_LOD0.SetActive(false);
      this.SWORD_BASTARD_LOD0.SetActive(false);
      this.SWORD_BOARD_01LOD0.SetActive(false);
      this.SWORD_SHORT_LOD0.SetActive(false);
      break;
   }
case 7:
   {
      this.AXE_01LOD0.SetActive(false);
      this.AXE_02LOD0.SetActive(false);
      this.CLUB_01LOD0.SetActive(false);
      this.CLUB_02LOD0.SetActive(false);
      this.FALCHION_LOD0.SetActive(false);
      this.GLADIUS_LOD0.SetActive(false);
      this.MACE_LOD0.SetActive(true);
      this.MAUL_LOD0.SetActive(false);
      this.SCIMITAR_LOD0.SetActive(false);
      this.SPEAR_LOD0.SetActive(false);
      this.SWORD_BASTARD_LOD0.SetActive(false);
      this.SWORD_BOARD_01LOD0.SetActive(false);
      this.SWORD_SHORT_LOD0.SetActive(false);
      break;
   }
case 8:
   {
      this.AXE_01LOD0.SetActive(false);
      this.AXE_02LOD0.SetActive(false);
      this.CLUB_01LOD0.SetActive(false);
      this.CLUB_02LOD0.SetActive(false);
      this.FALCHION_LOD0.SetActive(false);
      this.GLADIUS_LOD0.SetActive(false);
      this.MACE_LOD0.SetActive(false);
```

```
            this.MAUL_LOD0.SetActive(true);
            this.SCIMITAR_LOD0.SetActive(false);
            this.SPEAR_LOD0.SetActive(false);
            this.SWORD_BASTARD_LOD0.SetActive(false);
            this.SWORD_BOARD_01LOD0.SetActive(false);
            this.SWORD_SHORT_LOD0.SetActive(false);
            break;
        }
    case 9:
        {
            this.AXE_01LOD0.SetActive(false);
            this.AXE_02LOD0.SetActive(false);
            this.CLUB_01LOD0.SetActive(false);
            this.CLUB_02LOD0.SetActive(false);
            this.FALCHION_LOD0.SetActive(false);
            this.GLADIUS_LOD0.SetActive(false);
            this.MACE_LOD0.SetActive(false);
            this.MAUL_LOD0.SetActive(false);
            this.SCIMITAR_LOD0.SetActive(true);
            this.SPEAR_LOD0.SetActive(false);
            this.SWORD_BASTARD_LOD0.SetActive(false);
            this.SWORD_BOARD_01LOD0.SetActive(false);
            this.SWORD_SHORT_LOD0.SetActive(false);
            break;
        }
    case 10:
        {
            this.AXE_01LOD0.SetActive(false);
            this.AXE_02LOD0.SetActive(false);
            this.CLUB_01LOD0.SetActive(false);
            this.CLUB_02LOD0.SetActive(false);
            this.FALCHION_LOD0.SetActive(false);
            this.GLADIUS_LOD0.SetActive(false);
            this.MACE_LOD0.SetActive(false);
            this.MAUL_LOD0.SetActive(false);
            this.SCIMITAR_LOD0.SetActive(false);
            this.SPEAR_LOD0.SetActive(true);
            this.SWORD_BASTARD_LOD0.SetActive(false);
            this.SWORD_BOARD_01LOD0.SetActive(false);
            this.SWORD_SHORT_LOD0.SetActive(false);
            break;
        }
    case 11:
        {
            this.AXE_01LOD0.SetActive(false);
            this.AXE_02LOD0.SetActive(false);
            this.CLUB_01LOD0.SetActive(false);
            this.CLUB_02LOD0.SetActive(false);
```

```
            this.FALCHION_LOD0.SetActive(false);
            this.GLADIUS_LOD0.SetActive(false);
            this.MACE_LOD0.SetActive(false);
            this.MAUL_LOD0.SetActive(false);
            this.SCIMITAR_LOD0.SetActive(false);
            this.SPEAR_LOD0.SetActive(false);
            this.SWORD_BASTARD_LOD0.SetActive(true);
            this.SWORD_BOARD_01LOD0.SetActive(false);
            this.SWORD_SHORT_LOD0.SetActive(false);
            break;
        }
    case 12:
        {
            this.AXE_01LOD0.SetActive(false);
            this.AXE_02LOD0.SetActive(false);
            this.CLUB_01LOD0.SetActive(false);
            this.CLUB_02LOD0.SetActive(false);
            this.FALCHION_LOD0.SetActive(false);
            this.GLADIUS_LOD0.SetActive(false);
            this.MACE_LOD0.SetActive(false);
            this.MAUL_LOD0.SetActive(false);
            this.SCIMITAR_LOD0.SetActive(false);
            this.SPEAR_LOD0.SetActive(false);
            this.SWORD_BASTARD_LOD0.SetActive(false);
            this.SWORD_BOARD_01LOD0.SetActive(true);
            this.SWORD_SHORT_LOD0.SetActive(false);
            break;
        }
    case 13:
        {
            this.AXE_01LOD0.SetActive(false);
            this.AXE_02LOD0.SetActive(false);
            this.CLUB_01LOD0.SetActive(false);
            this.CLUB_02LOD0.SetActive(false);
            this.FALCHION_LOD0.SetActive(false);
            this.GLADIUS_LOD0.SetActive(false);
            this.MACE_LOD0.SetActive(false);
            this.MAUL_LOD0.SetActive(false);
            this.SCIMITAR_LOD0.SetActive(false);
            this.SPEAR_LOD0.SetActive(false);
            this.SWORD_BASTARD_LOD0.SetActive(false);
            this.SWORD_BOARD_01LOD0.SetActive(false);
            this.SWORD_SHORT_LOD0.SetActive(true);
            break;
        }

    }
}
```

```
public void SetHelmetType(Toggle id)
{
  try
  {
    PC.HELMET_TYPE name =
(PC.HELMET_TYPE)Enum.Parse(typeof(PC.HELMET_TYPE), id.name, true);
    if (id.isOn)
    {
      this.PC_CC.selectedHelmet = name;
      Debug.Log(string.Format("{0} was turned on", name));
    }
    else
    {
      this.PC_CC.selectedHelmet = PC.HELMET_TYPE.none;
      Debug.Log(string.Format("{0} was turned off", name));
    }
  }
  catch
  {
    // if the value passed is not in the enumeration set it to none
    this.PC_CC.selectedHelmet = PC.HELMET_TYPE.none;
    Debug.Log("Helmet Type Enumeration Not Found!");
  }

  switch (id.name)
  {
    case "HL01":
      {
        this.HELMET_01LOD0.SetActive(id.isOn);
        this.HELMET_02LOD0.SetActive(false);
        this.HELMET_03LOD0.SetActive(false);
        this.HELMET_04LOD0.SetActive(false);
        break;
      }
    case "HL02":
      {
        this.HELMET_01LOD0.SetActive(false);
        this.HELMET_02LOD0.SetActive(id.isOn);
        this.HELMET_03LOD0.SetActive(false);
        this.HELMET_04LOD0.SetActive(false);
        break;
      }
    case "HL03":
      {
        this.HELMET_01LOD0.SetActive(false);
        this.HELMET_02LOD0.SetActive(false);
        this.HELMET_03LOD0.SetActive(id.isOn);
        this.HELMET_04LOD0.SetActive(false);
```

```
        break;
      }
  case "HL04":
    {
      this.HELMET_01LOD0.SetActive(false);
      this.HELMET_02LOD0.SetActive(false);
      this.HELMET_03LOD0.SetActive(false);
      this.HELMET_04LOD0.SetActive(id.isOn);
      break;
    }
  default:
    {
      this.HELMET_01LOD0.SetActive(false);
      this.HELMET_02LOD0.SetActive(false);
      this.HELMET_03LOD0.SetActive(false);
      this.HELMET_04LOD0.SetActive(false);
      break;
    }
  }
}

public void SetShieldType(Toggle id)
{
  try
  {
    PC.SHIELD_TYPE name =
(PC.SHIELD_TYPE)Enum.Parse(typeof(PC.SHIELD_TYPE), id.name, true);
    if (id.isOn)
    {
      this.PC_CC.selectedShield = name;
      Debug.Log(string.Format("{0} was turned on", name));
    }
    else
    {
      this.PC_CC.selectedShield = PC.SHIELD_TYPE.none;
      Debug.Log(string.Format("{0} was turned off", name));
    }
  }
  catch
  {
    // if the value passed is not in the enumeration set it to none
    this.PC_CC.selectedShield = PC.SHIELD_TYPE.none;
    Debug.Log("Shield Type Enumeration Not Found!");
  }

  switch (id.name)
  {
    case "SL01":
```

Game Master and Game Mechanics

```csharp
        {
          this.SHIELD_01LOD0.SetActive(id.isOn);
          this.SHIELD_02LOD0.SetActive(false);
          break;
        }
      case "SL02":
        {
          this.SHIELD_01LOD0.SetActive(false);
          this.SHIELD_02LOD0.SetActive(id.isOn);
          break;
        }
      default:
        {
          this.SHIELD_01LOD0.SetActive(false);
          this.SHIELD_02LOD0.SetActive(false);
          break;
        }
    }
  }

  public void SetSkinType(Slider id)
  {
    this.PC_CC.SKIN_ID = System.Convert.ToInt32(id.value);
    Debug.Log(string.Format("Skin ID is {0}", this.PC_CC.SKIN_ID));

    this.SKN_LOD0.GetComponent<Renderer>().material =
this.PLAYER_SKIN[System.Convert.ToInt32(id.value)];
    this.FAT_LOD0.GetComponent<Renderer>().material =
this.PLAYER_SKIN[System.Convert.ToInt32(id.value)];
    this.RGL_LOD0.GetComponent<Renderer>().material =
this.PLAYER_SKIN[System.Convert.ToInt32(id.value)];
  }

  public void SetBootType(Toggle id)
  {
    try
    {
      PC.BOOT_TYPE name = (PC.BOOT_TYPE)Enum.Parse(typeof(PC.BOOT_TYPE),
id.name, true);
      if (id.isOn)
      {
        this.PC_CC.selectedBoot = name;
        Debug.Log(string.Format("{0} was turned on", name));
      }
      else
      {
        this.PC_CC.selectedBoot = PC.BOOT_TYPE.none;
        Debug.Log(string.Format("{0} was turned off", name));
```

```
            }
        }
        catch
        {
            // if the value passed is not in the enumeration set it to none
            this.PC_CC.selectedBoot = PC.BOOT_TYPE.none;
            Debug.Log("Boot Type Enumeration Not Found!");
        }

        switch (id.name)
        {
            case "BT01":
                {
                    this.BOOT_01LOD0.SetActive(id.isOn);
                    this.BOOT_02LOD0.SetActive(false);
                    break;
                }
            case "BT02":
                {
                    this.BOOT_01LOD0.SetActive(false);
                    this.BOOT_02LOD0.SetActive(id.isOn);
                    break;
                }
            default:
                {
                    this.BOOT_01LOD0.SetActive(false);
                    this.BOOT_02LOD0.SetActive(false);
                    break;
                }
        }
    }
}
```

In the preceding code, what we have done is added a new variable of type *PC* named
PC_CC. The *PC* class is the player character class we defined an enhanced to contain the
data for our player character.

The next logic we need to implement is to detect which option the player has selected
through the character customization UI and appropriately set the data in the *PC* object. The
implementation concept is the same for all the different parts of the player character that
can be customized. I will be listing one of them here.

```
public void SetBodyType(Toggle id)
{
try
{
PC.BODY_TYPE name = (PC.BODY_TYPE)Enum.Parse(typeof(PC.BODY_TYPE), id.name,
```

Game Master and Game Mechanics

```
true);
if(id.isOn)
{
this.PC_CC.selectedBodyType = name;
Debug.Log(string.Format("{0} was turned on", name));
}
else
{
this.PC_CC.selectedBodyType = PC.BODY_TYPE.normal;
Debug.Log(string.Format("{0} was turned off", name));
}
}
catch
{
// if the value passed is not in the enumeration set it to none
this.PC_CC.selectedBodyType= PC.BODY_TYPE.normal;
Debug.Log("Body Type Enumeration Not Found!");
}
...
}
```

The preceding code is for the customization of the body type of the player character. The first thing it tries to do is to parse and convert the value passed to the function by the UI component. Next, it sets the `selectedBodyType` variable in the *PC* object. If for some reason, the value passed does not exist in the enumeration, we will assign the default value to the `selectedBodyType` variable. There is also debug statements to give you feedback about the current value.

Changes to UI Controller

The UI Controller will also need to be updated now to make the necessary changes to the `GameMaster` object. We would need to update the `LoadLevel()` function to the following:

```
public void LoadLevel()
{
if(GameObject.FindGameObjectWithTag("BASE"))
{
GameMaster.instance.PC_CC =
GameObject.FindGameObjectWithTag("BASE").GetComponent<CharacterCustomizatio
n>().PC_CC;
}
GameMaster.instance.LEVEL_CONTROLLER.LEVEL = 1;
GameMaster.instance.LoadLevel();
}
```

This will make sure that GameMaster is updated with the proper player character data. Let's go ahead and test the code.

Testing

Starting from the Main Menu scene, make sure that you have the following GameObjects in the scene: `uiController` and `_GameMaster`. The `uiController` game object should have `UIController.cs` attached and `_GameMaster` should have the following components attached: `GameMaster.cs` and an `AudioSource` component that will be used for the background music.

Have the `_GameMaster` GameObject selected in the `Hierarchy Window`; run the game. Select the *Start Game* button. This will load the character customization scene. The `_GameMaster` GameObject should still be selected, if not, go ahead and select it from the *Hierarchy Window*, do some of the character customization and click on the **Save** button.

Game Master and Game Mechanics

The first level should have been loaded with your character and the customization you have made to your character in the previous step. So visually, your character has retained all of the customization you have done, and from a data point of view, when you look at the `_GameMaster` GameObject in the Inspector Window, you will notice that the data has been saved properly as shown in the preceding figure.

Summary

Chapter 5 was mostly code. We enhanced the `GameMaster` Class to handle the game settings and scene management. We began the chapter by making the `GameMaster` handle the user interface, the player character data, and the game settings, which currently is just the volume for the background music.

We added a new UI element that displays the settings panel for the game. At the moment, it only contains the main volume control. Next, we added the necessary code in the `UIController` class and the `GameMaster` class to handle the display of the settings window and also the slider value passed from the UI component to the `UIController` to the `GameMaster` class.

We also made the `GameMaster` class into a singleton. A singleton in software engineering is a design pattern that restricts the instantiation of a class to one object. This pattern fits perfectly for the `GameMaster` as we only need to have one instance of it active at any given time throughout the lifespan of the game.

We also looked how to perform scene management. We defined a static class named `SceneName` that contains constant string variables identifying the scene references in our game.

We then took the next step to improve our `GameMaster` and the internal structure for our code. We created a new class called `LevelController.cs` that handles the scene management who in turn is driven by the `GameMaster`. We practically took the logic for level handling from within the `GameMaster` class and reworked and improved it in the `LevelController` class.

Next, we developed an `AudioController` class that basically manages the audio for our game. This class also is driven by the `GameMaster`. By this time, our `GameMaster` is a lean script that manages all of the other components.

Chapter 5

The next big challenge was how to handle the player character data. Specifically speaking, how to save the character customization data for the player character internally after the player had customized the character. In order to save the data, we had to modify the PC.cs class.

We created several enumerations representing each part of the character that could be customized, such as the shoulder pad, the body type, the weapon type, the helmet type and so on. We used enumeration to make it easier to reference them within the code.

This approached forced us to make some modifications to the existing character customization setup that we have had implemented previously. So we had to update the UI components, to reflect the enumeration defined for each customizable type and we also had to modify the `CharacterCustomization.cs` class to handle the new changes.

The `CharacterCustomization` class implemented a *PC* type variable to keep track of the customizations and finally pass the data along to the `GameMaster`. During the process, we also improved the case handling of the `CharacterCustomization` class for default values and so on.

Finally, we had a test run of the game to double check that everything worked as designed and implemented.

We created a lot of code in this chapter. In the next chapter, we are going to start building our inventory system, and yes, that is going to involve more code!

6
Inventory System

The inventory system is one of the most critical components of an RPG. It will be used to store all important game elements that the player will need in your game environment. This chapter will guide you on how to create a simple generic Inventory System that can be utilized and extended as you see fit.

Here is a breakdown of the chapter:

- Inventory system
    - Weighted inventory
    - Determining item types
- Creating inventory items
    - Creating the prefab
    - Adding Inventory Item Agent
    - Inventory items defined as prefabs
- Inventory interface
    - Creating the inventory UI framework
    - Designing a dynamic item viewer
        - Adding a Scroll View
        - Adding elements to PanelItem and Scroll View
        - Adding txtItemElement dynamically
    - Building the final inventory item UI
- Integrating the UI with the actual inventory system
    - Hooking the category buttons and displaying the data
    - Testing the inventory system

- Inventory items and the player character
  - Applying inventory items
  - How it looks

There is a lot of work ahead of us in this chapter. Let's get started!

Inventory system

As with everything else we have discussed thus far, designing your Inventory System is also going to be heavily dependent on your game. There are many different types of Inventory System mechanics that you can study and choose based on the relevance of it to your game.

Weighted Inventory

I am going to be leaning towards implementing what is called the Weighted Inventory. In this type of inventory system, each item or piece of equipment is assigned a numerical value that represents the weight of the item. This in turn is used to determine how much inventory the player can carry at any given time during game play. This makes sense for our RPG, if you think about it.

Consider the following as an example: assume you are a hiker who wants to climb Mount Ararat. The climb itself is going to require some time and during the journey you will need to carry with you the necessary equipment to be able to complete the journey. Realistically, there are several crucial items that you as the hiker will need to carry with you. Here is a simplified list:

- Clothing
- Tents
- Sleeping bags
- Boots
- Icebreakers
- Food
- Light source
- Personal items

Chapter 6

Each one of the categories listed has a specific weight associated to it in real life. Therefore, when you are planning your hike, you will need to plan ahead and see how you can meet your climbing needs while in the meantime also reducing the number of items and the total weight of the items you will need to carry on your back during the journey. The actual logistics are a little more involved, but you get the picture.

It is no different in our RPG. The player character can only carry certain number of items and or equipment with them for their journey. For instance, the player character cannot be carrying 20 different types of weapons at any given time! It would be just impossible, realistically speaking. So it would be a nice touch to put in some realism in the gameplay.

Also, just like in real life, the heavier the equipment one has to carry, the more energy it will use. So we can also incorporate such a system for our game. For instance, carrying too many weapons will have a major effect on the player character over a long period of time. First of all, it will reduce its speed and movement drastically, and secondly, it can have a major impact on the health of the player. This is where your creativity and design skills will come into play. You are the master of the game, and you determine how you want to implement it!

I am going to keep it simple for demonstration's sake!

Determining item types

For starters, we are going to concentrate on some of the basic item types that we would like to define in our game. These are going to be weapons, armour, and clothing. On top of this, we can also add the following: health packets, potions, and collectables.

We are going to create three new scripts named `BaseItem.cs`, `InventoryItem.cs` and `InventorySystem.cs`. The `BaseItem` class will hold the generic properties for all items, just like the `BaseCharacter` class we defined previously. The `InventoryItem` class will inherit the `BaseItem` class and define the item type.

Here is a listing of `BaseItem.cs`:

```
using System;
using UnityEngine;
using System.Collections;


[Serializable]
public class BaseItem
{
  public enum ItemCategory
```

[189]

```
{
  WEAPON = 0,
  ARMOUR = 1,
  CLOTHING = 2,
  HEALTH = 3,
  POTION = 4
}

[SerializeField]
private string name;
[SerializeField]
private string description;

public string NAME
{
  get { return this.name; }
  set { this.name = value; }
}

public string DESCRIPTION
{
  get { return this.description; }
  set { this.description = value; }
}

}
```

The main idea in the preceding code is the `ItemCategory`. At the moment, I have kept it to only five different types of categories that the Inventory would keep track of.

A category could have multiple item types. For instance, there are different types of weapons, such as swords, hammers, and spears.

Here is the listing of `InventoryItem.cs`:

```
using System;
using UnityEngine;
using System.Collections;


[Serializable]
public class InventoryItem : BaseItem
{
  [SerializeField]
  private ItemCategory category;
```

```csharp
[SerializeField]
private float strength;
[SerializeField]
private float weight;

public ItemCategory CATEGORY
{
  get { return this.category; }
  set { this.category = value; }
}

public float STRENGTH
{
  get { return this.strength; }
  set { this.strength = value; }
}

public float WEIGHT
{
  get { return this.weight; }
  set { this.weight = value; }
}
}
```

The preceding code implements more properties or attributes for the items to be used in the inventory. For now, let's just keep it the way it is. We can always change it in the future.

The next important script is the actual script that will be used to manage the inventory. There are many ways to implement the logic for the inventory system. Again keeping things simple, the current script will have five `List` datatypes of type `InventoryItem`, one for each item category.

Here is the listing of `InventorySystem.cs`:

```csharp
 using System;
using UnityEngine;
using System.Collections.Generic;

[Serializable]
public class InventorySystem
{
  [SerializeField]
  private List<InventoryItem> weapons = new List<InventoryItem>();
  [SerializeField]
  private List<InventoryItem> armour = new List<InventoryItem>();
  [SerializeField]
  private List<InventoryItem> clothing = new List<InventoryItem>();
```

Inventory System

```csharp
[SerializeField]
private List<InventoryItem> health = new List<InventoryItem>();
[SerializeField]
private List<InventoryItem> potion = new List<InventoryItem>();

private InventoryItem selectedWeapon;
private InventoryItem selectedArmour;

public InventoryItem SELECTED_WEAPON
{
  get { return this.selectedWeapon; }
  set { this.selectedWeapon = value; }
}
public InventoryItem SELECTED_ARMOUR
{
  get { return this.selectedArmour; }
  set { this.selectedArmour = value; }
}

public InventorySystem()
{
  this.ClearInventory();
}

public void ClearInventory()
{
  this.weapons.Clear();
  this.armour.Clear();
  this.clothing.Clear();
  this.health.Clear();
  this.potion.Clear();
}

// this function will add an inventory item
public void AddItem(InventoryItem item)
{
  switch(item.CATEGORY)
  {
    case BaseItem.ItemCategory.ARMOUR:
      {
        this.armour.Add(item);
        break;
      }
    case BaseItem.ItemCategory.CLOTHING:
      {
        this.clothing.Add(item);
        break;
      }
```

```
      case BaseItem.ItemCategory.HEALTH:
        {
          this.health.Add(item);
          break;
        }
      case BaseItem.ItemCategory.POTION:
        {
          this.potion.Add(item);
          break;
        }
      case BaseItem.ItemCategory.WEAPON:
        {
          this.weapons.Add(item);
          break;
        }
    }
  }


// this function will remove an inventory item
public void DeleteItem(InventoryItem item)
{
  switch (item.CATEGORY)
  {
    case BaseItem.ItemCategory.ARMOUR:
      {
        this.armour.Remove(item);
        break;
      }
    case BaseItem.ItemCategory.CLOTHING:
      {
        this.clothing.Remove(item);
        break;
      }
    case BaseItem.ItemCategory.HEALTH:
      {
        this.health.Remove(item);
        break;
      }
    case BaseItem.ItemCategory.POTION:
      {
        this.potion.Remove(item);
        break;
      }
    case BaseItem.ItemCategory.WEAPON:
      {
        this.weapons.Remove(item);
        break;
      }
```

Inventory System

```
    }
  }
}
```

We won't have direct access to the lists that will be used to contain the inventory items. For now, we have implemented two functions, `AddItem()` and `DeleteItem()`, which will handle the two basic features of the inventory, adding an item to it and removing an item from it. These two functions will take an `InventoryItem` object and, based on the `ItemCategory`, be added or removed from the appropriate list within the inventory.

The basics are in place. Now we will need to integrate this with the `GameMaster.cs` script. To do so, we will need to create a new variable of type `InventorySystem` named `INVENTORY` and initialized in the `Awake()` function of the `GameMaster.cs` script.

The following listing will illustrate just the new addition:

```csharp
// reference to player Character Customization
public PC PC_CC;
public InventorySystem INVENTORY;

public GameObject START_POSITION;

public GameObject CHARACTER_CUSTOMIZATION;

public LevelController LEVEL_CONTROLLER;
public AudioController AUDIO_CONTROLLER;

// Ref to UI Elements ...
public bool DISPLAY_SETTINGS = false;
public UIController UI;

void Awake()
{
  // simple singleton
  if (instance == null)
  {
    instance = this;

    // initialize Level Controller
    instance.LEVEL_CONTROLLER = new LevelController();

    // initialize Audio Controller
    instance.AUDIO_CONTROLLER = new AudioController();
    instance.AUDIO_CONTROLLER.AUDIO_SOURCE =
GameMaster.instance.GetComponent<AudioSource>();
    instance.AUDIO_CONTROLLER.SetDefaultVolume();
```

[194]

```
  // initialize Inventory System
  instance.INVENTORY = new InventorySystem();
  InventoryItem tmp = new InventoryItem();
  tmp.CATEGORY = BaseItem.ItemCategory.CLOTHING;
  tmp.NAME = "Testing";
  tmp.DESCRIPTION = "Testing the item type";
  tmp.STRENGTH = 0.5f;
  tmp.WEIGHT = 0.2f;
  instance.INVENTORY.AddItem(tmp);
}
else if (instance != this)
{
  Destroy(this);
}

// keep the game object when moving from
// one scene to the next scene
DontDestroyOnLoad(this);
}
```

Notice that we are actually creating an `InventoryItem` and inserting it into the `InventorySystem` for testing purposes. Another great feature is the fact that you can see the `InventorySystem` within the designer, in the *Inspector Window*, since we have serialized the classes and the fields:

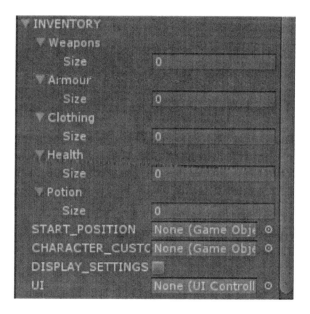

Inventory System

The preceding screenshot displays the Inventory System as seen in the **Inspector Window** when you select the **GameMaster** object. When you run the game to test it, you will see the following update:

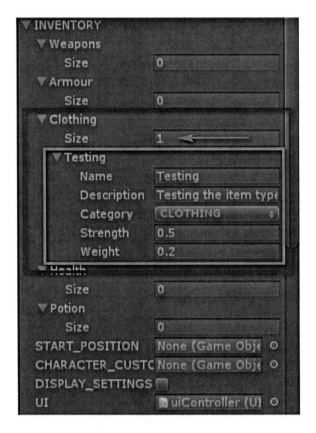

Notice in the preceding screenshot how the data reflects appropriately in the Inventory System as expected! The **Clothing** list has now increased its size to 1, and the `InventoryItem` within the list is properly stored and displayed for testing and debugging. We have one Clothing item named **Testing**, with the given description and a **Strength** *of* 0.5 and a **Weight** *of* 0.2.

So far so good, now we need to actually create the items that will be used to visually represent our Inventory Items! This is discussed in the next section.

Chapter 6

Creating inventory item

It is now time to actually create the items we are going to use for our inventory system. I will be creating one item type from each item category to keep things simple. This section will really be again highly dependent on how you have modeled your character models. In my particular model, as discussed earlier in the book, all of the character's essential parts are embedded within the **fbx**. In this case, you will need to navigate down your model's hierarchy and extract the mesh for the specific armour or weapon or anything else that you are going to be using for the inventory:

You can also use independent models representing your inventory items that may or may not be related to your character model's mesh. These items are just used for visual representation within the world, so that the player can pick them up.

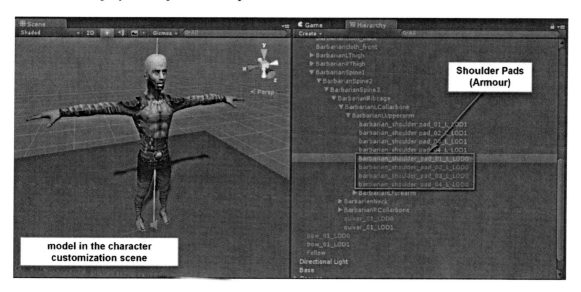

If you recall from the character customization scene, we have already gone through the model and identified the parts we want to have the player be able to enable or disable based on the selection they make through the interface.

[197]

Creating the Prefab

If you have not already done so, go ahead and create a folder in your **Project Window** named **Prefabs**. Within this folder, go ahead and create a new folder and name it **InventoryItems**, and then a subfolder named **ShoulderPads**. You are welcome to use a different naming and folder structure if you choose, as long as you are comfortable with it and it is organized for you to work with.

To create a prefab, you simply need to take an existing GameObject that is present in the **Scene Window** and drag it into the **Project Window**. To keep things organized, we will be using the structure defined in the previous paragraph. So you will need to navigate to the **ShoulderPads** folder in the Project Window and then perform the following: simply drag one of the shoulder pad meshes from your model and drop it into the **ShoulderPads** folder:

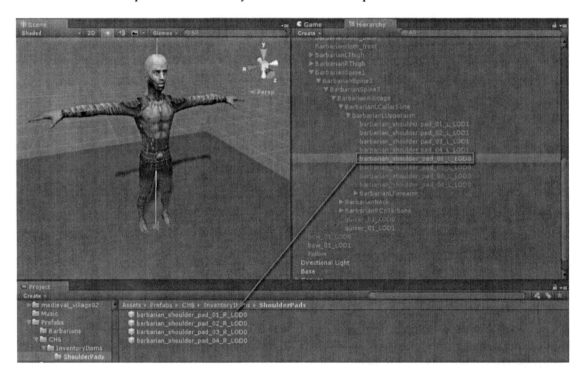

Chapter 6

Observe, when you create a prefab, the prefab will be an exact copy of the GameObject in the active scene! In this case, my mesh is disabled in the scene, therefore when I create a prefab of the mesh, it will also be disabled! Since it is disabled, when you drag the newly created prefab into the scene as a new GameObject, it will be invisible; you will need to enable it.

Adding Inventory Item Agent

We need a means to interact with our inventory items. In order to do this, we will need to create a new script that will handle our interaction with the inventory items during game play. This will be coded in the `InventoryItemAgent.cs` script. At the moment, the script will just enable us to interact with the `InventoryItem` object through the IDE.

Here is the listing of the script:

```
using UnityEngine;
using System.Collections;

public class InventoryItemAgent : MonoBehaviour
{
  public InventoryItem ItemDescription;
}
```

Inventory System

Very simply, in order for us to be able to interact with the GameObject, we would need to use a script that inherits *MonoBehaviour*. Go ahead and attach this script to your prefab. Now you can easily set up your inventory items visually:

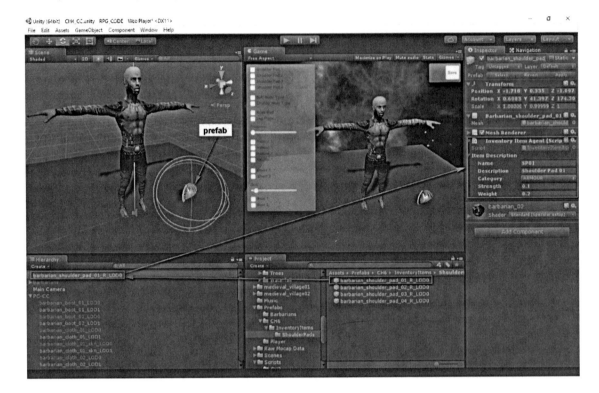

In the preceding screenshot, you can see that we have created a GameObject from the prefab and using the **InventoryItemAgent** component, we have access to the properties of the **InventoryItem** object. Utilizing this concept, you can now create your prefabs for the different types of inventory items.

If you are applying your changes in the scene window, make sure you apply them to the original prefab so that it keeps it in memory.
Caution: When you apply changes to a prefab, all instances of the prefab get updated with the new attributes.

Chapter 6

At the moment, we have implemented an easy way to define our inventory items, but we still need to implement use interaction with the items. The logic for the interaction will be implemented in the `InventoryItemAgent.cs` script. First, we need to identify who we are colliding with; in this case, we want to make sure it is the player that is going to collect the item. Second, we need to store the data into the `GameMaster` and also remove the `GameObject` from the active scene. The last two parts will be handled by the `GameMaster`, as you will see.

Here is the new code listing for `InventoryItemAgent.cs`:

```
using UnityEngine;
using System.Collections;

public class InventoryItemAgent : MonoBehaviour
{
    public InventoryItem ItemDescription;

    public void OnTriggerEnter(Collider c)
    {
        // make sure we are colliding with the player
        if(c.gameObject.tag.Equals("Player"))
        {
            // Make a copy of the Inventory Item Object
            InventoryItem myItem = new InventoryItem();
            myItem.CopyInventoryItem(this.ItemDescription);

            // Add the item to our inventory
            GameMaster.instance.INVENTORY.AddItem(myItem);

            // Destroy the GameObject from the scene
            GameMaster.instance.RPG_Destroy(this.gameObject);
        }
    }

}
```

I have created a new function in the `InventoryItem.cs` script called `CoptInventoryItem()`. This function is used to make a copy of one `InventoryItem` object into another one. Here is the code for the newly added function in the `InventoryItem` class:

```
public void CopyInventoryItem(InventoryItem item)
{
    this.CATEGORY = item.CATEGORY;
    this.DESCRIPTION = item.DESCRIPTION;
    this.NAME = item.NAME;
```

```
    this.STRENGTH = item.STRENGTH;
    this.WEIGHT = item.WEIGHT;
}
```

We already saw how to add an item to the inventory using the `GameMaster`. However, we needed to add a new function that would handle the destruction of `GameObject`s in our game. This is done by the `RPG_Destroy()` function.

You cannot use `Destroy()`, `DestroyImmediate()`, or `DestroyObject()` since they are part of all `GameObject`s in Unity. Therefore, be cautious with your naming convention within your own classes.

Here is the listing of the new function:

```
public void RPG_Destroy(GameObject obj)
{
   Destroy(obj);
}
```

One final component that needs to be added to your prefabs representing the inventory items is a *Collider*:

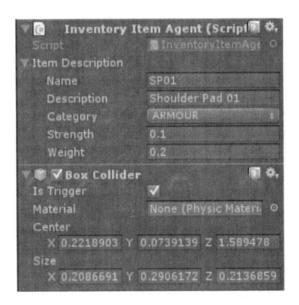

I used a **Box Collider** to keep things simple. A collider can be added by selecting **Add Component | Physics | Box Collider** from the **Inspector Window**.

Inventory Items Defined as Prefabs

The following screenshot will demonstrate some of the inventory item prefabs I have created for demonstration:

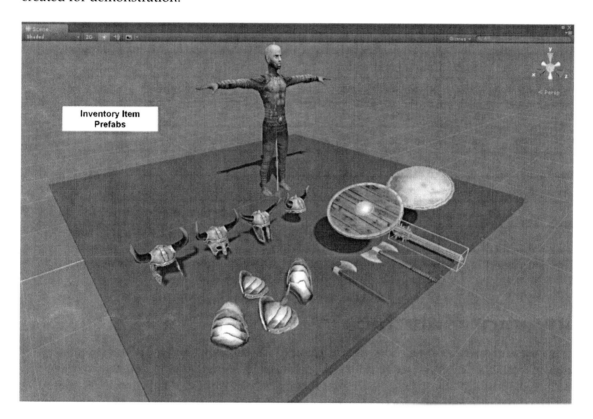

The key for all of this to work is to make sure that your prefabs have the `InventoryItemAgent.cs` script as well as a `Collider` component attached to the prefabs. Then you will need to provide the Inventory Item data through the IDE, uniquely identifying each one.

Inventory System

The following table lists the data for each inventory item defined:

Prefab	Name	Description	Category	Strength	Weight
Helmet	HL01	Brass Helmet with Two Horns	ARMOUR	0.2	0.2
	HL02	Brass Helmet Face Protection	ARMOUR	0.3	0.25
	HL03	Bronze Helmet Protecting Face	ARMOUR	0.3	0.3
	HL04	Bronze Helmet	ARMOUR	0.2	0.25
Shield	SL01	Iron Shield	ARMOUR	0.3	0.3
	SL02	Wooden Shield	ARMOUR	0.2	0.2
Shoulder Pads	SP01	Shoulder Pad 01	ARMOUR	0.1	0.2
	SP02	Shoulder Pad 02	ARMOUR	0.1	0.2
	SP03	Shoulder Pad 03	ARMOUR	0.15	0.25
	SP04	Shoulder Pad 04	ARMOUR	0.2	0.25
Weapons	Axe1	Single Head	WEAPON	0.2	0.1
	Axe2	Double Head	WEAPON	0.25	0.2
	Club1	Wooden Club	WEAPON	0.2	0.1

The data again is arbitrary; you decide what best suits your game and game design.

Inventory Interface

It is now time to think about how we are going to visualize our inventory during game play. Creating a user interface (UI) for any game is a challenging task. You need to have a balanced approach about the amount of information you want to display on the screen at playtime without interfering with the game play. In the meantime, you want to make sure that the player has the most crucial and important information necessary to complete their mission at hand.

With that said, let's see how we can design a simple user interface to enable the player with the basics of interacting with the inventory system. Here is a list of minimum features that the player should be able to perform:

- Display the Inventory at any time during game play
- Navigate based on category

- See what items are listed under each category
- Be able to remove an item from the inventory
- Be able to consume an item from the inventory
- See what inventory items are already in use by the player

This list will give us a good start for implementing our inventory interface. Let's start by identifying the categories that will need to be displayed. The categories are defined as an **enum** named `ItemCategory` in the `BaseItem` class.

We have the following: weapons, armour, clothing, health, and potions:

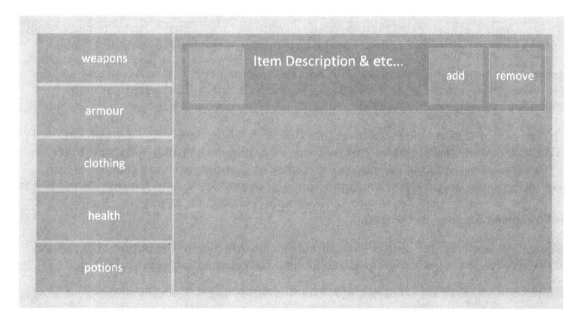

The preceding diagram is a concept I am leaning towards for the implementation of the inventory interface. The interface can be constructed by utilizing the following UI elements:

- Buttons
- Panels
- Text
- Images

Inventory System

Each category will have a button and there will be one main panel that will contain the list of items per category as illustrated in the preceding diagram. Each item will be contained in its own panel that will contain an image of the inventory item, the item description, and two buttons that can be used to add or remove the item from the inventory system.

Creating the inventory UI framework

Let's start by first implementing the initial framework for our inventory system graphical interface. In the main scene of your project, go ahead and create a new *Canvas* GameObject if you have not done so already.

To do so, right-click on the **Hierarchy** *Window* and select **UI | Panel**. This will automatically create a **Canvas** GameObject and a Panel UI Element as a child to the canvas.

Rename this panel **PanelInventory**. This will be the main panel that will contain everything else. Now, let's go ahead and start building the buttons that will represent our main categories.

Similarly, right-click on the **PanelInventory** GameObject and select **UI | Button**. This will make sure that the newly created button becomes a child of the **PanelInventory**. If, for whatever reason, this is not the case in the **Hierarchy Window** after the creation of the button(s), simply drag the newly created button(s) under the **PanelInventory** panel. Do this for all the five categories. Rename the buttons appropriately, for example, **butWeaponsCategory** and so on.

Change the caption of the button so that it reflects the function of the button. Also, rename the **Text** element to something like the following: **txtWeaponsCategory** and so on.

Finally, add a new **Panel** element to the **PanelInventory** again by selecting the **PanelInventory** GameObject and right-clicking and selecting **UI | Panel**. Rename the newly created panel **PanelCategory**:

[206]

Your inventory user interface should look something like the screenshot shown. Before we get more involved, let's go ahead and hook up some of the basics for showing and hiding the inventory interface for the player. To do this, we will need to modify the UIController.cs, LevelController.cs, and also the GameMaster.cs scripts.

I will not be listing the whole source file, as we will do that later on in the chapter. These are the changes for each script for now:

- UIController.cs: Added a new function named DisplayInventory() and a new variable to reference the inventory canvas named InventoryCanvas:

```
public void DisplayInventory()
{
this.InventoryCanvas.gameObject.SetActive(GameMaster.instance.DISPLAY_INVENTORY);
    Debug.Log("Display Inventory Function");
}
```

Inventory System

- `LevelController.cs`: Updated the `OnlevelWasLoaded()` function to assign the `uiController` GameObject to the `GameMaster` instance if one is present:

```
if(GameObject.FindGameObjectWithTag("UI"))
{
   GameMaster.instance.UI = 
GameObject.FindGameObjectWithTag("UI").GetComponent<UIController>();
}
```

- `GameMaster.cs`: Modified the `Update()` function to check and see if the J key was pressed and released. This in turn toggled a Boolean variable to see if we are supposed to show or hide the inventory interface:

```
void Update()
{
  // only when we are in the game level
  if(instance.LEVEL_CONTROLLER.CURRENT_SCENE.name==SceneName.Level_1)
  {
    if (Input.GetKeyUp(KeyCode.J))
    {
      Debug.Log("Pressing J");
      instance.DISPLAY_INVENTORY = !instance.DISPLAY_INVENTORY;
      instance.UI.DisplayInventory();
    }
  }
}
```

If you test your scene from the main menu, you will be able to test out the interface and toggle it on and off.

> Don't forget that you will need to disable the Canvas for the Inventory System at design time or at runtime when the game loads initially.

Chapter 6

Designing a Dynamic Item Viewer

The next challenge for us is to create a method to dynamically populate the inventory items and displaying them properly on the user interface. We are going to use two new UI elements that we have not used before. We will be using a *ScrollView* to give us the ability to scroll through the items when needed. We are also going to take a look at some of the *Layout* UI elements that are available out of the box in Unity 5.x.

Let's first get the scroll view set up and also be able to add a simple UI prefab to the scroll view. Once this is done, we can go ahead and enhance the UI prefab to handle what we have outlined in the previous section.

Adding a Scroll View

We need to make a way to display multiple inventory items on the screen. We now need to learn how to create a scrollable view for the Inventory UI:

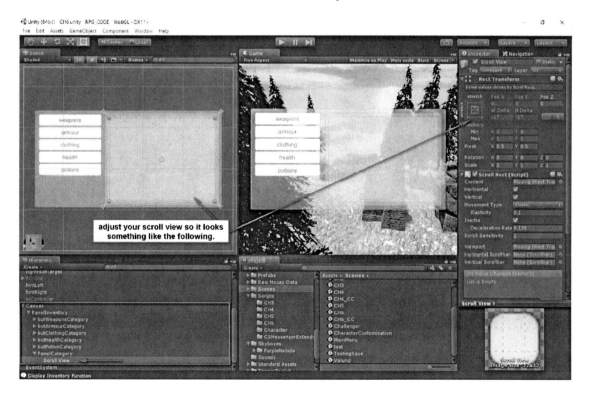

Inventory System

Go to the scene where you have created your Inventory UI, and select *PanelCategory* in the *Canvas*. Right-click and select *UI | Scroll View* to add a scroll view UI element. You should now have a scroll view UI element with the associated children under your *PanelCategory* panel. The children are going to be *Viewport*, *Scrollbar Horizontal*, and *Scrollbar Vertical*.

 Make your adjustment to the Scroll View UI element before you delete the children.

We are going to make some modifications to the default Scroll View. Go ahead and delete the following from the *Scroll View*: the *Scrollbar Horizontal*, *Scrollbar Vertical*, and *Viewport* child elements. After you are done, your screen should look something like in the screenshot shown.

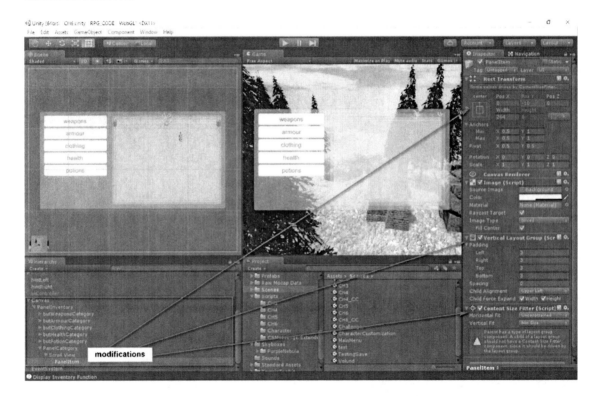

[210]

Chapter 6

Next, we need to add a **Panel** element as a child to our **Scroll View**. Go ahead and select the scroll view and right-click and select **UI | Panel**. Rename the newly added panel **PanelItem**. We need to add two Layout components to our **PanelItem**. To do this, select the **PanelItem**, and from the **Inspector Window**, select **Add Component | Layout | Vertical Layout Group** and once more select **Add Component | Layout | Content Size Filter**.

Go ahead and modify the following attributes under the **Vertical Layout Group** components. Set the **Left, Right, Top and Bottom Padding** to 3. Set the **Spacing** to , change the **Child Alignment** to **Upper Left**, and check the **Child Force Expand** to **True** for both **Width** and **Height**.

For the Content Size Filter component, set the **Horizontal Fit** to **Unconstrained** and the **Vertical Fit** to **Min Size**.

Finally, in the **Rect Transform** component, change the **Anchor Point** to **Top Center**, and modify the **Pos Y** to **-10**.

At this point, we have the basic framework in place. The next step it to populate our newly created **ScrollView**!

Adding Elements to PanelItem and Scroll View

For starters, let's go ahead and add a *Text* element under the **PanelItem** panel. Again, select the **PanelItem** element and right-click and select **UI | Text**. Next, select the text element and rename it **txtItemElement**. We need to add a new component to the Text element; from the **Inspector Window**, go ahead and select **Add Component | Layout | Layout Element**.

Inventory System

Modify the **Min Height** attribute of the **Layout Element** component to **20**:

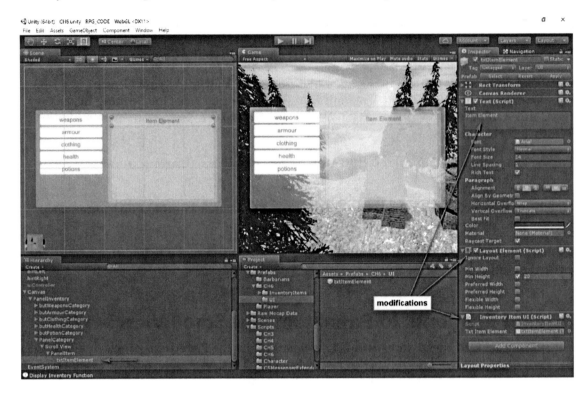

We need a means to access and modify the **Text** attribute of the new Text UI element. In order to do this, we need to create a new script called **InventoryItemUI.cs**. The code will just have a public variable that will reference the Text element. Here is the listing:

```
using UnityEngine;
using UnityEngine.UI;

public class InventoryItemUI : MonoBehaviour {
  public Text txtItemElement;
}
```

Finally, drag and drop the Text element from the Hierarchy Window into the **TextItemElement** attribute of the **InventoryItemUI** component attached to the **txtItemElement** object. Refer to the preceding screenshot.

Chapter 6

 The script is used to self-reference. We will use it to modify the text component of the Text UI element.

Now we will need to create a **Prefab** of the **txtItemElement** by dragging and dropping it into a designated folder. I have created a new folder under my **Prefabs** folder, named it *UI*, and created the prefab in that folder. Refer to the previous screenshot.

You can now delete the **txtItemElement** from the **Hierarchy Window** under the **PanelItem** object. We will be adding them dynamically during runtime.

There is one last configuration you will need to do before we move forward. You will need to add a Mask component to the Scroll View UI element. Select the Scroll View from the **Hierarchy Window** and from the **Inspector Window**, select **Add Component | UI | Mask**. After the addition of the **Mask** component, make sure that **the Show Mask Graphics** attribute is *unchecked*.

Adding txtItemElement Dynamically

Now it is time to add our inventory item placeholder dynamically to the `PanelItem` UI element. To do so, we will use the `UIController.cs` scrip. Go ahead and open up the scrip and add the following variable to the class:

```
public Transform PanelItem;
public GameObject InventoryItemElement;
```

In the designer, you will need to assign the `PanelItem` UI element from the *Canvas* GameObject and the `txtItemElement` prefab from the prefab folder.

Next, we are going to modify the `Update()` function so that when we press the H key on the keyboard, it will go ahead and instantiate a new `InventoryItemElement` and make it a child element of the `PanelItem` object.

Here is the listing of the code:

```
public void Update()
{
   if(Input.GetKeyUp(KeyCode.H))
   {
      GameObject newButton =
GameObject.Instantiate(this.InventoryItemElement) as GameObject;
      InventoryItemUI txtItem = newButton.GetComponent<InventoryItemUI>();
      txtItem.txtItemElement.text = string.Format("Adding New Item {0}",
```

[213]

Inventory System

```
Time.deltaTime);
     newButton.transform.SetParent(this.PanelItem);
  }
}
```

The preceding code listing simply instantiates the prefab and makes it a child of the `PanelItem` element. We are also changing the caption of the element and placing it with a timestamp to see the uniqueness of each UI element.

The outcome is shown in the following screenshot:

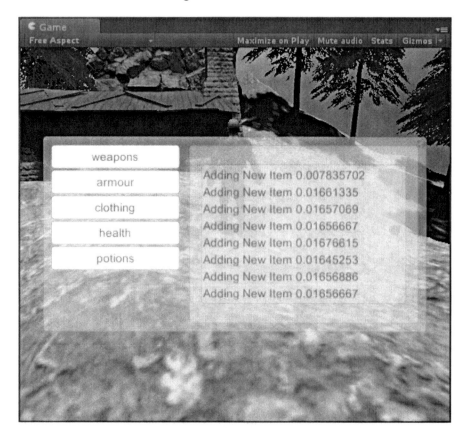

At this point, we have put together the main elements to have our inventory interface list items dynamically and be able to scroll through them.

Chapter 6

Building the Final Inventory Item UI

To create the actual Inventory Item user interface, we are going to need to use several UI elements. We will need a panel to be the container of the item. Within the *Panel*, we are going to need to use an *Image*, a *Text*, and two *Button* UI elements:

I will not be going through the steps of how to put the Panel together. You should know how to create user interfaces by now.

Just make sure that you add the *Layout Element* component and *Inventory Item UI* script to the Panel that will be the base for the Inventory Item.

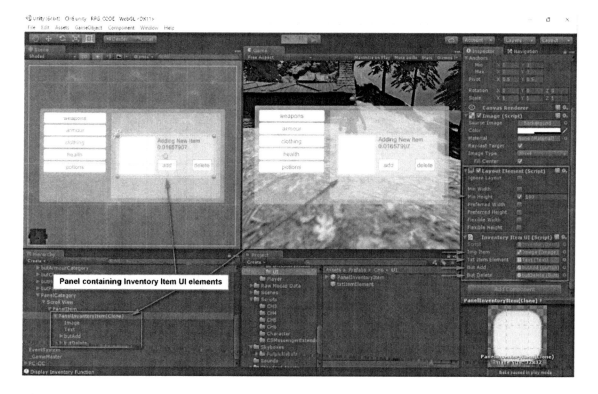

The preceding screenshot illustrates the UI component that has been developed for displaying the Inventory Item. Since the UI component has been modified, we also have to update the `InventoryItemUI.cs` script to contain a reference to all of the new UI elements in the *Panel*.

Inventory System

Here is the listing of the new `InventoryItemUI.cs`:

```
using UnityEngine;
using UnityEngine.UI;

public class InventoryItemUI : MonoBehaviour {
  public Image   imgItem;
  public Text    txtItemElement;
  public Button butAdd;
  public Button butDelete;
}
```

We also need to update the `UIController.cs` script to handle the new prefab accordingly.

Here is the listing for the new UI prefab in `UIController.cs`:

```
public void Update()
{
  if(Input.GetKeyUp(KeyCode.H))
  {
    GameObject newItem =
GameObject.Instantiate(this.InventoryItemElement) as GameObject;
    InventoryItemUI txtItem = newItem.GetComponent<InventoryItemUI>();
    txtItem.txtItemElement.text = string.Format("Adding New Item {0}",
Time.deltaTime);

    // button triggers
txtItem.butAdd.GetComponent<Button>().onClick.AddListener(() => {
      Debug.Log(string.Format("You have clicked button add for {0}",
txtItem.txtItemElement.text));
    });

    txtItem.butDelete.GetComponent<Button>().onClick.AddListener(() =>
    {
      Debug.Log(string.Format("You have clicked button delete for {0}",
txtItem.txtItemElement.text));
      Destroy(newItem);
      Debug.Log("Item removed from inventory ...");
    });

    newItem.transform.SetParent(this.PanelItem);
  }
}
```

In the preceding listing, the main concept I want to point out is the implementation of the `onClick()` event handler for the buttons within the prefab.

Chapter 6

Since we are dynamically generating our UI and hence the buttons, we need to be able to trigger the `onClick()` function somewhere; this is done by adding a listener as shown in the code.

For now, when you click the **butAdd** button, you will get an output on the **Console Window** with the appropriate caption. When you click the **butDelete** button, you will get another output on the **Console Window** with the appropriate caption. Then the item will be destroyed, in other words, removed from the inventory.

Integrating the UI with the actual inventory system

We have seen and implemented the concepts necessary to make our Inventory System UI work properly. Now it is time to actually fill the user interface with the actual data that is stored in the GameMaster.

Hooking the category buttons and displaying the data

Using the `UIController.cs` script, we are going to create five new methods that will handle the proper visualization of our Inventory System. We are going to add the following five functions:

- `DisplayWeaponsCategory()`
- `DisplayArmourCategory()`
- `DisplayClothingCategory()`
- `DisplayHealthCategory()`
- `DisplayPotionsCategory()`

We also need to clear the existing inventory items from the panel when the user switches from one category to the next. This will require a private function named `ClearInventoryItemPanel()` that will just do that.

[217]

Inventory System

Here is the listing for the new `UIController.cs` script:

```
using UnityEngine;
using UnityEngine.UI;
using System.Collections;
using System.Collections.Generic;

public class UIController : MonoBehaviour
{
  public Canvas SettingsCanvas;
  public Slider ControlMainVolume;

  // the canvas object for inventory system
  public Canvas InventoryCanvas;

  public Transform PanelItem;
  public GameObject InventoryItemElement;

  public void Update()
  {
  }

  public void DisplaySettings()
  {
    GameMaster.instance.DISPLAY_SETTINGS =
!GameMaster.instance.DISPLAY_SETTINGS;
this.SettingsCanvas.gameObject.SetActive(GameMaster.instance.DISPLAY_SETTIN
GS);
  }

  public void MainVolume()
  {
    GameMaster.instance.MasterVolume(ControlMainVolume.value);
  }

  public void StartGame()
  {
    GameMaster.instance.StartGame();
  }

  public void LoadLevel()
  {
    if (GameObject.FindGameObjectWithTag("BASE"))
    {
      GameMaster.instance.PC_CC =
GameObject.FindGameObjectWithTag("BASE").GetComponent<CharacterCustomizatio
n>().PC_CC;
    }
```

[218]

Chapter 6

```
    GameMaster.instance.LEVEL_CONTROLLER.LEVEL = 1;
    GameMaster.instance.LoadLevel();
  }

  public void DisplayInventory()
  {
this.InventoryCanvas.gameObject.SetActive(GameMaster.instance.DISPLAY_INVEN
TORY);
    Debug.Log("Display Inventory Function");
  }

  private void ClearInventoryItemsPanel()
  {
    while(this.PanelItem.childCount>0)
    {
      Transform t = this.PanelItem.GetChild(0).transform;
      t.parent = null;
      Destroy(t.gameObject);
    }
  }

  public void DisplayWeaponsCategory()
  {
    if(GameMaster.instance.DISPLAY_INVENTORY)
    {
      this.ClearInventoryItemsPanel();

      foreach (InventoryItem item in GameMaster.instance.INVENTORY.WEAPONS)
      {
        GameObject newItem =
GameObject.Instantiate(this.InventoryItemElement) as GameObject;
        InventoryItemUI txtItem = newItem.GetComponent<InventoryItemUI>();
        txtItem.txtItemElement.text =
          string.Format("Name: {0}, Description: {1}, Strength: {2},
Weight: {3}",
                                    item.NAME,
                                    item.DESCRIPTION,
                                    item.STRENGTH,
                                    item.WEIGHT);

        // button triggers
        txtItem.butAdd.GetComponent<Button>().onClick.AddListener(() =>
        {
          Debug.Log(string.Format("You have clicked button add for {0}",
txtItem.txtItemElement.text));
        });

        txtItem.butDelete.GetComponent<Button>().onClick.AddListener(() =>
```

[219]

Inventory System

```
        {
            Debug.Log(string.Format("You have clicked button delete for {0}",
txtItem.txtItemElement.text));
            Destroy(newItem);
        });

        newItem.transform.SetParent(this.PanelItem);
    }


    }
 }


  public void DisplayArmourCategory()
  {
    if (GameMaster.instance.DISPLAY_INVENTORY)
    {
      this.ClearInventoryItemsPanel();

      foreach (InventoryItem item in GameMaster.instance.INVENTORY.ARMOUR)
      {
        GameObject newItem =
GameObject.Instantiate(this.InventoryItemElement) as GameObject;
        InventoryItemUI txtItem = newItem.GetComponent<InventoryItemUI>();
        txtItem.txtItemElement.text =
          string.Format("Name: {0}, Description: {1}, Strength: {2},
Weight: {3}",
                                      item.NAME,
                                      item.DESCRIPTION,
                                      item.STRENGTH,
                                      item.WEIGHT);

        // button triggers
        txtItem.butAdd.GetComponent<Button>().onClick.AddListener(() =>
        {
            Debug.Log(string.Format("You have clicked button add for {0}",
txtItem.txtItemElement.text));
        });

        txtItem.butDelete.GetComponent<Button>().onClick.AddListener(() =>
        {
            Debug.Log(string.Format("You have clicked button delete for {0}",
txtItem.txtItemElement.text));
            Destroy(newItem);
        });

        newItem.transform.SetParent(this.PanelItem);
      }
    }
```

Chapter 6

```csharp
  }

  public void DisplayClothingCategory()
  {
    if (GameMaster.instance.DISPLAY_INVENTORY)
    {
      this.ClearInventoryItemsPanel();

      foreach (InventoryItem item in
GameMaster.instance.INVENTORY.CLOTHING)
      {
        GameObject newItem =
GameObject.Instantiate(this.InventoryItemElement) as GameObject;
        InventoryItemUI txtItem = newItem.GetComponent<InventoryItemUI>();
        txtItem.txtItemElement.text =
          string.Format("Name: {0}, Description: {1}, Strength: {2},
Weight: {3}",
                                   item.NAME,
                                   item.DESCRIPTION,
                                   item.STRENGTH,
                                   item.WEIGHT);

        // button triggers
        txtItem.butAdd.GetComponent<Button>().onClick.AddListener(() =>
        {
          Debug.Log(string.Format("You have clicked button add for {0}",
txtItem.txtItemElement.text));
        });

        txtItem.butDelete.GetComponent<Button>().onClick.AddListener(() =>
        {
          Debug.Log(string.Format("You have clicked button delete for {0}",
txtItem.txtItemElement.text));
          Destroy(newItem);
        });

        newItem.transform.SetParent(this.PanelItem);
      }
    }
  }

  public void DisplayHealthCategory()
  {
    if (GameMaster.instance.DISPLAY_INVENTORY)
    {
      this.ClearInventoryItemsPanel();

      foreach (InventoryItem item in GameMaster.instance.INVENTORY.HEALTH)
```

[221]

Inventory System

```
    {
        GameObject newItem =
GameObject.Instantiate(this.InventoryItemElement) as GameObject;
        InventoryItemUI txtItem = newItem.GetComponent<InventoryItemUI>();
        txtItem.txtItemElement.text =
            string.Format("Name: {0}, Description: {1}, Strength: {2},
Weight: {3}",
                                    item.NAME,
                                    item.DESCRIPTION,
                                    item.STRENGTH,
                                    item.WEIGHT);

        // button triggers
        txtItem.butAdd.GetComponent<Button>().onClick.AddListener(() =>
        {
            Debug.Log(string.Format("You have clicked button add for {0}",
txtItem.txtItemElement.text));
        });

        txtItem.butDelete.GetComponent<Button>().onClick.AddListener(() =>
        {
            Debug.Log(string.Format("You have clicked button delete for {0}",
txtItem.txtItemElement.text));
            Destroy(newItem);
        });

        newItem.transform.SetParent(this.PanelItem);
    }

    }
}

public void DisplayPotionsCategory()
{
    if (GameMaster.instance.DISPLAY_INVENTORY)
    {
        this.ClearInventoryItemsPanel();

        foreach (InventoryItem item in GameMaster.instance.INVENTORY.POTIONS)
        {
            GameObject newItem =
GameObject.Instantiate(this.InventoryItemElement) as GameObject;
            InventoryItemUI txtItem = newItem.GetComponent<InventoryItemUI>();
            txtItem.txtItemElement.text =
                string.Format("Name: {0}, Description: {1}, Strength: {2},
Weight: {3}",
                                    item.NAME,
                                    item.DESCRIPTION,
```

Chapter 6

```
                        item.STRENGTH,
                        item.WEIGHT);

        // button triggers
        txtItem.butAdd.GetComponent<Button>().onClick.AddListener(() =>
        {
          Debug.Log(string.Format("You have clicked button add for {0}",
 txtItem.txtItemElement.text));
        });

        txtItem.butDelete.GetComponent<Button>().onClick.AddListener(() =>
        {
          Debug.Log(string.Format("You have clicked button delete for {0}",
 txtItem.txtItemElement.text));
          Destroy(newItem);
        });

        newItem.transform.SetParent(this.PanelItem);
      }

    }
  }

}
```

We had to also make some modifications to the `InventorySystem.cs` script to make it possible for us to access properties storing the data easier.

Here is the new listing of the script:

```
using System;
using UnityEngine;
using System.Collections.Generic;

[Serializable]
public class InventorySystem
{
  [SerializeField]
  private List<InventoryItem> weapons = new List<InventoryItem>();
  [SerializeField]
  private List<InventoryItem> armour = new List<InventoryItem>();
  [SerializeField]
  private List<InventoryItem> clothing = new List<InventoryItem>();
  [SerializeField]
  private List<InventoryItem> health = new List<InventoryItem>();
  [SerializeField]
  private List<InventoryItem> potion = new List<InventoryItem>();
```

[223]

Inventory System

```
public List<InventoryItem> WEAPONS
{
  get { return this.weapons; }
}

public List<InventoryItem> ARMOUR
{
  get { return this.armour; }
}

public List<InventoryItem> CLOTHING
{
  get { return this.clothing; }
}

public List<InventoryItem> HEALTH
{
  get { return this.health; }
}

public List<InventoryItem> POTIONS
{
  get { return this.potion; }
}

//[SerializeField]
private InventoryItem selectedWeapon;
//[SerializeField]
private InventoryItem selectedArmour;

public InventoryItem SELECTED_WEAPON
{
  get { return this.selectedWeapon; }
  set { this.selectedWeapon = value; }
}
public InventoryItem SELECTED_ARMOUR
{
  get { return this.selectedArmour; }
  set { this.selectedArmour = value; }
}

public InventorySystem()
{
  this.ClearInventory();
}

public void ClearInventory()
{
```

[224]

```
    this.weapons.Clear();
    this.armour.Clear();
    this.clothing.Clear();
    this.health.Clear();
    this.potion.Clear();
}

// this function will add an inventory item
public void AddItem(InventoryItem item)
{
  switch(item.CATEGORY)
  {
    case BaseItem.ItemCategory.ARMOUR:
      {
        this.armour.Add(item);
        break;
      }
    case BaseItem.ItemCategory.CLOTHING:
      {
        this.clothing.Add(item);
        break;
      }
    case BaseItem.ItemCategory.HEALTH:
      {
        this.health.Add(item);
        break;
      }
    case BaseItem.ItemCategory.POTION:
      {
        this.potion.Add(item);
        break;
      }
    case BaseItem.ItemCategory.WEAPON:
      {
        this.weapons.Add(item);
        break;
      }
  }
}

// this function will remove an inventory item
public void DeleteItem(InventoryItem item)
{
  switch (item.CATEGORY)
  {
    case BaseItem.ItemCategory.ARMOUR:
      {
        this.armour.Remove(item);
```

Inventory System

```
          break;
        }
    case BaseItem.ItemCategory.CLOTHING:
        {
          this.clothing.Remove(item);
          break;
        }
    case BaseItem.ItemCategory.HEALTH:
        {
          this.health.Remove(item);
          break;
        }
    case BaseItem.ItemCategory.POTION:
        {
          this.potion.Remove(item);
          break;
        }
    case BaseItem.ItemCategory.WEAPON:
        {
          this.weapons.Remove(item);
          break;
        }
    }
  }

}
```

Notice that I have removed the code from the *Update()* function in the *UIController.cs* script as it was only for testing reasons.

Testing the Inventory System

For testing purposes, I have placed a number of Inventory Item Prefabs I have created earlier in this chapter:

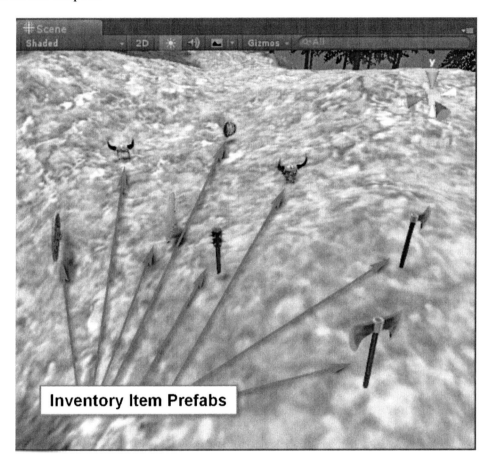

Inventory System

Start the game from the Main Menu and go through the Character Customization scene to save the character player and start the game. Once you are in the playable scene, go ahead and collect a few of the items that have been placed over the scene:

Notice in the preceding screenshot that I have selected the **_GameMaster** GameObject to display the **INVENTORY** data in the **Inspector Window**.

We have picked up two weapon types and two armour types. The weapon items we have picked up are **axe1** and **club1**. The armour items we have picked up are **HL02** and **SP01** as indicated in the **Inspector Window**.

Notice that in the *Game Window*, when we bring up the *Inventory Window* for display and click the *weapons* button, we get two listings. The listing displays the proper data for each inventory item in the category.

To list the armour items in the inventory, we will click the armour button. The following screenshot will display the items in the armour category in the inventory based on our data:

Chapter 6

To illustrate the **onClick()** event for the add button, please see the following screenshot from the **Console Window**:

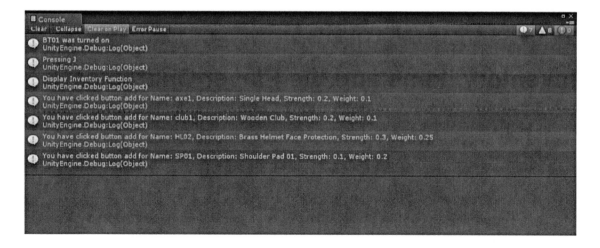

[229]

Inventory System

We have come a long way. Let's take a moment to put things in perspective.

We first created the following scripts to lay the foundation for our Inventory System in the game:

- BaseItem.cs
- InventoryItem.cs
- InventoryItemAgent.cs
- InventorySystem.cs

The next step was to create the prefab for each inventory item and add to it the `InventoryItemAgent.cs` script. This would in turn allow us to assign the necessary data to identify the prefab as an inventory item during game play.

Next, we started work on the design and development of the user interface for the inventory system. We created a sketch of how we would like the inventory window to look, and implemented the framework using the build in UI architecture.
Slowly adding to the UI and applying different concepts and new elements, we built the final user interface for the inventory system.

Finally, we used the prefabs to test the complete addition and removal of the inventory items from the user interface.

The next challenge we face is how to actually apply the inventory items to the player character.

Inventory items and the Player Character

Now that we have seen how to create the Inventory System, we need to be able to utilize it during game play to apply changes to our player character. In this section, we are going to examine how to do just that!

Here are some of the new features we need to work on:

- Applying selected inventory items to the player character
- Performing accounting on both the player character and the inventory system
- Updating the game state accordingly

Chapter 6

Applying inventory items

We need to make some design decisions about how we are going to handle applying the inventory items to the player character, and in turn how the system will handle the event. For instance, let's assume the player character has acquired several weapons, let's say weapons A, B, and C.

Let's also assume that, initially, the player does not have any active weapons. Now, the player selects to activate weapon A. For this scenario, we would just use the inventory item data and activate weapon A for the player, taking into consideration all of the accounting that comes with the weapon.

Now, the player wants to change his/her weapon to B because it is more powerful and they would need it to defeat the boss. Since the player already has Weapon A active, what are we going to do with it before we activate Weapon B? Do we put it back into the game world, or do we put it back into our inventory for later consumption?

In our case, once you have an item in the inventory, it will stay with you until you actually delete it from the inventory, in which case it will be destroyed. We need to make a few code modifications and also some prefab modifications to have everything working together.

Let's start with the *InventoryItem.cs* script. We are going to add new data to store the type of the Inventory Item. This is necessary because we have a category and within the category we have different types of items. This is specifically true for the Armour category! For instance, we have a Helmet, a Shield, a Shoulder Pad, and so on.

Here is the code listing:

```
using System;
using UnityEngine;
using System.Collections;


[Serializable]
public class InventoryItem : BaseItem
{
  public enum ItemType
  {
    HELMET = 0,
    SHIELD = 1,
    SHOULDER_PAD = 2,
    KNEE_PAD = 3,
    BOOTS = 4,
    WEAPON = 5
  }
```

[231]

Inventory System

```
[SerializeField]
private ItemCategory category;
[SerializeField]
private ItemType type;
[SerializeField]
private float strength;
[SerializeField]
private float weight;

public ItemCategory CATEGORY
{
  get { return this.category; }
  set { this.category = value; }
}

public ItemType TYPE
{
  get { return this.type; }
  set { this.type = value; }
}

public float STRENGTH
{
  get { return this.strength; }
  set { this.strength = value; }
}

public float WEIGHT
{
  get { return this.weight; }
  set { this.weight = value; }
}

public void CopyInventoryItem(InventoryItem item)
{
  this.CATEGORY = item.CATEGORY;
  this.TYPE = item.TYPE;
  this.DESCRIPTION = item.DESCRIPTION;
  this.NAME = item.NAME;
  this.STRENGTH = item.STRENGTH;
  this.WEIGHT = item.WEIGHT;
}
}
```

When you make the update to your script, make sure to go back into the IDE and select the proper type for each prefab we have created, to represent your inventory items:

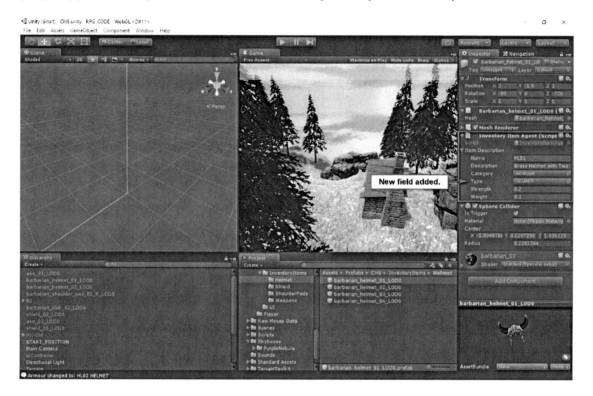

You will need to update the **Type** field for each prefab you have created for your inventory items.

We would also need to update the `PC.cs` script. We are going to make private the original data variables and create public properties to access them. This way, if we need to perform any extra work prior to or after setting or getting the property value, we can do so easily.

Here is the listing for the `PC.cs` script:

```
using System;
using UnityEngine;

public delegate void WeaponChangedEventHandler(PC.WEAPON_TYPE weapon);

[Serializable]
public class PC : BaseCharacter
{
```

Inventory System

```csharp
//public event WeaponChangedEventHandler PlayerWeaponChanged;

public enum SHOULDER_PAD
{
  none = 0,
  SP01 = 1,
  SP02 = 2,
  SP03 = 3,
  SP04 = 4
};

public enum BODY_TYPE { normal = 1, BT01 = 2, BT02 = 3 };

// Shoulder Pad
[SerializeField]
private SHOULDER_PAD selectedShoulderPad = SHOULDER_PAD.none;
public SHOULDER_PAD SELECTED_SHOULDER_PAD
{
  get { return this.selectedShoulderPad; }
  set { this.selectedShoulderPad = value; }
}

[SerializeField]
private BODY_TYPE selectedBodyType = BODY_TYPE.normal;
public BODY_TYPE SELECTED_BODY_TYPE
{
  get { return this.selectedBodyType; }
  set { this.selectedBodyType = value; }
}

// Do we have a knee pad?
private bool kneePad = false;
public bool KNEE_PAD
{
  get { return this.kneePad; }
  set { this.kneePad = value; }
}

// Do we have a leg plate?
private bool legPlate = false;
public bool LEG_PLATE
{
  get { return this.legPlate; }
  set { this.legPlate = value; }
}

public enum WEAPON_TYPE
{
```

```
    none = 0,
    axe1 = 1,
    axe2 = 2,
    club1 = 3,
    club2 = 4,
    falchion = 5,
    gladius = 6,
    mace = 7,
    maul = 8,
    scimitar = 9,
    spear = 10,
    sword1 = 11,
    sword2 = 12,
    sword3 = 13
  };

  // Store the selected weapon. In the future we might want to create a
  // event handler to raise an even when the weapon is being changed in the
setter
  [SerializeField]
  private WEAPON_TYPE selectedWeapon = WEAPON_TYPE.none;
  public WEAPON_TYPE SELECTED_WEAPON
  {
    get { return this.selectedWeapon; }
    set
    {
      this.selectedWeapon = value;
      //if (PlayerWeaponChanged != null)
      //{
      //  // All listeners will be invoked
      //  PlayerWeaponChanged(this.selectedWeapon);
      //}
    }
  }


  public enum HELMET TYPE { none = 0, HL01 = 1, HL02 = 2, HL03 = 3, HL04 =
4 };

  // do we have any helmet? Which one is selected if any?
  [SerializeField]
  private HELMET_TYPE selectedHelmet = HELMET_TYPE.none;
  public HELMET_TYPE SELECTED_HELMET
  {
    get { return this.selectedHelmet; }
    set { this.selectedHelmet = value; }
  }
```

Inventory System

```
public enum SHIELD_TYPE { none = 0, SL01 = 1, SL02 = 2 };

// Do we have a shield on? Which shiled is active?
[SerializeField]
private SHIELD_TYPE selectedShield = SHIELD_TYPE.none;
public SHIELD_TYPE SELECTED_SHIELD
{
  get { return this.selectedShield; }
  set { this.selectedShield = value; }
}

public int SKIN_ID = 1;

public enum BOOT_TYPE { none = 0, BT01 = 1, BT02 = 2 };

[SerializeField]
private BOOT_TYPE selectedBoot = BOOT_TYPE.none;
public BOOT_TYPE SELECTED_BOOT
{
  get { return this.selectedBoot; }
  set { this.selectedBoot = value; }
}

[SerializeField]
private InventoryItem selectedArmour;
public InventoryItem SELECTED_ARMOUR
{
  get { return this.selectedArmour; }
  set { this.selectedArmour = value; }
}
}
```

The next code modification will be on the `CharacterCustomization.cs` script. Since this script has been used in the character customization scene, we can utilize the same script and expand it to apply the visual changes to our player character. But before we can utilize this script, we will need to copy the actual component from the `Base` GameObject defined in our Character Customization scene, and paste it into the `PC_CC` GameObject representing our player character!

Chapter 6

 When you copy a component using the gear menu in the *Inspector Window*, all the configurations, links, and references stay intact! When you paste the component using again the gear menu in the *Inspector Window*, you will have an exact copy of the component. This will eliminate the need for us to rewire all of the GameObjects to their references in the script.

The following two screenshots will illustrate the copy of the component from the Base GameObject to the `PC_CC` GameObject:

[237]

Inventory System

This works because the script is actually referencing the different parts of the PC_CC GameObject hierarchy in the first place. The difference was that it used to be attached to the Base GameObject for the customization.

 Can they both be active at the same time in the same scene, at this point? Yes! However, if you have the time, you might want to redo your UI event triggers to use the PC_CC GameObject and then you can remove the CharacterCustomization.cs script from the Base GameObject.

Now we actually need to modify the CharacterCustomization.cs script to activate the different parts of the player character model using the data it will receive from the GameMaster.cs script.

Chapter 6

Here is a partial listing of the `CharacterCustomization.cs` script:

```
public void SetWeaponType(PC.WEAPON_TYPE id)
  {
    switch (System.Convert.ToInt32(id))
    {
      case 0:
        {
          this.AXE_01LOD0.SetActive(false);
          this.AXE_02LOD0.SetActive(false);
          this.CLUB_01LOD0.SetActive(false);
          this.CLUB_02LOD0.SetActive(false);
          this.FALCHION_LOD0.SetActive(false);
          this.GLADIUS_LOD0.SetActive(false);
          this.MACE_LOD0.SetActive(false);
          this.MAUL_LOD0.SetActive(false);
          this.SCIMITAR_LOD0.SetActive(false);
          this.SPEAR_LOD0.SetActive(false);
          this.SWORD_BASTARD_LOD0.SetActive(false);
          this.SWORD_BOARD_01LOD0.SetActive(false);
          this.SWORD_SHORT_LOD0.SetActive(false);
          break;
        }
      case 1:
        {
          this.AXE_01LOD0.SetActive(true);
          this.AXE_02LOD0.SetActive(false);
          this.CLUB_01LOD0.SetActive(false);
          this.CLUB_02LOD0.SetActive(false);
          this.FALCHION_LOD0.SetActive(false);
          this.GLADIUS_LOD0.SetActive(false);
          this.MACE_LOD0.SetActive(false);
          this.MAUL_LOD0.SetActive(false);
          this.SCIMITAR_LOD0.SetActive(false);
          this.SPEAR_LOD0.SetActive(false);
          this.SWORD_BASTARD_LOD0.SetActive(false);
          this.SWORD_BOARD_01LOD0.SetActive(false);
          this.SWORD_SHORT_LOD0.SetActive(false);
          break;
        }
      case 2:
        {
          this.AXE_01LOD0.SetActive(false);
          this.AXE_02LOD0.SetActive(true);
          this.CLUB_01LOD0.SetActive(false);
          this.CLUB_02LOD0.SetActive(false);
          this.FALCHION_LOD0.SetActive(false);
          this.GLADIUS_LOD0.SetActive(false);
```

[239]

```
            this.MACE_LOD0.SetActive(false);
            this.MAUL_LOD0.SetActive(false);
            this.SCIMITAR_LOD0.SetActive(false);
            this.SPEAR_LOD0.SetActive(false);
            this.SWORD_BASTARD_LOD0.SetActive(false);
            this.SWORD_BOARD_01LOD0.SetActive(false);
            this.SWORD_SHORT_LOD0.SetActive(false);
            break;
        }
    case 3:
        {
            this.AXE_01LOD0.SetActive(false);
            this.AXE_02LOD0.SetActive(false);
            this.CLUB_01LOD0.SetActive(true);
            this.CLUB_02LOD0.SetActive(false);
            this.FALCHION_LOD0.SetActive(false);
            this.GLADIUS_LOD0.SetActive(false);
            this.MACE_LOD0.SetActive(false);
            this.MAUL_LOD0.SetActive(false);
            this.SCIMITAR_LOD0.SetActive(false);
            this.SPEAR_LOD0.SetActive(false);
            this.SWORD_BASTARD_LOD0.SetActive(false);
            this.SWORD_BOARD_01LOD0.SetActive(false);
            this.SWORD_SHORT_LOD0.SetActive(false);
            break;
        }
    case 4:
        {
            this.AXE_01LOD0.SetActive(false);
            this.AXE_02LOD0.SetActive(false);
            this.CLUB_01LOD0.SetActive(false);
            this.CLUB_02LOD0.SetActive(true);
            this.FALCHION_LOD0.SetActive(false);
            this.GLADIUS_LOD0.SetActive(false);
            this.MACE_LOD0.SetActive(false);
            this.MAUL_LOD0.SetActive(false);
            this.SCIMITAR_LOD0.SetActive(false);
            this.SPEAR_LOD0.SetActive(false);
            this.SWORD_BASTARD_LOD0.SetActive(false);
            this.SWORD_BOARD_01LOD0.SetActive(false);
            this.SWORD_SHORT_LOD0.SetActive(false);
            break;
        }
    case 5:
        {
            this.AXE_01LOD0.SetActive(false);
            this.AXE_02LOD0.SetActive(false);
            this.CLUB_01LOD0.SetActive(false);
```

```
            this.CLUB_02LOD0.SetActive(false);
            this.FALCHION_LOD0.SetActive(true);
            this.GLADIUS_LOD0.SetActive(false);
            this.MACE_LOD0.SetActive(false);
            this.MAUL_LOD0.SetActive(false);
            this.SCIMITAR_LOD0.SetActive(false);
            this.SPEAR_LOD0.SetActive(false);
            this.SWORD_BASTARD_LOD0.SetActive(false);
            this.SWORD_BOARD_01LOD0.SetActive(false);
            this.SWORD_SHORT_LOD0.SetActive(false);
            break;
        }
    case 6:
        {
            this.AXE_01LOD0.SetActive(false);
            this.AXE_02LOD0.SetActive(false);
            this.CLUB_01LOD0.SetActive(false);
            this.CLUB_02LOD0.SetActive(false);
            this.FALCHION_LOD0.SetActive(false);
            this.GLADIUS_LOD0.SetActive(true);
            this.MACE_LOD0.SetActive(false);
            this.MAUL_LOD0.SetActive(false);
            this.SCIMITAR_LOD0.SetActive(false);
            this.SPEAR_LOD0.SetActive(false);
            this.SWORD_BASTARD_LOD0.SetActive(false);
            this.SWORD_BOARD_01LOD0.SetActive(false);
            this.SWORD_SHORT_LOD0.SetActive(false);
            break;
        }
    case 7:
        {
            this.AXE_01LOD0.SetActive(false);
            this.AXE_02LOD0.SetActive(false);
            this.CLUB_01LOD0.SetActive(false);
            this.CLUB_02LOD0.SetActive(false);
            this.FALCHION_LOD0.SetActive(false);
            this.GLADIUS_LOD0.SetActive(false);
            this.MACE_LOD0.SetActive(true);
            this.MAUL_LOD0.SetActive(false);
            this.SCIMITAR_LOD0.SetActive(false);
            this.SPEAR_LOD0.SetActive(false);
            this.SWORD_BASTARD_LOD0.SetActive(false);
            this.SWORD_BOARD_01LOD0.SetActive(false);
            this.SWORD_SHORT_LOD0.SetActive(false);
            break;
        }
    case 8:
        {
```

Inventory System

```
        this.AXE_01LOD0.SetActive(false);
        this.AXE_02LOD0.SetActive(false);
        this.CLUB_01LOD0.SetActive(false);
        this.CLUB_02LOD0.SetActive(false);
        this.FALCHION_LOD0.SetActive(false);
        this.GLADIUS_LOD0.SetActive(false);
        this.MACE_LOD0.SetActive(false);
        this.MAUL_LOD0.SetActive(true);
        this.SCIMITAR_LOD0.SetActive(false);
        this.SPEAR_LOD0.SetActive(false);
        this.SWORD_BASTARD_LOD0.SetActive(false);
        this.SWORD_BOARD_01LOD0.SetActive(false);
        this.SWORD_SHORT_LOD0.SetActive(false);
        break;
    }
case 9:
    {
        this.AXE_01LOD0.SetActive(false);
        this.AXE_02LOD0.SetActive(false);
        this.CLUB_01LOD0.SetActive(false);
        this.CLUB_02LOD0.SetActive(false);
        this.FALCHION_LOD0.SetActive(false);
        this.GLADIUS_LOD0.SetActive(false);
        this.MACE_LOD0.SetActive(false);
        this.MAUL_LOD0.SetActive(false);
        this.SCIMITAR_LOD0.SetActive(true);
        this.SPEAR_LOD0.SetActive(false);
        this.SWORD_BASTARD_LOD0.SetActive(false);
        this.SWORD_BOARD_01LOD0.SetActive(false);
        this.SWORD_SHORT_LOD0.SetActive(false);
        break;
    }
case 10:
    {
        this.AXE_01LOD0.SetActive(false);
        this.AXE_02LOD0.SetActive(false);
        this.CLUB_01LOD0.SetActive(false);
        this.CLUB_02LOD0.SetActive(false);
        this.FALCHION_LOD0.SetActive(false);
        this.GLADIUS_LOD0.SetActive(false);
        this.MACE_LOD0.SetActive(false);
        this.MAUL_LOD0.SetActive(false);
        this.SCIMITAR_LOD0.SetActive(false);
        this.SPEAR_LOD0.SetActive(true);
        this.SWORD_BASTARD_LOD0.SetActive(false);
        this.SWORD_BOARD_01LOD0.SetActive(false);
        this.SWORD_SHORT_LOD0.SetActive(false);
        break;
```

```
      }
case 11:
   {
      this.AXE_01LOD0.SetActive(false);
      this.AXE_02LOD0.SetActive(false);
      this.CLUB_01LOD0.SetActive(false);
      this.CLUB_02LOD0.SetActive(false);
      this.FALCHION_LOD0.SetActive(false);
      this.GLADIUS_LOD0.SetActive(false);
      this.MACE_LOD0.SetActive(false);
      this.MAUL_LOD0.SetActive(false);
      this.SCIMITAR_LOD0.SetActive(false);
      this.SPEAR_LOD0.SetActive(false);
      this.SWORD_BASTARD_LOD0.SetActive(true);
      this.SWORD_BOARD_01LOD0.SetActive(false);
      this.SWORD_SHORT_LOD0.SetActive(false);
      break;
   }
case 12:
   {
      this.AXE_01LOD0.SetActive(false);
      this.AXE_02LOD0.SetActive(false);
      this.CLUB_01LOD0.SetActive(false);
      this.CLUB_02LOD0.SetActive(false);
      this.FALCHION_LOD0.SetActive(false);
      this.GLADIUS_LOD0.SetActive(false);
      this.MACE_LOD0.SetActive(false);
      this.MAUL_LOD0.SetActive(false);
      this.SCIMITAR_LOD0.SetActive(false);
      this.SPEAR_LOD0.SetActive(false);
      this.SWORD_BASTARD_LOD0.SetActive(false);
      this.SWORD_BOARD_01LOD0.SetActive(true);
      this.SWORD_SHORT_LOD0.SetActive(false);
      break;
   }
case 13:
   {
      this.AXE_01LOD0.SetActive(false);
      this.AXE_02LOD0.SetActive(false);
      this.CLUB_01LOD0.SetActive(false);
      this.CLUB_02LOD0.SetActive(false);
      this.FALCHION_LOD0.SetActive(false);
      this.GLADIUS_LOD0.SetActive(false);
      this.MACE_LOD0.SetActive(false);
      this.MAUL_LOD0.SetActive(false);
      this.SCIMITAR_LOD0.SetActive(false);
      this.SPEAR_LOD0.SetActive(false);
      this.SWORD_BASTARD_LOD0.SetActive(false);
```

Inventory System

```
            this.SWORD_BOARD_01LOD0.SetActive(false);
            this.SWORD_SHORT_LOD0.SetActive(true);
            break;
        }


    }
}
```

I have not listed the whole script as it will take a lot of pages. But the basic concept is to overload the `SetXXXXX()` functions so that they will perform the necessary tasks based on the parameters coming in, such as, for the previous example, `PC.WEAPON_TYPE`.

The next scrip that needs to be modified is the `UIController.cs` script. This is where we are going to modify the five functions we created previously to actually apply the changes to the player character. Let's look at one of the functions that have been modified without listing the whole code:

```
    public void DisplayWeaponsCategory()
    {
      if(GameMaster.instance.DISPLAY_INVENTORY)
      {
        this.ClearInventoryItemsPanel();

        foreach (InventoryItem item in GameMaster.instance.INVENTORY.WEAPONS)
        {
          GameObject objItem =
  GameObject.Instantiate(this.InventoryItemElement) as GameObject;
          InventoryItemUI invItem = objItem.GetComponent<InventoryItemUI>();
          invItem.txtItemElement.text =
            string.Format("Name: {0}, Description: {1}, Strength: {2},
  Weight: {3}",
                                      item.NAME,
                                      item.DESCRIPTION,
                                      item.STRENGTH,
                                      item.WEIGHT);


          invItem.item = item;

          // add button triggers
          invItem.butAdd.GetComponent<Button>().onClick.AddListener(() =>
          {
            Debug.Log(string.Format("You have clicked button add for {0},
  {1}", invItem.txtItemElement.text, invItem.item.NAME));

            // let's apply the selected item to the player character
            GameMaster.instance.PC_CC.SELECTED_WEAPON =
```

Chapter 6

```
(PC.WEAPON_TYPE)Enum.Parse(typeof(PC.WEAPON_TYPE), invItem.item.NAME);
        GameMaster.instance.PlayerWeaponChanged();
      });

      // delete button triggers
      invItem.butDelete.GetComponent<Button>().onClick.AddListener(() =>
      {
        Debug.Log(string.Format("You have clicked button delete for {0}",
invItem.txtItemElement.text));
        Destroy(objItem);
      });

      objItem.transform.SetParent(this.PanelItem);
    }

  }
}
```

If you notice, we are also saving the *item* from the `foreach` loop into the `invItem.item` variable. This is important to make sure the `OnClick()` listener is picking up the current `InventoryItem` from the list.

The bulk of the work is being done in the `onClick.AddListener()` for each button. We are basically setting the selected weapon using the `GameMaster.instance` to store and then we are calling the `PlayerWeaponChanged()` function to handle some more features. You will see that in the next code listing.

You will need to handle each add button listener in similar fashion, based on how you have designed and implemented your code and your prefabs.

Finally, we are going to make some modifications to the `GameMaster.cs` script. Here is the listing:

```
using UnityEngine;
using UnityEngine.UI;
using UnityEngine.SceneManagement;

using System.Collections;
using System;

public class GameMaster : MonoBehaviour
{
  public static GameMaster instance;
```

Inventory System

```csharp
        // let's have a reference to the player character GameObject
        public GameObject PC_GO;

        // reference to player Character Customization
        public PC PC_CC;
        public InventorySystem INVENTORY;

        public GameObject START_POSITION;

        public GameObject CHARACTER_CUSTOMIZATION;

        public LevelController LEVEL_CONTROLLER;
        public AudioController AUDIO_CONTROLLER;

        // Ref to UI Elements ...
        public bool DISPLAY_SETTINGS = false;
        public bool DISPLAY_INVENTORY = false;

        public UIController UI;

        void Awake()
        {
          // simple singleton
          if (instance == null)
          {
            instance = this;

            instance.DISPLAY_INVENTORY = false;
            instance.DISPLAY_SETTINGS = false;

            // initialize Level Controller
            instance.LEVEL_CONTROLLER = new LevelController();

            // initialize Audio Controller
            instance.AUDIO_CONTROLLER = new AudioController();
            instance.AUDIO_CONTROLLER.AUDIO_SOURCE =
      GameMaster.instance.GetComponent<AudioSource>();
            instance.AUDIO_CONTROLLER.SetDefaultVolume();

            // initialize Inventory System
            instance.INVENTORY = new InventorySystem();

          }
          else if (instance != this)
          {
            Destroy(this);
          }
```

```
   // keep the game object when moving from
   // one scene to the next scene
   DontDestroyOnLoad(this);
 }

 #region Player Inventory Items Applied
 public void PlayerWeaponChanged()
 {
   Debug.Log(string.Format("Weapon changed to: {0}",
instance.PC_CC.SELECTED_WEAPON.ToString()));
GameMaster.instance.PC_GO.GetComponent<CharacterCustomization>().SetWeaponT
ype(GameMaster.instance.PC_CC.SELECTED_WEAPON);
 }

 public void PlayerArmourChanged(InventoryItem item)
 {
   Debug.Log(string.Format("Armour changed to: {0} {1}",
instance.PC_CC.SELECTED_ARMOUR.NAME, instance.PC_CC.SELECTED_ARMOUR.TYPE));
   switch (item.TYPE.ToString())
   {
     case "HELMET":
       {
         GameMaster.instance.PC_CC.SELECTED_HELMET =
(PC.HELMET_TYPE)Enum.Parse(typeof(PC.HELMET_TYPE),
instance.PC_CC.SELECTED_ARMOUR.NAME);
GameMaster.instance.PC_GO.GetComponent<CharacterCustomization>().SetHelmetT
ype(GameMaster.instance.PC_CC.SELECTED_HELMET);
         break;
       }
     case "SHIELD":
       {
         GameMaster.instance.PC_CC.SELECTED_SHIELD =
(PC.SHIELD_TYPE)Enum.Parse(typeof(PC.SHIELD_TYPE),
instance.PC_CC.SELECTED_ARMOUR.NAME);
GameMaster.instance.PC_GO.GetComponent<CharacterCustomization>().SetShieldT
ype(GameMaster.instance.PC_CC.SELECTED_SHIELD);
         break;
       }
     case "SHOULDER_PAD":
       {
         GameMaster.instance.PC_CC.SELECTED_SHOULDER_PAD =
(PC.SHOULDER_PAD)Enum.Parse(typeof(PC.SHOULDER_PAD),
instance.PC_CC.SELECTED_ARMOUR.NAME);
GameMaster.instance.PC_GO.GetComponent<CharacterCustomization>().SetShoulde
rPad(GameMaster.instance.PC_CC.SELECTED_SHOULDER_PAD);
         break;
       }
     case "KNEE_PAD":
```

Inventory System

```
            {
               break;
            }
         case "BOOTS":
            {
               break;
            }


      }
   }


   #endregion

   // for each level/scene that has been loaded
   // do some of the preparation work
   void OnLevelWasLoaded()
   {
      GameMaster.instance.LEVEL_CONTROLLER.OnLevelWasLoaded();
   }

   // Use this for initialization
   void Start()
   {
      // let's find a reference to the UI controller of the loaded scene
      if (GameObject.FindGameObjectWithTag("UI") != null)
      {
         GameMaster.instance.UI =
GameObject.FindGameObjectWithTag("UI").GetComponent<UIController>();
      }

GameMaster.instance.UI.SettingsCanvas.gameObject.SetActive(GameMaster.insta
nce.DISPLAY_SETTINGS);
   }

   // Update is called once per frame
   void Update()
   {
      // only when we are in the game level
      if(instance.LEVEL_CONTROLLER.CURRENT_SCENE.name==SceneName.Level_1)
      {
         if (Input.GetKeyUp(KeyCode.J))
         {
            //Debug.Log("Pressing J");
            instance.DISPLAY_INVENTORY = !instance.DISPLAY_INVENTORY;
            instance.UI.DisplayInventory();
         }
      }
   }
```

Chapter 6

```
public void MasterVolume(float volume)
{
   GameMaster.instance.AUDIO_CONTROLLER.MasterVolume(volume);
}

public void StartGame()
{
   GameMaster.instance.LoadLevel();
}

public void LoadLevel()
{
   GameMaster.instance.LEVEL_CONTROLLER.LoadLevel();
}

public void RPG_Destroy(GameObject obj)
{
   Destroy(obj);
}
}
```

The only function I want to have you take note of is the `PlayerArmourChanged()` function. It was because of this function that we have to add the new *Type* data variable and datatype to the *InventoryItem* class. We have a lot of different types of armour, and we needed a way to distinguish between them. Based on the armour type, we would then call the appropriate function to active them on the player character.

How It Looks

This chapter was a bit involved in regard to configuring your GameObjects and prefabs, and more importantly the code that went along to glue everything together. I have tried to keep things as simple as possible.

[249]

Inventory System

Here is a screenshot illustrating the player character prior to picking up the inventory items placed on the level. Notice that the `INVENTORY` is empty in the `GameMaster` object and also there are no selected items in the `PC_CC` object:

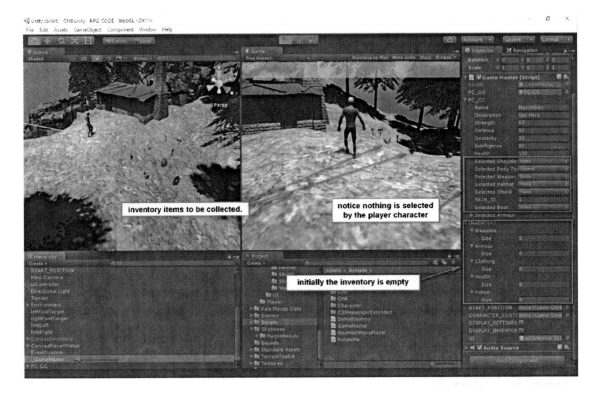

Chapter 6

After I move the player character to pick up the inventory items, I will use the hot key programmed to bring up the Inventory Window, in my case, the J key. The following screenshot captures the interaction:

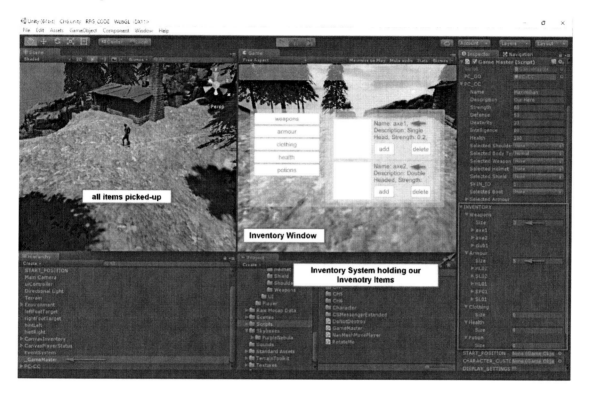

[251]

Inventory System

And now let's see how things change when we apply a few of the inventory items to the player character:

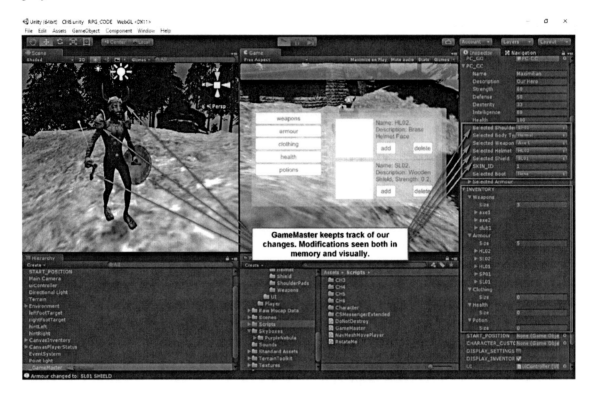

Summary

There is a lot covered in this chapter. The core of the chapter was to create a usable Inventory System. We began the chapter by discussing the Weighted Inventory and gave a brief overview of its concept. Then we determined the item types we are going to be using for our game.

We created the scripts BaseItem.cs, InventoryItem.cs, and InventorySystem.cs. These scripts were then utilized as a starting point to design and develop our inventory. We then updated the GameMaster.cs script to test the basics of the newly created scripts and be able to view the data within the Unity IDE by serializing the attributes. We did this by instantiating an InventoryItem and inserting it into the InventorySystem and validated the operation visually through the IDE.

Chapter 6

The next step was to actually create the inventory item prefabs. This section covered how to navigate and find your customizable inventory items if your model included everything on the actual fbx model, how to extract it from the model and convert into a Prefab for later use. Then we created a new script called `InventoryItemAgent.cs` which was attached to every prefab created to represent an inventory item. This script basically gives us the ability to set the data for each Inventory Item from within the IDE. Very useful! We also had to attach a collider to each prefab to handle collision and trigger a pick-up call when the player collided with the object.

Once we had the basics in place, we started looking at how to design and implement the user interface for our inventory system. We discussed the categories that we want to represent and how the items within each category will be listed / displayed for the player during game play. We implemented the initial framework for the Inventory Window and integrated it with the game.

Now we were ready to discuss how to create a dynamic item viewer that can be populated during runtime and represent the inventory items we have collected correctly. We introduced some new user interface concepts such as scroll view and how to utilize layouts in our interface. We did a quick test with a simple placeholder to just display the name of the item. Once we got the mechanics working, we implemented the main inventory item control panel and converted it into a prefab to be used instantiated at runtime when needed.

At the end, we worked on the integration of the Inventory System with the Inventory UI with the GameMaster and Player Character to have the final implementation. This required that we update and modify more scripts.

By the end of the chapter, you have a fully functional Inventory System that can be expanded as needed. In the next two chapters, we are going to see how to enhance our user interface by adding an HUD and finally cover the concepts of multiplayer programming.

7
User Interface and System Feedback

Have you ever seen the tip of an iceberg? Well, so far that's what we have done throughout the previous six chapters. In this chapter we are going to keep on improving on our game's user interface and feedback system. We are going to create a Heads Up Display that will be responsible for managing the user interaction with the system menus and also the system giving feedback to the player.

Here is a breakdown of the chapter:

- Heads Up Display
- Basic information for a HUD
- Our design
- HUD framework
- Completing HUD design
- Panel character info
- Panel active items
- Panel special items
- Integrating the code
- Enemy stats in the HUD
- NPC stats user interface
- Creating the NPC canvas
- NPC taking a hit
- Enhancing the code

Let's get started!

User Interface and System Feedback

Designing a Heads Up Display

Designing a Heads Up Display (HUD) is going to be a very challenging task. The HUD is the interface through which your players can interact with the virtual world and also receive feedback from the virtual world environment. As with everything else that we have designed so far, the HUD design is also heavily related to the type and the needs of the game you are trying to make.

For instance, an RTS (Real Time Strategy) will have a very different type of HUD design then an FPS (First Person Shooter), and than an RPG (Role Playing Game). They will have some things in common, but the way they are designed is going to be very distinct, as well as some of the features and functionality.

We could have a whole book just on the design and development of user interfaces and how to approach them in a scientific manner. But that is outside the scope of this book, and we are concerned with the theories.

Basic information for a HUD

Any simple heads up display will have, at a minimum, a way to display the following information:

- Basics information about the player character
- Health
- Mana
- Strength
- Level, etc
- Current inventory items consumed by the player character
- Current weapon used by the player
- Current armour used by the player
- Available potions and/or health
- Feedback from the game environment
- Anything useful pertaining to the game
- Power ups
- Level ups, etc

Let's go ahead and design our HUD. Once again we will start with a simple framework and slowly build on top of it, as we need to.

Our design

Taking everything into consideration, let's go ahead and design a HUD that will be useful for our game, and at the same time we will keep it simple but useful. We should have a HUD that will display the basic player character information in a manner in which it does not block the gameplay, but at the same time gives critical information to the player regarding their character's state.

We should also design a way to display the current inventory items that the player has activated to be used, such as the weapon, or the armour. Finally, we should also have a simple way for the player to use any health packets and or potions they might have during gameplay.

Here is a quick sketch of what I want my HUD to look like. Again, you are free and in fact I encourage you to come up with your own design.

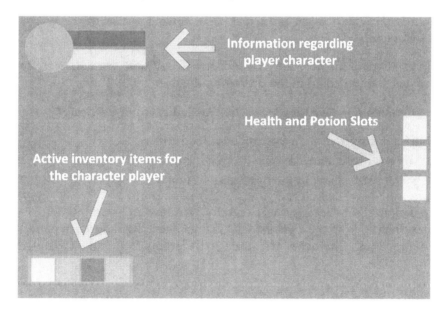

User Interface and System Feedback

I have roughly marked what I would like my HUD to look like during gameplay.

Notice that I have kept it simple. In the top left corner, I have placed the immediate information that the player will need to have, such as their health and perhaps their strength.

In the bottom left corner, I have placed a scrollable panel that will list all of the active inventory items that the player may have active on their player character, and on the right side of the screen I have three slots that will be used for immediate access to things such as health packets and or potions that the player might need to use during their gameplay.

HUD framework

Now that we have an understanding of what we want our UI to look like, let's actually start implementing it in Unity. We need to create a new canvas to hold our HUD. To create this, right-click in the *Hierarchy Window* and select *UI | Canvas*. Rename the new *Canvas* GameObject to *CanvasHUD*.

Go ahead and implement the necessary UI sections as outlined. We will need three main panels for each section indicated in the preceding diagram.

These are the three main panels for each section, as indicated in the design:

- Character information in the top left screen corner
- Active inventory items in the bottom left corner of the screen
- A special items panel in the right mid-section of the screen

Create each panel by right-clicking the **Hierarchy Window** and selecting **UI | Panel**. Make sure the panels are a child of the **CanvasHUD** GameObject. Rename each panel accordingly. I have named mine **PanelCharacterInfo**, **PanelActiveItems**, and **PanelSpecialItems**.

Chapter 7

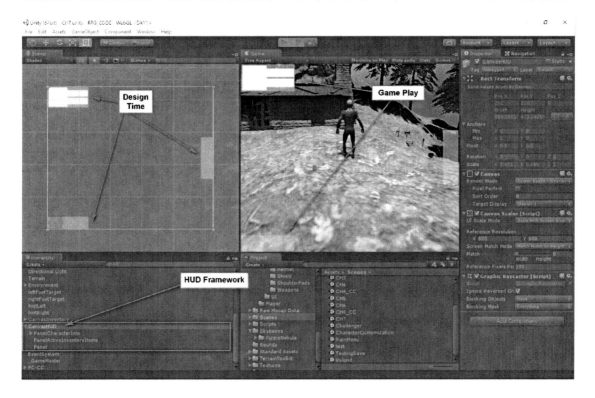

Take a look at the preceding screenshot to get a feeling for the HUD framework.

Completing HUD design

Now that we have the framework in place, let's go ahead and complete each section individually. I would like to start with the *PanelCharacterInfo*.

Panel character Info

From a design point of view, the panel that will contain the visual components for the character is not going to be very complex. The panel will consist of five images.

The main image will be used to hold an avatar of the character. The other four images will be used to display the health and mana of the character. Since these values are going to be displayed in a bar format, we are using two images for each item. One of the images is going to host the border, and the other the representation of the actual value.

To come up with the images, I am going to use external tools such as Photoshop. Microsoft Expression Design is a good tool for creating frames and so on.

In the preceding screenshot, I have made a nice image portraying the avatar of the player character. You should take into consideration the actual size of the image you will be placing inside the *PanelCharacterInfo* panel. The image size I have generated is 301 x 301 pixels.

To create the graphics for the bars representing the health and the mana for our character player, we will actually need to have three images. One image will represent the negative value of the bar, one image will represent the positive value of the bar and the third will be the border image for the bar. They will be overlaid on top of each other to create the illusion of our graphic bars.

Chapter 7

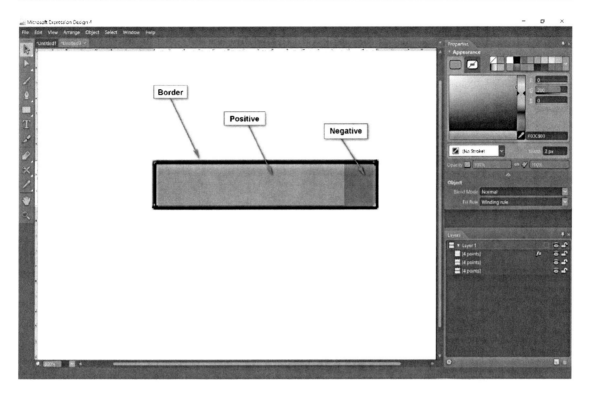

Creating the three distinct sprites and overlaying them will give you a good illusion of what are looking for.

After exporting our images, we need to import them into Unity. Use your file system to move your images from their original location to the *Assets* folder under your Unity project.

I have placed my textures in the following directory: **Assets | Textures | CH7.**

User Interface and System Feedback

Once you have moved them into the desired location within your Unity project, you will need to convert the images to sprites. Select all of the images that will be used for the GUI and from the **Inspector Window**, change the **Texture Type to Sprite (2D and UI)**.

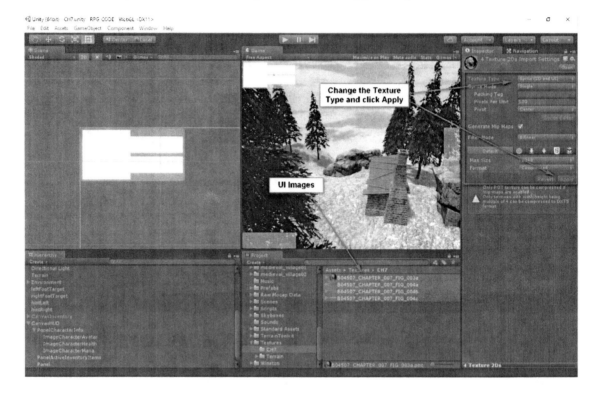

It's time to apply our textures to the actual UI elements we have defined under the *PanelCharacterInfo* panel within the *Canvas* object.

There are a few steps that need to be performed before we can fully apply the UI elements to the HUD.

The first thing you should do, if you have not done so already, is create three new UI image elements under the *PanelCharacterInfo* panel by right-clicking the panel and selecting *UI | Image*.

Chapter 7

I have named my three images: *imgHealthRebBackground*, *imgHealthGreenBackground* and *imgHealthBorder*. The order of the images does matter, and you should take a note of it when you are designing the UI. Generally speaking, if a UI element is lower in the hierarchy, it will be rendered on top of the other elements.

See the following screenshot for details:

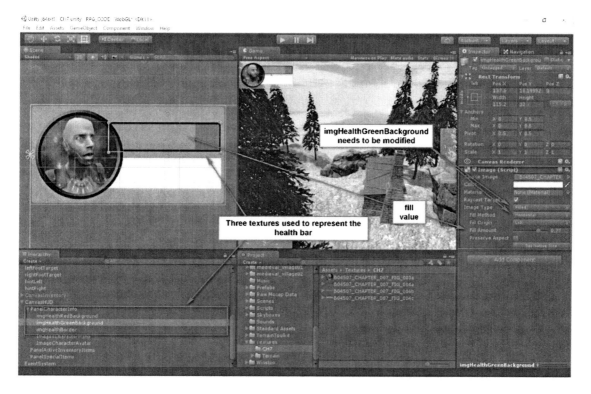

Notice the order of the images representing the health bar. The image that is representing the green bar will need to be modified using the *Inspector Window*. Select it, and change the *Image Type* to *Filled*, change the *Fill Method* to *Horizontal* and the *Fill Origin* to *Left*. We are going to be using the *Fill Amount* to control the visual part of our health bar. Notice that I have set it to *0.77* for demonstration purposes.

By default, when the game starts, we will be starting at a *Fill Amount* of *1*, which is equivalent to 100 percent, for the player character's health. 0.77 is equivalent to 77 percent and so on.

[263]

User Interface and System Feedback

We are going to apply the same technique to our mana bar. Go ahead and create two more images that will represent the two backgrounds for our mana bar.

 We will be using the same border image for both bars.

Again, don't forget you will need to make the appropriate changes to the imported textures within Unity. Convert them to *Sprite (2D and UI) Texture Type*.

Create the necessary image UI elements under the panel, and apply the textures to the image element within the canvas. You should have something like the following screenshot:

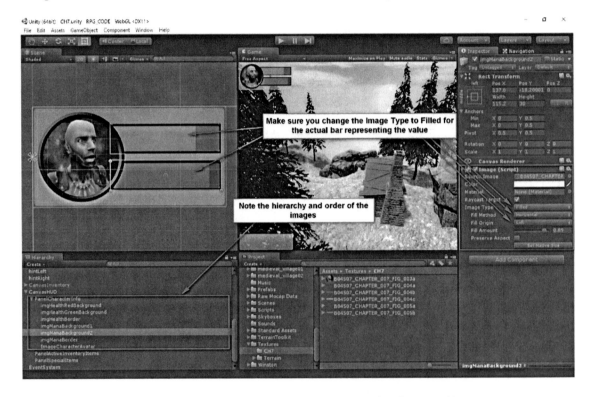

That's all there is to it! Not bad for a person with no artistic background!

[264]

Chapter 7

Panel active inventory items

Creating the UI for active inventory items is going to be similar to what we have done in Chapter 6, *Inventory System*. The difference will be that we are only going to be listing the items that have been consumed by the player character using the inventory system.

In other words, the Active Inventory Items display is a visual indication of the items that have been activated within the inventory. It is important to keep in mind that we are more interested in learning the concepts and applying them in a simple example that you can expand upon and improve on your own.

The basic idea is to create a scrollable panel that will be used to add items as needed. We have already seen how to set up the scrollable view and how to configure the UI components to support what we are trying to achieve. I won't be getting into the details here again, please refer to Chapter 6, *Inventory System*, for the necessary steps if needed.

From the *Hierarchy Window*, right-click on *PanelActiveInventoryItems* and select *UI | Scroll View*. Go ahead and remove the *Viewport, Scrollbar Horizontal* and *Scrollbar Vertical* children that have been created with the *Scroll View* element.

[265]

User Interface and System Feedback

You just need to make sure that the layout configuration you are applying is for horizontal and not vertical, as we did in Chapter 6, *Inventory System*.

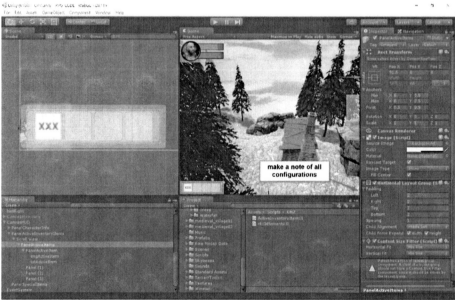

Chapter 7

And finally, the following:

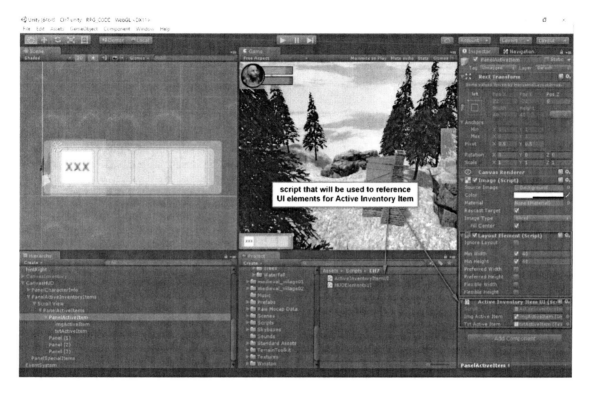

The three preceding screenshots illustrate the different parts of the configuration for the Active Inventory Items panel. If you are unsure about how to put this together, please go back to Chapter 6, *Inventory System* and read *Designing a Dynamic Item Viewer* section.

Don't forget to make a prefab of the UI element that will be representing your active inventory item in the panel.

You will also need a script to reference the UI elements designated for your items. I have called this script *ActiveInventoryItemUI.cs*, and currently there are two attributes: one is a reference to the *Image* element and the other a reference to the *Text* element.

Here is the listing for the script:

```
using UnityEngine;
using UnityEngine.UI;
using System.Collections;

public class ActiveInventoryItemUI : MonoBehaviour {
```

[267]

User Interface and System Feedback

```
        public Image imgActiveItem;
        public Text txtActiveItem;
}
```

We will need to eventually integrate all of these scripts together to make things work properly.

Special items panel

Now we are going to look at the design of our last panel. The main difference between this panel and the last one that we developed is the orientation. Everything else will be exactly the same. However, for this panel our orientation is going to be vertical instead of horizontal.

Here is a screenshot capturing everything at once:

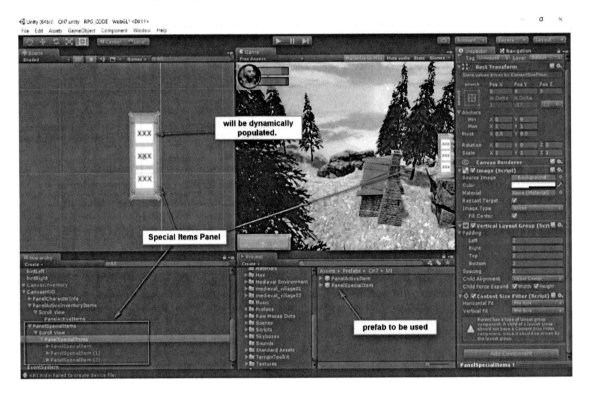

Chapter 7

The procedure to create the panel has already been discussed several times, and you should not have any trouble creating it.

 I have let you make your own textures and images to be applied to the UI elements.

As I was designing the special items panel, I came up with a better idea for how to improve the panel UI. You might want to have a static icon representing each special item, and have a counter attached to the UI representing how many you have of each item. Each time you collect one it will increase, and each time you consume one it will decrease.

Here is what the current HUD looks like based on our design:

We need to now start thinking about integrating the HUD user interface with the code base we have developed so far.

[269]

User Interface and System Feedback

Integrating the code

Now that we have our HUD design up and running, we will need to integrate the UI elements with the actual code that will be deriving them. There are a few scripts that are going to be created to support the new UI features, and a few that will be updated to glue everything together.

The following scripts have been created: *ActiveInventoryItemUI.cs*, *ActiveSpecialItemUI.cs* and *HUDElementsUI.cs*.

The listing of these scripts is as follows:

```
using UnityEngine;
using UnityEngine.UI;
using System.Collections;

public class ActiveInventoryItemUI : MonoBehaviour
{
  public InventoryItem item;

  public Image imgActiveItem;
  public Text txtActiveItem;

}

using UnityEngine;
using UnityEngine.UI;
using System.Collections;
using UnityEngine.EventSystems;

public class ActiveSpecialItemUI : EventTrigger
{

  public override void OnPointerClick(PointerEventData data)
  {
    InventoryItem iia =
this.gameObject.GetComponent<ActiveInventoryItemUI>().item;

    switch(iia.CATEGORY)
    {
      case BaseItem.ItemCategory.HEALTH:
        {
          // add the item to the special items panel
        GameMaster.instance.UI.ApplySpecialInventoryItem(iia);
          Destroy(this.gameObject);

          break;
```

[270]

```
        }
      case BaseItem.ItemCategory.POTION:
        {
          break;
        }
    }

  }

}
using UnityEngine;
using UnityEngine.UI;
using System.Collections;

public class HUDElementsUI : MonoBehaviour
{
  public Image imgHealthBar;
  public Image imgManaBar;

  public GameObject activeInventoryItem;
  public GameObject activeSpecialItem;

  public Transform panelActiveInventoryItems;
  public Transform panelActiveSpecialItems;

}
```

User Interface and System Feedback

These scripts are going to be used in the HUD user interface to give us access to the elements. For instance, you will need to attach the HUDElementsUI.cs script to the CanvasHUD GameObject.

The preceding screenshot illustrates how the HUD Canvas is configured with the *HUDElementsUI.cs* script.

Now let's take a look at the prefabs we have created to represent the UI elements to be used for the panels. There are two; I have named them *PanelActiveItem* and *PanelSpecialItem*.

I will discuss *PanelSpecialItem*, as it contains everything *PanelActiveItem* contains plus an additional script that is attached to it for event handling.

Chapter 7

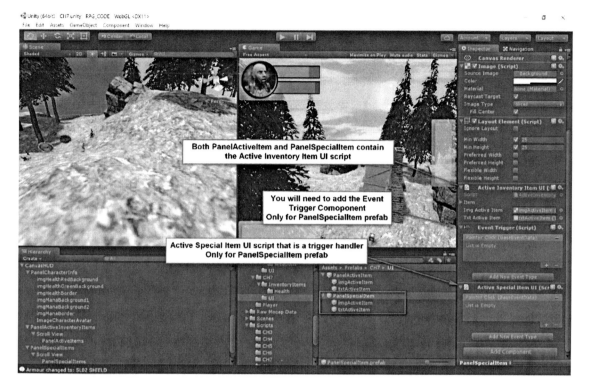

What we have just covered was the implementation of the scripts that are used to get access to the proper UI elements within the HUD canvas.

You will notice that for the *PanelSpecialItem* prefab there are two new and very important components that we have attached to it. One is the *Event Trigger* within Unity, and the other is the *ActiveSpecialItemUI.cs* script, which is used to handle the *PointerClick* event for the special item.

What this means is that we are basically making the item clickable, and when the player clicks on the item, something happens. In this case, it applies the special item to the player character.

Now we are ready to update the other scripts we have already developed to incorporate the HUD functionality. The scripts that will need to be modified are *InventorySystem.cs* and *UIController.cs*.

Here is a listing of *InventorySystem.cs*:

```
using System;
using UnityEngine;
```

User Interface and System Feedback

```csharp
using System.Collections.Generic;

[Serializable]
public class InventorySystem
{
  [SerializeField]
  private List<InventoryItem> weapons = new List<InventoryItem>();
  [SerializeField]
  private List<InventoryItem> armour = new List<InventoryItem>();
  [SerializeField]
  private List<InventoryItem> clothing = new List<InventoryItem>();
  [SerializeField]
  private List<InventoryItem> health = new List<InventoryItem>();
  [SerializeField]
  private List<InventoryItem> potion = new List<InventoryItem>();

  public List<InventoryItem> WEAPONS
  {
    get { return this.weapons; }
  }

  public List<InventoryItem> ARMOUR
  {
    get { return this.armour; }
  }

  public List<InventoryItem> CLOTHING
  {
    get { return this.clothing; }
  }

  public List<InventoryItem> HEALTH
  {
    get { return this.health; }
  }

  public List<InventoryItem> POTIONS
  {
    get { return this.potion; }
  }

  private InventoryItem selectedWeapon;
  private InventoryItem selectedArmour;

  public InventoryItem SELECTED_WEAPON
  {
    get { return this.selectedWeapon; }
    set { this.selectedWeapon = value; }
```

[274]

```csharp
}
public InventoryItem SELECTED_ARMOUR
{
  get { return this.selectedArmour; }
  set { this.selectedArmour = value; }
}

public InventorySystem()
{
  this.ClearInventory();
}

public void ClearInventory()
{
  this.weapons.Clear();
  this.armour.Clear();
  this.clothing.Clear();
  this.health.Clear();
  this.potion.Clear();
}

// this function will add an inventory item
public void AddItem(InventoryItem item)
{
  switch(item.CATEGORY)
  {
    case BaseItem.ItemCategory.ARMOUR:
      {
        this.armour.Add(item);
        break;
      }
    case BaseItem.ItemCategory.CLOTHING:
      {
        this.clothing.Add(item);
        break;
      }
    case BaseItem.ItemCategory.HEALTH:
      {
        this.health.Add(item);

        // add the item to the special items panel
        GameMaster.instance.UI.AddSpecialInventoryItem(item);

        break;
      }
    case BaseItem.ItemCategory.POTION:
      {
        this.potion.Add(item);
```

```
          break;
        }
    case BaseItem.ItemCategory.WEAPON:
        {
          this.weapons.Add(item);
          break;
        }
    }
}

// this function will remove an inventory item
public void DeleteItem(InventoryItem item)
{
  switch (item.CATEGORY)
  {
    case BaseItem.ItemCategory.ARMOUR:
        {
          this.armour.Remove(item);
          break;
        }
    case BaseItem.ItemCategory.CLOTHING:
        {
          this.clothing.Remove(item);
          break;
        }
    case BaseItem.ItemCategory.HEALTH:
        {
          // let's find the item and mark it for removal
          InventoryItem tmp = null;
          foreach(InventoryItem i in this.health)
          {
if(item.CATEGORY.Equals(i.CATEGORY)&&item.NAME.Equals(i.NAME)&&item.STRENGT
H.Equals(i.STRENGTH))
            {
              tmp = i;
            }
          }

          this.health.Remove(tmp);

          break;
        }
    case BaseItem.ItemCategory.POTION:
        {
          // let's find the item and mark it for removal
          InventoryItem tmp = null;
          foreach (InventoryItem i in this.health)
          {
```

```csharp
                if (item.CATEGORY.Equals(i.CATEGORY) &&
item.NAME.Equals(i.NAME) && item.STRENGTH.Equals(i.STRENGTH))
                {
                    tmp = i;
                }
            }

            this.potion.Remove(item);
            break;
        }
      case BaseItem.ItemCategory.WEAPON:
        {
            this.weapons.Remove(item);
            break;
        }
    }
  }

}

using UnityEngine;
using UnityEngine.UI;
using System;

public class UIController : MonoBehaviour
{
  public Canvas SettingsCanvas;
  public Slider ControlMainVolume;

  // the canvas object for inventory system
  public Canvas InventoryCanvas;

  public Transform PanelItem;
  public GameObject InventoryItemElement;

  public HUDElementsUI hudUI;

  public void Update()
  {

  }

  public void DisplaySettings()
  {
    GameMaster.instance.DISPLAY_SETTINGS =
!GameMaster.instance.DISPLAY_SETTINGS;
this.SettingsCanvas.gameObject.SetActive(GameMaster.instance.DISPLAY_SETTIN
GS);
```

User Interface and System Feedback

```csharp
  }

  public void MainVolume()
  {
    GameMaster.instance.MasterVolume(ControlMainVolume.value);
  }

  public void StartGame()
  {
    GameMaster.instance.StartGame();
  }

  public void LoadLevel()
  {
    if (GameObject.FindGameObjectWithTag("BASE"))
    {
      GameMaster.instance.PC_CC =
GameObject.FindGameObjectWithTag("BASE").GetComponent<CharacterCustomizatio
n>().PC_CC;
    }
    GameMaster.instance.LEVEL_CONTROLLER.LEVEL = 1;
    GameMaster.instance.LoadLevel();
  }

  public void DisplayInventory()
  {
this.InventoryCanvas.gameObject.SetActive(GameMaster.instance.DISPLAY_INVEN
TORY);
  }

  private void ClearInventoryItemsPanel()
  {
    while(this.PanelItem.childCount>0)
    {
      Transform t = this.PanelItem.GetChild(0).transform;
      t.parent = null;
      Destroy(t.gameObject);
    }
  }


  public void DisplayWeaponsCategory()
  {
    if(GameMaster.instance.DISPLAY_INVENTORY)
    {
      this.ClearInventoryItemsPanel();

      foreach (InventoryItem item in GameMaster.instance.INVENTORY.WEAPONS)
```

[278]

```
      {
         GameObject objItem =
GameObject.Instantiate(this.InventoryItemElement) as GameObject;
         InventoryItemUI invItem = objItem.GetComponent<InventoryItemUI>();
         invItem.txtItemElement.text =
            string.Format("Name: {0}, Description: {1}, Strength: {2},
Weight: {3}",
                                    item.NAME,
                                    item.DESCRIPTION,
                                    item.STRENGTH,
                                    item.WEIGHT);


         invItem.item = item;

         // add button triggers
         invItem.butAdd.GetComponent<Button>().onClick.AddListener(() =>
         {
            Debug.Log(string.Format("You have clicked button add for {0},
{1}", invItem.txtItemElement.text, invItem.item.NAME));

            // let's apply the selected item to the player character
            GameMaster.instance.PC_CC.SELECTED_WEAPON =
(PC.WEAPON_TYPE)Enum.Parse(typeof(PC.WEAPON_TYPE), invItem.item.NAME);
            GameMaster.instance.PlayerWeaponChanged(invItem.item);
            this.AddActiveInventoryItem(invItem.item);
         });

         // delete button triggers
         invItem.butDelete.GetComponent<Button>().onClick.AddListener(() =>
         {
            Debug.Log(string.Format("You have clicked button delete for {0}",
invItem.txtItemElement.text));
            Destroy(objItem);
         });

         objItem.transform.SetParent(this.PanelItem);
      }


   }
  }

  public void DisplayArmourCategory()
  {
    if (GameMaster.instance.DISPLAY_INVENTORY)
    {
      this.ClearInventoryItemsPanel();
```

User Interface and System Feedback

```csharp
            foreach (InventoryItem item in GameMaster.instance.INVENTORY.ARMOUR)
            {
                GameObject objItem =
GameObject.Instantiate(this.InventoryItemElement) as GameObject;
                InventoryItemUI invItem = objItem.GetComponent<InventoryItemUI>();
                invItem.txtItemElement.text =
                    string.Format("Name: {0}, Description: {1}, Strength: {2},
Weight: {3}",
                                                item.NAME,
                                                item.DESCRIPTION,
                                                item.STRENGTH,
                                                item.WEIGHT);

                invItem.item = item;

                // add button triggers
                invItem.butAdd.GetComponent<Button>().onClick.AddListener(() =>
                {
                    Debug.Log(string.Format("You have clicked button add for {0},
{1}", invItem.txtItemElement.text, invItem.item.NAME));

                    // let's apply the selected item to the player character
                    GameMaster.instance.PC_CC.SELECTED_ARMOUR = invItem.item;
                    GameMaster.instance.PlayerArmourChanged(invItem.item);
                    this.AddActiveInventoryItem(invItem.item);
                });

                // delete button triggers
                invItem.butDelete.GetComponent<Button>().onClick.AddListener(() =>
                {
                    Debug.Log(string.Format("You have clicked button delete for {0}",
invItem.txtItemElement.text));
                    Destroy(objItem);
                });

                objItem.transform.SetParent(this.PanelItem);
            }
        }
    }

    public void DisplayClothingCategory()
    {
        if (GameMaster.instance.DISPLAY_INVENTORY)
        {
            this.ClearInventoryItemsPanel();

            foreach (InventoryItem item in
GameMaster.instance.INVENTORY.CLOTHING)
```

[280]

```
        {
            GameObject objItem =
GameObject.Instantiate(this.InventoryItemElement) as GameObject;
            InventoryItemUI invItem = objItem.GetComponent<InventoryItemUI>();
            invItem.txtItemElement.text =
                string.Format("Name: {0}, Description: {1}, Strength: {2},
Weight: {3}",
                                    item.NAME,
                                    item.DESCRIPTION,
                                    item.STRENGTH,
                                    item.WEIGHT);

            invItem.item = item;

            // add button triggers
            invItem.butAdd.GetComponent<Button>().onClick.AddListener(() =>
            {
                Debug.Log(string.Format("You have clicked button add for {0}",
invItem.txtItemElement.text));

            });

            // delete button triggers
            invItem.butDelete.GetComponent<Button>().onClick.AddListener(() =>
            {
                Debug.Log(string.Format("You have clicked button delete for {0}",
invItem.txtItemElement.text));
                Destroy(objItem);
            });

            objItem.transform.SetParent(this.PanelItem);
        }
    }
}

    public void DisplayHealthCategory()
    {
        if (GameMaster.instance.DISPLAY_INVENTORY)
        {
            this.ClearInventoryItemsPanel();

            foreach (InventoryItem item in GameMaster.instance.INVENTORY.HEALTH)
            {
                GameObject objItem =
GameObject.Instantiate(this.InventoryItemElement) as GameObject;
                InventoryItemUI invItem = objItem.GetComponent<InventoryItemUI>();
                invItem.txtItemElement.text =
                    string.Format("Name: {0}, Description: {1}, Strength: {2},
```

```
Weight: {3}",
                                    item.NAME,
                                    item.DESCRIPTION,
                                    item.STRENGTH,
                                    item.WEIGHT);

        invItem.item = item;

        // add button triggers
        invItem.butAdd.GetComponent<Button>().onClick.AddListener(() =>
        {
            Debug.Log(string.Format("You have clicked button add for {0}",
invItem.txtItemElement.text));

            // let's apply the selected item to the player character
            GameMaster.instance.PC_CC.HEALTH += invItem.item.STRENGTH * 100;
//(PC.WEAPON_TYPE)Enum.Parse(typeof(PC.WEAPON_TYPE), invItem.item.NAME);
            if(GameMaster.instance.PC_CC.HEALTH>100f)
            {
                GameMaster.instance.PC_CC.HEALTH = 100f;
            }

            GameMaster.instance.INVENTORY.DeleteItem(invItem.item);

            Destroy(objItem);
            //GameMaster.instance.PlayerWeaponChanged(invItem.item);
            //this.AddActiveInventoryItem(invItem.item);

        });

        // delete button triggers
        invItem.butDelete.GetComponent<Button>().onClick.AddListener(() =>
        {
            Debug.Log(string.Format("You have clicked button delete for {0}",
invItem.txtItemElement.text));
            Destroy(objItem);
        });

        objItem.transform.SetParent(this.PanelItem);
    }

  }
}

public void DisplayPotionsCategory()
{
    if (GameMaster.instance.DISPLAY_INVENTORY)
    {
```

```
        this.ClearInventoryItemsPanel();

        foreach (InventoryItem item in GameMaster.instance.INVENTORY.POTIONS)
        {
            GameObject objItem =
GameObject.Instantiate(this.InventoryItemElement) as GameObject;
            InventoryItemUI invItem = objItem.GetComponent<InventoryItemUI>();
            invItem.txtItemElement.text =
                string.Format("Name: {0}, Description: {1}, Strength: {2},
Weight: {3}",
                                        item.NAME,
                                        item.DESCRIPTION,
                                        item.STRENGTH,
                                        item.WEIGHT);

            invItem.item = item;

            // add button triggers
            invItem.butAdd.GetComponent<Button>().onClick.AddListener(() =>
            {
                Debug.Log(string.Format("You have clicked button add for {0}",
invItem.txtItemElement.text));
            });

            // delete button triggers
            invItem.butDelete.GetComponent<Button>().onClick.AddListener(() =>
            {
                Debug.Log(string.Format("You have clicked button delete for {0}",
invItem.txtItemElement.text));
                Destroy(objItem);
            });

            objItem.transform.SetParent(this.PanelItem);
        }

    }
}

#region Adding Active Inventory Item to the UI
public void AddActiveInventoryItem(InventoryItem item)
{
    // Make a copy of the Inventory Item Object
    InventoryItem myItem = new InventoryItem();
    myItem.CopyInventoryItem(item);

    GameObject objItem =
GameObject.Instantiate(this.hudUI.activeInventoryItem) as GameObject;
    ActiveInventoryItemUI aeUI =
```

```
objItem.GetComponent<ActiveInventoryItemUI>();
    aeUI.txtActiveItem.text = myItem.NAME.ToString();

    aeUI.item = myItem;

    objItem.transform.SetParent(this.hudUI.panelActiveInventoryItems);

LayoutRebuilder.MarkLayoutForRebuild(this.hudUI.panelActiveInventoryItems
as RectTransform);
  }

  public void AddSpecialInventoryItem(InventoryItem item)
  {
    // Make a copy of the Inventory Item Object
    InventoryItem myItem = new InventoryItem();
    myItem.CopyInventoryItem(item);

    GameObject objItem =
GameObject.Instantiate(this.hudUI.activeSpecialItem) as GameObject;
    ActiveInventoryItemUI aeUI =
objItem.GetComponent<ActiveInventoryItemUI>();
    aeUI.txtActiveItem.text = myItem.NAME.ToString();
    aeUI.item = myItem;

    objItem.transform.SetParent(this.hudUI.panelActiveSpecialItems);

    LayoutRebuilder.MarkLayoutForRebuild(this.hudUI.panelActiveSpecialItems
as RectTransform);
  }

  public void ApplySpecialInventoryItem(InventoryItem item)
  {
    GameMaster.instance.PC_CC.HEALTH += item.STRENGTH * 100;
//(PC.WEAPON_TYPE)Enum.Parse(typeof(PC.WEAPON_TYPE), invItem.item.NAME);
    if (GameMaster.instance.PC_CC.HEALTH > 100f)
    {
      GameMaster.instance.PC_CC.HEALTH = 100f;
    }

    GameMaster.instance.INVENTORY.DeleteItem(item);
  }
  #endregion

}
```

Chapter 7

Now that you have everything in place, you can go ahead and test run the game to make sure everything is working as expected. This is also a good time to test/debug your code and your project settings if you have not done so already.

I have to make the following point once again; the idea is to grasp the concept. We are looking at one way to implement what we want to achieve; you might come up with a better way along the way, or decide to do something totally different. I encourage that!

The preceding screenshot illustrates the state of the player character and that of the inventory when the level initially loads. I have indicated the critical parts that we are testing and that we are going to track to make sure our code is working properly.

In the next screenshot, the player character has picked up a few of the inventory items we have placed in the level. When you bring up the inventory window and click on any one of the categories defined, i.e., weapons, you will get a listing of all the weapons that we have in our inventory and so forth.

[285]

User Interface and System Feedback

We have collected one weapon type, one health packet, and a couple of defensive items. Notice that our special items panel is displaying an item. This is the health packet we have picked up.

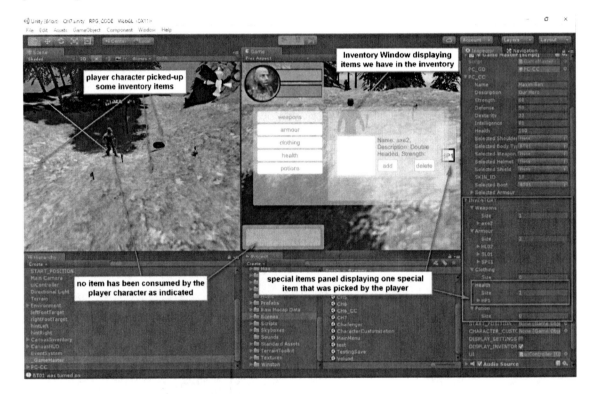

The next screenshot will illustrate how the HUD updates itself when the player starts consuming some of the inventory items by adding them using the inventory window during gameplay.

Notice that we have activated three inventory items: a weapon named *axe2* and two armours of type helmet and shield named *HL02* and *SL01* respectively.

Chapter 7

You can see them on the player character as well as in the panel holding the active inventory items. Pretty cool.

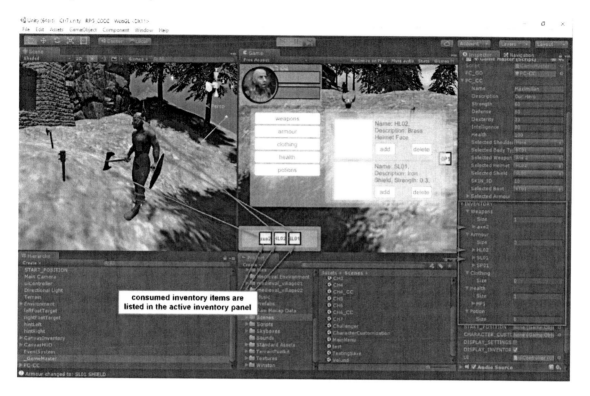

It's time to go and meet the enemy. We have not discussed the interaction between the player character and the non-player characters (NPCs) much. We will do this shortly.

We have applied some of the inventory items from our inventory to the player character, and now we can actually go and face the enemy. We are going to allow the enemy to attack us to see how our health reduces. Then we will use the health packet from our special items panel to increase our health once more.

[287]

User Interface and System Feedback

The next two screenshots will illustrate this scenario:

We are going to run away and apply our health packet!

Chapter 7

Notice how, when we apply the health packet, it removes itself from the inventory system as well as the special items panel. You might take note and say, but hold on, if we have applied the health packet, then how come our health bar is actually less then when we started? Well, unfortunately, when I resumed gameplay and started running away, the enemy got the opportunity to give my player character a few more hard blows! Therefore, by the time I had applied the health packet, and the initial screenshot, my health had dropped another 20 points!

How do I know this? Well, the health packet has a strength and weight of 0.2, translating to 20 points on a scale from 0 to 100, which is the representation of our health.

[289]

User Interface and System Feedback

Enemy stats in the HUD

We have not really discussed how to handle and manage the statistics and the visual representation of the NPC with the player. It is now time to do just that! So we need to decide what it is that we want to display as information to the player. For the moment, let's keep it simple and just display the basic health and strength of the enemy.

The question is, what is the best way to display this information? Should we display the information based on a distance threshold between the player character and the NPC, or should we display it when the player requests it at some time during gameplay?

Let's go ahead and take the first scenario. We will display the information for the NPC upon reaching a certain distance between the player character and the NPC. We can even make this distance the same as the line of sight we have set for the NPC! This is good because, if they can see us, then they are close enough for us to see their stats! Let's get to work!

NPC stats user interface

We are going to be using some of the existing textures that we have created for our player character. Like the textures for the health bar and strength bar, we just need to create a canvas that is going to be in the World Space and attached to the NPC character.

Creating the NPC canvas

The main difference between the canvas we are going to create for the NPC and the one we have been creating for the player is some of the configurations.

One of the main differences is going to be the *Render Mode* of the canvas. The NPC canvas is going to have a *World Space Render Mode*. This will allow us to position the canvas as another GameObject within the scene. The next important difference will be the *Rect Transform* attributes, and more importantly the *Scale* and *Rotation* attributes.

Chapter 7

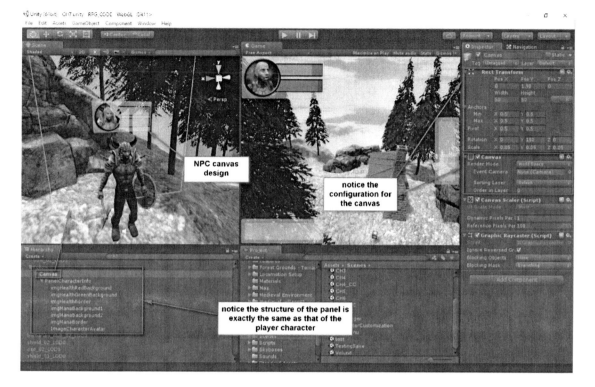

To make life easier, all you need to do is create the canvas and change its properties as shown in the preceding screenshot. For the next step, you can copy the whole *PanelCharacterInfo* we have developed in the previous sections, and paste it as a child of the new canvas.

This way, you will not have to re-create each UI element one by one and this will help save a lot of time. However, you will need to change the *Scale* and the *Transform* properties in the *PanelCharacterInfo* panel, the new one, to arrange it so that it renders above the NPC's head!

User Interface and System Feedback

The next step is for us to be able to control the values of the stat bars from the code. For this, we are going to create a new script called *NPCStatUI.cs* and attach it to the canvas object we just created for the NPC stats.

I have renamed the canvas to *CanvasNPCStats*.

Here is a listing of the script:

```
using UnityEngine;
using UnityEngine.UI;
using System.Collections;

public class NPCStatUI : MonoBehaviour
{
  public Image imgHealthBar;
  public Image imgManaBar;
}
```

The script we just created will only give us a reference to the image elements. We still need to be able to have a method to update the values.

We need to find a way to reference all of the NPC characters in a given scene. Once that is determined, we will need to set the initial values of the health and strength bar. Then, during gameplay, we will need to be able to update each NPC's stats according to the state of the game.

In order for us to identify the NPCs in a given scene, we are going to use the *Tag* element defined in each GameObject. We need to create a new *Tag* named *ENEMY*, and every NPC that is of enemy type will need to be tagged as such. This is an easy way to do a quick search and get a list of GameObjects based on their *Tag* value.

You should also start thinking about how are you going to dynamically attach the NPC stat canvas to the NPC on runtime. At the moment, for testing purposes, I am going to leave it attached to the model. But the question is, where do you actually attach it? Well, we have an empty GameObject named *Follow* attached to our model prefab. Since this is driven from our player character model, we have embedded the *Follow* as a placeholder for the main camera during gameplay. For the NPC, we are going to use it to attach the NPC canvas as a child GameObject to the *Follow* GameObject in the model hierarchy. You can see these in the preceding screenshots.

Chapter 7

We are going to use the *NPC_Agent.cs* script to initialize the NPC Status canvas prefab and the appropriate values of the UI elements. This is the best place to place the initialization because it will be self-contained. Here is the new listing for the script:

```
using UnityEngine;
using UnityEngine.UI;

using System;
using System.Collections;

[Serializable]
public class NPC_Agent : MonoBehaviour
{

  [SerializeField]
  public NPC npcData;

  [SerializeField]
  public Transform canvasNPCStatsAttachment;

  [SerializeField]
  public Canvas canvasNPCStats;

  [SerializeField]
  public GameObject canvasNPCStatsPrefab;

  public void SetHealthValue(float value)
  {
    this.canvasNPCStats.GetComponent<NPCStatUI>().imgHealthBar.fillAmount -
= value;
  }

  public void SetStrengthValue(float value)
  {
    this.canvasNPCStats.GetComponent<NPCStatUI>().imgManaBar.fillAmount -=
value;
  }

  //// Use this for initialization
  void Start()
  {
    // let's go ahead and instantiate our stats
    GameObject tmpCanvasGO = GameObject.Instantiate(
      this.canvasNPCStatsPrefab,
      this.canvasNPCStatsAttachment.transform.position +
this.canvasNPCStatsPrefab.transform.position,
      this.canvasNPCStatsPrefab.transform.rotation) as GameObject;
```

[293]

```
            tmpCanvasGO.transform.SetParent(this.canvasNPCStatsAttachment);

            this.canvasNPCStats = tmpCanvasGO.GetComponent<Canvas>();
            this.canvasNPCStats.GetComponent<NPCStatUI>().imgHealthBar.fillAmount = 1f;
            this.canvasNPCStats.GetComponent<NPCStatUI>().imgManaBar.fillAmount = 1f;

    }
}
```

Note that you will need to assign *canvasNPCStatsAttachment*, which will be used to store a reference to the GameObject we are going to attach to the NCP canvas, and *canvasNPCStatsPrefab* will be used to assign the prefab representing the NPC status canvas at design time. If you run the game now, you will have the prefab instantiated dynamically and attached to the *Follow* GameObject in the hierarchy, with the fill values set to 1f, that is, 100 percent.

NPC health

We need to take a moment and go back to some of the initial scripts and configurations we created in the early chapters, where we defined the player character's *Animator Controller* and *CharacterController.cs* script.

> Please refer to `Chapter 3`, *Character Design*, to refresh your memory about Animator Controller and Curves.

Open the Animator Controller we created in `Chapter 3`, *Character Design*, named *CH3_Animator_Controller*. Select the *Parameters* tab and create a new parameter called *Attack1C* of *float* datatype.

Chapter 7

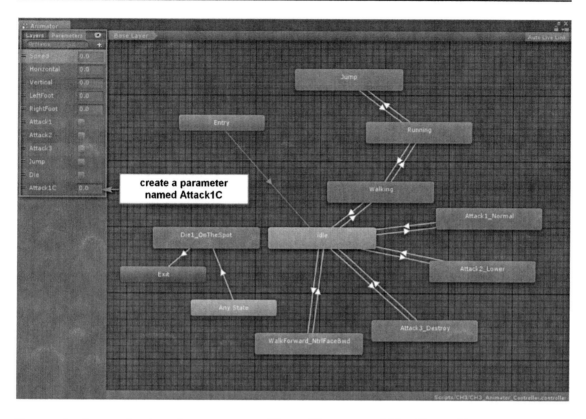

For a refresher, go back to the `Chapter 4`, *Player Character and Non-Player Character Design*, section, *PC and NPC Interaction*, and you will recall how we defined and configured the Curve to assign the parameter based on the animation.

 We have defined the Curve only for one of the attack animations.

Once you have configured the parameter in the *Animator Controller* for the player character, we have to update the *CharacterController.cs* script to trigger an attack based on the parameter value.

The following listing is a partial listing of the script displaying just the modified portion:

```
void FixedUpdate()
{
    // The Inputs are defined in the Input Manager
    h = Input.GetAxis("Horizontal"); // get value for horizontal axis
```

User Interface and System Feedback

```
    v = Input.GetAxis("Vertical");    // get value for vertical axis

    speed = new Vector2(h, v).sqrMagnitude;

    animator.SetFloat("Speed", speed);
    animator.SetFloat("Horizontal", h);
    animator.SetFloat("Vertical", v);

    // We have three different attack modes, we have only implemented the
curve parameter for attack1
    // therefore, during game play if you use attack2/attack3 you will see
the visual attack happening
    // but the data will not reflect
    if (this.attack1 || this.attack2 || this.attack3)
    {
      if (animator.GetFloat("Attack1C") == 1.0f)
      {
        GameMaster.instance.PlayerAttackEnemy();

        // reset the timer
        this.attackTimer = Time.timeSinceLevelLoad + this.attackThreashold;
      }
    }
  }
```

In the code, we check to see if any of the attack modes are active, and if so we check to see what the curve parameter *Attack1C* is at the moment of the animation. If we are at *1.0f*, then we call the *GameMaster* object to perform the rest.

Now, we need to take a look at a few functions we have defined/modified in the *GameMaster.cs* script:

```
// for each level/scene that has been loaded
// do some of the preparation work
void OnLevelWasLoaded()
{
GameMaster.instance.LEVEL_CONTROLLER.OnLevelWasLoaded();
// find all NPC GameObjects of Enemy type
if(GameObject.FindGameObjectsWithTag("ENEMY").Length>0)
{
var tmpGONPCEnemy = GameObject.FindGameObjectsWithTag("ENEMY");
GameMaster.instance.goListNPCEnemy.Clear();
foreach(GameObject goTmpNPCEnemy in tmpGONPCEnemy)
{
instance.goListNPCEnemy.Add(goTmpNPCEnemy);
instance.closestNPCEnemy = goTmpNPCEnemy;
}
}
```

[296]

```
}
public void PlayerAttackEnemy()
{
NPC npc = instance.closestNPCEnemy.GetComponent<NPC_Agent>().npcData;
npc.HEALTH -= 1;
}
```

Some explanation is needed here. The function *OnLevelWasLoaded()* is called each time a new scene is being loaded at runtime. This is where we query all GameObjects that are tagged *ENEMY*. We then store them internally for further processing down the line.

For testing purposes and due to the simplicity of the scene, there is only one enemy present for testing, I am also setting the *closestNPCEnemy* object to the last GameObject tagged *ENEMY*. This variable is later used in the *PlayerAttachEnemy()* function to set the NPCs *HEALTH* property.

When the *PlayerAttackEnemy()* function is called, we get a reference to the NPC component of the NPC character, and reduce the health based on the attack.

Now, this also forces us to update the *BaseCharacter.cs* script; here is a listing of the modification:

```
public float HEALTH
{
get { return this.health; }
set
{
this.health = value;
if(this.tag.Equals("Player"))
{
if (GameMaster.instance.UI.hudUI != null)
{
GameMaster.instance.UI.hudUI.imgHealthBar.fillAmount = this.health / 100.0f;
}
}
else
{
this.characterGO.GetComponent<NPC_Agent>().SetHealthValue(this.health / 100.0f);
}
}
}
```

In the *HEALTH* property, we check to see if we are the player or an NPC. If we are the player, we need to use the GameMaster to update our Stats UI, if we are going to update our own NPC Stats UI.

User Interface and System Feedback

This mean that when you are creating your player character and/or NPC, you will need to make sure you are assigning the data elements properly, see here:

```
void Awake()
{
PC tmp = new PC();
tmp.TAG = this.transform.gameObject.tag;
tmp.characterGO = this.transform.gameObject;
tmp.NAME = "Maximilian";
tmp.HEALTH = 100.0f;
tmp.DEFENSE = 50.0f;
tmp.DESCRIPTION = "Our Hero";
tmp.DEXTERITY = 33.0f;
tmp.INTELLIGENCE = 80.0f;
tmp.STRENGTH = 60.0f;
this.playerCharacterData = tmp;
}
```

The preceding code snippet is the *Awake()* from the *PlayerAgent.cs* script. You will need to perform the same for the *NPC_Agent.cs* script.

The code and scripts we have looked at have been used to test the ideas we have put forward. The results are positive. You might have noticed that when the player character is attacking, we are not taking into consideration its position relative to that of the enemy. We are also automatically assigning the closest NPC character in the GameMaster to eventually be the last element of the query we do each time a level loads.

Enhancing the code

One last code implementation I would like to make, before I close out the chapter, is to make sure that when we are in attack mode for the player character, the hit points are going to affect the NPC that it is intended for automatically. In other words, determine which NPC is closest to us based on distance and also our view angle toward the NPC.

We have already created the logic to determine these quantities for the NPC character, and we need to implement something similar for the player character. Let's take a look at a partial listing of the code changes we need to make for the *CharacterMovement.cs* script:

```
using UnityEngine;
using System.Collections;

public class CharacterController : MonoBehaviour
{
```

[298]

Chapter 7

```csharp
public Animator animator;

public float speed = 6.0f;
public float h = 0.0f;
public float v = 0.0f;

public bool attack1 = false; // used for attack mode 1
public bool attack2 = false; // used for attack mode 2
public bool attack3 = false; // used for attack mode 3

public bool jump = false;     // used for jumping
public bool die = false;      // are we alive?

public bool DEBUG = false;

// Reference to the sphere collider trigger component.
private SphereCollider col;

// where is the player character in relation to NPC
public Vector3 direction;

// how far away is the player character from NPC
public float distance = 0.0f;

// what is the angle between the PC and NPC
public float angle = 0.0f;

// is the PC in sight?
public bool enemyInSight;

// what is the field of view for our NPC?
// currently set to 110 degrees
public float fieldOfViewAngle = 110.0f;

// calculate the angle between PC and NPC
public float calculatedAngle;

// Use this for initialization
void Start()
{
  this.animator = GetComponent<Animator>() as Animator;
  //this.attackTimer = 0.0f;

  // we don't see the player by default
  this.enemyInSight = false;
}

// Update is called once per frame
```

[299]

User Interface and System Feedback

```
private Vector3 moveDirection = Vector3.zero;

Quaternion startingAngle = Quaternion.AngleAxis(-60, Vector3.up);
Quaternion stepAngle = Quaternion.AngleAxis(5, Vector3.up);
Vector3 viewDistance = new Vector3(0, 0, 30);

Quaternion startingAttackAngle = Quaternion.AngleAxis(-25, Vector3.up);
Quaternion stepAttackAngle = Quaternion.AngleAxis(5, Vector3.up);
Vector3 attackDistance = new Vector3(0, 0, 2);

void Update()
{
  ...

  if (Input.GetKeyDown(KeyCode.I))
  {
    this.die = true;
    SendMessage("Died");
  }
  animator.SetBool("Die", die);

}

void FixedUpdate()
{
  // The Inputs are defined in the Input Manager
  // get value for horizontal axis
  h = Input.GetAxis("Horizontal");
  // get value for vertical axis
  v = Input.GetAxis("Vertical");

  speed = new Vector2(h, v).sqrMagnitude;

  if (DEBUG)
    Debug.Log(string.Format("H:{0} - V:{1} - Speed:{2}", h, v, speed));

  animator.SetFloat("Speed", speed);
  animator.SetFloat("Horizontal", h);
  animator.SetFloat("Vertical", v);

  // We have three different attack modes, we have only implemented the
curve parameter for attack1
  // therefore, during game play if you use attack2/attack3 you will see
the visual attack happening
  // but the data will not reflect
  if (this.attack1 || this.attack2 || this.attack3)
  {
    #region used for attack range
```

[300]

```
        RaycastHit hitAttack;
        var angleAttack = transform.rotation * startingAttackAngle;
        var directionAttack = angleAttack * attackDistance;
        var posAttack = transform.position + Vector3.up;
        for (var i = 0; i < 10; i++)
        {
           Debug.DrawRay(posAttack, directionAttack, Color.yellow);
           if (Physics.Raycast(posAttack, directionAttack, out hitAttack,
1.0f))
           {
              var enemy = hitAttack.collider.GetComponent<NPC_Agent>();
              if (enemy)
              {
                //Enemy was seen
                if(DEBUG)
                   Debug.Log(string.Format("Detected: {0}",
enemy.npcData.NAME));
                 this.enemyInSight = true;
                 GameMaster.instance.closestNPCEnemy =
hitAttack.collider.gameObject;
              }
              else
              {
                 this.enemyInSight = false;
              }
           }
           directionAttack = stepAngle * directionAttack;
        }
        #endregion

        if (enemyInSight)
        {
           if (animator.GetFloat("Attack1C") == 1.0f)
           {
              PC pc =
this.gameObject.GetComponent<PlayerAgent>().playerCharacterData;
              float impact = (pc.STRENGTH + pc.HEALTH) / 100.0f;
              GameMaster.instance.PlayerAttackEnemy(impact);
           }
        }

      }

   }
```

User Interface and System Feedback

The way we calculate the sighting and distance of the enemy NPCs is through raycasting. This is done only when we are in attack mode: we check to see if the NPC is in front of us, and if so, we set the *closestNPCEnemy* object in the GameMaster and set the flag *enemyInSight*, where we then perform the necessary subtraction from the health of the NPC.

Notice that I have also changed the way we are computing the impact of the hit based on a simple equation:

$$impact = \frac{pc.STRENGTH + pc.HEALTH}{100}$$

Where pc is the object reference to our Player Character. The same equation is used on the NPC objects. This is just a simple demonstration that the impact of the hit point of the player or the NPC is based on the strength and the health of the actors in the scene.

The preceding screenshot illustrates how we detect if an NPC is in attack range or not.

In turn you can derive the strength value from the components that the play or the NPC has activated throughout the gameplay.

Here is partial listing of *BaseCharacter.cs* illustrating the *HEALTH* property:

```
public float HEALTH
{
get { return this.health; }
set
{
this.health = value;
if(this.tag.Equals("Player"))
{
if (GameMaster.instance.UI.hudUI != null)
{
GameMaster.instance.UI.hudUI.imgHealthBar.fillAmount = this.health /
100.0f;
}
}
else
{
this.characterGO.GetComponent<NPC_Agent>().SetHealthValue(this.health /
100.0f);
}
}
}
```

There are more code changes and updates, please refer to the associated files provided.

User Interface and System Feedback

During the process of implementation I have modified a few other code locations that are not listed within the book due to physical limitations. Here are the scripts that have been modified: *BaseCharacter.cs, CharacterController.cs, GameMaster.cs, NPC_Agent.cs, PlayerAgent.cs* and *NPC_Movement.cs*.

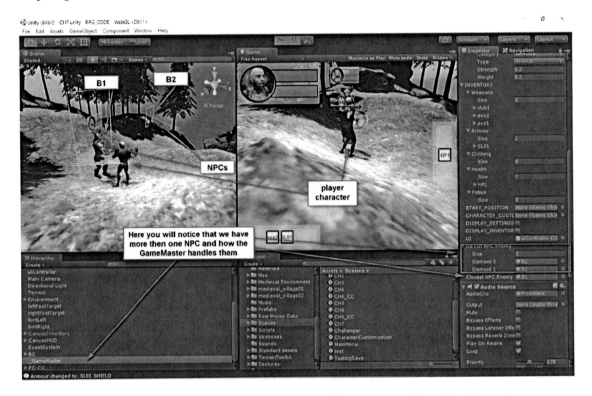

You are encouraged to do some research and try different types of mechanics and implementation to enhance your skills.

Summary

In this chapter we have expanded on our idea and seen how to integrate all of the major pieces together. The main objective of the chapter was to create a Heads Up Display (HUD) for our game.

We started out with a design concept that was of interest to us, and created a layout for our HUD before the actual implementation. Once we concluded what the HUD should look like, we started building the framework for it. We designed the three main sections of the HUD and referred to them as the following: *PanelCharacterInfo*, *PanelActiveItems* and *PanelSpecialItems*.

Next, we started building the UI elements and the code necessary to make the panels work with our code. We started with the *PanelCharacterInfo*, which represented the stats for our character player, which is a reference to the player's avatar, to the health and to the strength of the character. In the process, we had to create or update several of the scripts to work with the new UI.

Next we designed and developed the *PanelActiveItems* panel. The implementation and approach to this specific panel was a little more involved. The purpose of this panel is to display all of the current active inventory items that the player has consumed. We had to make the panel scrollable, since we don't know how many items at any given time the player will be consuming. We created the necessary prefabs to be placeholders for the inventory items, and also the scripts that would make them work together.

The design for *PanelSpecialItems* was very similar to that of the *PanelActiveItems*, with two main differences. First, we had to make sure that the panel was vertical instead of horizontal, so we had to make sure that the proper configuration was applied. Secondly, the main functionality was different for this panel. The items displayed were supposed to be intractable, which meant that we had to create custom event handlers, apply the necessary values to the player character, and update the whole game state.

User Interface and System Feedback

Once we were satisfied with the design of our HUD, we starting building the necessary scripts to integrate the UI elements with the GameMaster and other scripts. This was basically making sure that our UI was always reflecting the state of the object that was of interest to us. The health, stamina and inventory are the main items we used to communicate the concepts.

In the last section of the chapter, we concentrated on implementing the player's character movement and detecting the NPC's, and how to track the hit points between the player character and the NPC, which we had not done in previous chapters.

We also had to do some backtracking and make some adjustments to the Animation Controller we had defined for our player character, to have curves defined for our attack animation values based on the motion.

During the process, we had to solve the following challenges: How do we know if we are in close enough range that we can actually attack and hit the NPC character? How are we going to detect which NPC is closer to us? More importantly, how is the data going to be passed along from the action of attacking to the actual hit on the NPC?

We have done a lot in a short period of time, and in a small number of pages. Some of the functions have been left for the reader to solve on their own. For instance, we have not discussed how to delete an inventory item and so on. I felt that this was trivial, and that the reader will be sufficiently comfortable to implement the function on their own once they see the bigger scope and how to connect everything together.

With that said, let's move on to the next chapter.

8
Multiplayer Setup

The desire of every indie-game developer is to make a multiplayer game. The reality is that creating multiplayer games are difficult. There are a lot of scenarios that you need to take into consideration as a game designer/developer. Besides the technical complexities that are involved in the nature of creating online multiplayer games, there are also game play elements that you will need to consider.

The purpose of this chapter is to give you a good overview of the out of the box networking functionality using Unity 5. This is a complex topic and as such, we cannot cover everything in this chapter. A whole new book will be required to really dive into the details.

Having said that, I structured this chapter to include a simple project that will be used to illustrate the fundamentals of networking; I will then show you how to network enable our own game objects.

Here is a breakdown of the chapter:

- Heads Up Display
- Completing HUD Design
- Integrating the Code

Here we go!

Multiplayer Setup

Challenges of a Multiplayer Game

General rule of thumb is, if you don't need to enable your game to be multiplayer, don't! It just adds a whole lot of complexity and extra requirements and specifications that you will need to start worrying about. But if you must, then you must!

You probably know by now that creating even the simplest multiplayer game will have its own challenges that you will need to address as the game designer. There are different types of online multiplayer game design:

- Real-time multiplayer games
- Turn-based multiplayer games
- Asynchronous multiplayer games
- Local multiplayer games

The most challenging out of all the different types of multiplayer games is Real-time multiplayer gaming. This is because all players have to be synchronized in a proper and effective way with the latest game state at any given time.

That is, if we have Player A perform a specific action, Player B will see the action at the same time on his or her screen. Now, consider we have another player join, say Player C, Player A and B will need to synchronize with Player C and in turn Player C will need to synchronize its own environment with Player A's and Player B's state.

Not just the actual position/rotation of the players has to be synchronized, but also all of the player data will need to be synchronized. Now, imagine what happens when you multiply this by 100 or 1000 or 1,000,000 connected players.

For a real-world multiplayer game, what we are going to cover here is not enough, and what Unity provides out of the box is not enough either. Chances are that you will need to write your own server-side code to handle the player data.

Now, you can see the challenge involved in designing and developing multiplayer games, we can start by building our first multiplayer game.

Chapter 8

Initial Multiplayer Game

The best way to learn about multiplayer games is by doing a simple example. The following project is based on the Unity networking tutorial but has been extended to have some other features implemented that will be helpful in the implementation of networking in our RPG.

Fundamental Networking Components

We need to get familiar with some networking components that will be used for the creation of our network-enabled games. These components are:

- **Network Manager**: The NetworkManager is a higher level class that allows you to control the state of a networked game. It provides an interface in the editor to control the configuration of the network, the prefabs used for spawning, and the scenes to use for different network game states.
- **Network Manager HUD**: This provides a default user interface for controlling the network state of the game. It also shows information about the current state of the NetworkManager in the editor.
- **Network Identity**: The NetworkIdentity component is at the heart of the new networking system. This component controls an object's network identity and it makes the networking system aware of it.
- **Network Transform**: The NetworkTransform component synchronizes movement of game objects across the network. This component takes authority into account, so LocalPlayer objects synchronize their position from the client to server, then out to other clients. Other objects (with server authority) synchronize their position from the server to clients.

[309]

Networking Project

The following project is used to demonstrate the concepts of a multiplayer game. The concepts can then be applied to more complex scenarios.

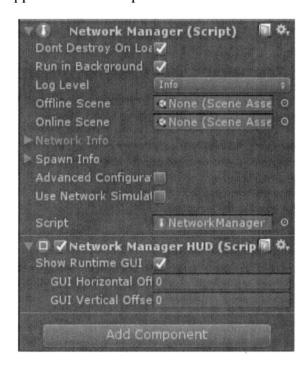

We will start by creating a new Unity project. All multiplayer games need to have a NetworkManager implemented. To do this, we are going to create an Empty GameObject and rename it to Network Manager; now attach the NetworkManager component to the newly created object using the Inspector Window and navigating to **Add Component** | **Network** | **NetworkManager**. We are also going to add the **Network Manager** HUD component to the selected GameObject. Again, from the InspectorWindow navigate to **Add Component** | **Network** | **NetworkManagerHUD**.

Adding Player Character

We are now going to be adding a simple character player. You can really use any primitive GameObject to represent your PC, I am going to create my player to take the shape of a simple tank. See the following figure:

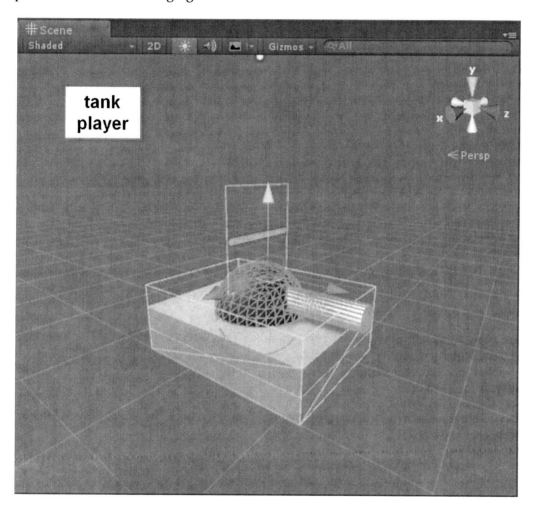

Multiplayer Setup

The following image will illustrate the hierarchy of the Tank GameObject:

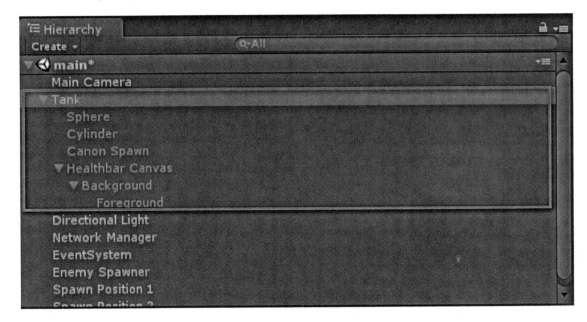

I am not going to cover how to create the GameObject, as you should be able to do that very easily by now. What I will cover, is how to enable the new Tank GameObject network enabled.

We are going to attach two network components to the Tank GameObject. The first one is going to be NetworkIdentity, which can be added by selecting the **Tank** GameObject and from within the Inspector Window navigating to **Add Component | Network | Network Identity.**

When you are done adding the component, make sure to check the **Local Player Authority** property checkbox.

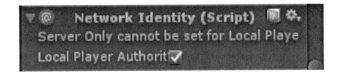

The Local Player Authority allows the object to be controlled by the client that owns it.

Next, we need to add the NetworkTransform component to the Tank GameObject. Again, selecting the **Tank** GameObject, from the *Inspector Window* and navigate to **Add Component** | **Network** | **NetworkTransform** to add the component:

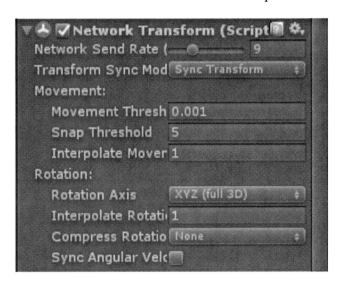

We are going to keep the default values for the **NetworkTransform** component. You can read more on the different properties on your own using the online documentation. The main attribute you may want to adjust is the **Network Send Rate**.

Next, we want to create a script that will allow us to control the movement of the Tank. Go ahead and create a new C# script and name it PlayerController.cs.

Here is a listing of the script:

```
using UnityEngine;
using UnityEngine.Networking;
using System.Collections;

public class PlayerController : NetworkBehaviour
{

  public GameObject bulletPrefab;
  public Transform bulletSpawn;

  public override void OnStartLocalPlayer()
  {
    GetComponent<MeshRenderer>().material.color = Color.blue;
  }
```

Multiplayer Setup

```csharp
void Update()
{
  // only execute the following code if local player ...
  if (!isLocalPlayer)
    return;

  var x = Input.GetAxis("Horizontal") * Time.deltaTime * 150.0f;
  var z = Input.GetAxis("Vertical") * Time.deltaTime * 3.0f;

  transform.Rotate(0, x, 0);
  transform.Translate(0, 0, z);

  if (Input.GetKeyDown(KeyCode.Space))
  {
    CmdFire();
  }
}

[Command]
void CmdFire()
{
  // Create the Bullet from the Bullet Prefab
  var bullet = (GameObject)Instantiate(
      bulletPrefab,
      bulletSpawn.position,
      bulletSpawn.rotation);

  // Add velocity to the bullet
  bullet.GetComponent<Rigidbody>().velocity = bullet.transform.forward *
6;

  if(isLocalPlayer)
    bullet.GetComponent<MeshRenderer>().material.color = Color.blue;

  // Spawn the bullet on the Clients
  NetworkServer.Spawn(bullet);

  // Destroy the bullet after 2 seconds
  Destroy(bullet, 2.0f);
}

}
```

The code is straightforward, but there are some important concepts that we need to discuss.
First and foremost, you will note that we are inheriting from `NetworkBehaviour`, instead
of `MonoBehaviour`.

Chapter 8

NetworkBehaviour is used to work with objects with the NetworkIdentiy component. This allows you to perform network-related functions such as Commands, ClientRPCs, SyncEvents, and SyncVars.

Variable Synchronization

Synchronizing variables is one of the important aspects of a multiplayer game. If you recall, one of the challenges of multiplayer games was the ability to make sure all of the key data for the game is synchronized across the server and the clients. This is accomplished by the `SyncVar`attribute. You will see how this is applied in the next script we are going to create for the health of the unity.

Network Callbacks

These are functions that are invoked on NetworkBehaviour script for various network events. Here is a list:

- `OnStartServer()`: This is called when an object is spawned on the server or when the server is started for objects in the scene.
- `OnStartClient()`: This is called when the object is spawned on the client or when the client connects to a server for objects in the scene.
- `OnSerialize()`: This is called to gather state to send from the server to clients.
- `OnDeSerialize()`: This is called to apply a state to objects on clients.
- `OnNetworkDestroy()`: This is called on clients when server told the object to be destroyed.
- `OnStartLocalPlayer()`: This is called on clients for player objects for the local client only.
- `OnRebuildObservers()`: This is called on the server when the set of observers for an object is rebuild.
- `OnSetLocalVisibility()`: This is called on a host when the visibility of an object changed for the local client.
- `OnCheckObserver()`: This is called on the server to check visibility state for a new client.

In the `PlayerController.cs` script, you will note that we are using the `OnStartClient()` to highlight the local player by changing its material color to blue.

[315]

Multiplayer Setup

Sending Commands

Commands are the way for clients to request a function to be performed on the server. In a server authoritative system, clients can only do things through commands. Commands are run on the player object on the server that corresponds to the client that sent the command. This routing happens automatically, so it is impossible for a client to send a command for a different player.

A command must begin with the prefix "Cmd" and have the [Command] custom attribute on them.

In our `PlayerController.cs` script, when the player fires, it send a command to the server using the `CmdFire()` function.

Client RPC Calls

Client RPC calls are a way for server objects to cause things to happen on client objects. This is the reverse direction to how commands send messages, but the concepts are the same. Client RPC calls, however, are not only invoked on player objects, they can be invoked on any NetworkIdentity object. They must begin with the prefix "Rpc" and have the [ClientRPC] custom attribute.

You will see an example of this on the `Health.cs` script, which we will be creating next.

We would need a way to also keep track of our player character's health. This will be done using a new script called `Health.cs`.

Here is a listing of the script:

```
using UnityEngine;
using UnityEngine.Networking;

public class Health : NetworkBehaviour {
  public const int maxHealth = 100;

  [SyncVar(hook = "OnChangeHealth")]
  public int currentHealth = maxHealth;

  public RectTransform healthBar;

  public bool destroyOnDeath;

  public override void OnStartClient()
  {
```

[316]

```
    healthBar.sizeDelta = new Vector2(currentHealth,
healthBar.sizeDelta.y);
  }

  public void TakeDamage(int amount)
  {
    currentHealth -= amount;
    if (currentHealth <= 0)
    {
      if (destroyOnDeath)
      {
        Destroy(gameObject);
      }
      else
      {
        currentHealth = maxHealth;

        // called on the Server, will be invoked on the Clients
        RpcRespawn();
      }
    }

  }

  void OnChangeHealth(int health)
  {
    healthBar.sizeDelta = new Vector2(health, healthBar.sizeDelta.y);
  }

  [ClientRpc]
  void RpcRespawn()
  {
    if (isLocalPlayer)
    {
      // move back to zero location
      transform.position = Vector3.zero;
    }
  }
}
```

Notice, in this script we are also inheriting from `NetworkBehaviour`. The two main items I want to bring to your attention are the `SyncVar`, the `ClientRpc`, and the `OnStartClient()` functions.

We want to synchronize the player's health across the network, to do this, we use the `SyncVar NetworkBehaviour`. `SyncVar` can be any basic type, not, classes, lists, or other collections.

[317]

Multiplayer Setup

When the value of a `SyncVar` is changed on the server, it will be sent to all of the ready clients in the game. When objects are spawned, they are created on the client with the latest state of all SyncVars from the server.

The `OnStartClient()` function makes sure that each object with the `Health.cs` script attached to it, will have the most up-to-date value to display on the health bar UI.

I want to take a moment and make sure I give you a crucial pointer here. Assume, we are running a networked game session, and we have the Host, PlayerA, and Player B connected and going about their business. During the gameplay, Player A and Player B have their health value changed. Now, we have a third player connect to the game, Player C. If the `OnStartClient()` is not implemented, the client for PlayerC will have the correct data synchronized for all of the GameObjects with the `Health.cs` script; however, the data will not reflect correctly on the UI because, we need to have a trigger for that to happen. This can be handled in the `OnStartClient()` function as shown in the code.

The next function is the `RpcRespawn()` function. In the `TakeDamage()` function, we check the health of the current GameObject; if the health drops below zero, we check to see if the `destroyOnDeath` Boolean variable is set. If it is not set, we go ahead and reset the `currentHealth` value to `maxHealth` value, and we use the `RpcRespawn()` method to respawn the player at the origin. Remember this function is executed on all clients!

Within the function, we check to see if the caller is the local player by checking the variable `isLocalPlayer`. Yes, creating a multiplayer game does get confusing! This will become apparent more, as you start experimenting with it more.

Creating the Canon Ball for the Tank

Ok, so we need to create a prefab that will represent our Canon Balls! Very simple, create a sphere, and make it the same size as the nozzle of your Tank Gun.

We are going to need to attach the following components to the Canon Ball GameObject: `NetworkIdentity`, `NetworkTransform`, `Rigidbody`, and a `Bullet.cs` scripts.

Make sure that you set the `Use Gravity` property is `False` on the `Rigidbody` component. Also, make sure that both `Server Only` and `Local Player Authority` properties are `False` on the `NetworkIdentity` component. On the `NetworkTransform` component, change the `Network Send Rate` to . Once we generate the object on the server, the physics will take care of the motion on each client.

Create a new C# script called `Bullet.cs`.

Chapter 8

Here is the listing for the script:

```
using UnityEngine;

public class Bullet : MonoBehaviour {

  void OnCollisionEnter(Collision collision)
  {
    var hit = collision.gameObject;
    var health = hit.GetComponent<Health>();
    if (health != null)
    {
      health.TakeDamage(10);
    }

    Destroy(gameObject);
  }
}
```

All we are doing here is detecting a collision. If there is a collision, we get the `Health` component. If the `Health` component is not null, we call the `TakeDamage()` function and pass is a value.

If you recall from the `Health.cs` script, the `TakeDamage()` function reduces the `currentHealth` of the player, which in return is a `SyncVar` that it gets updated on all active clients.

One item we did not discuss is the idea of a `hook`. A `SyncVar` can have a `hook`. Think of a hook as an event handler. The hook attribute can be used to specify a function to be called when the `SyncVar` changes value on the client.

```
[SyncVar(hook = "OnChangeHealth")]
public int currentHealth = maxHealth;
```

The `OnChangeHealth()` function is responsible to update the UI canvas for displaying our health value.

```
void OnChangeHealth(int health)
{
  healthBar.sizeDelta = new Vector2(health, healthBar.sizeDelta.y);
}
```

Go ahead and also make a prefab of the Canon Ball and delete the instance from the scene.

[319]

Multiplayer Setup

Make sure you have assigned the proper prefab association that are required on each script. For instance, the Tank GameObject's `PlayerController.cs` script needs a reference to the Canon Ball prefab and also the Canon Spawn Location. The `Health.cs` script needs a reference to the HealthBar foreground image and so on.

Creating Tank Prefab and Configuring NetworkManager

Now that we created our Tank GameObject and attached all of the necessary components and scripts to it. We need to make a Prefab of it. This is because we are going to let the NetworkManger spawn our Player Character, and in order for it to be able to do so, it needs to refer to a prefab that is a representation of your player character.

The **NetworkManager** has a Spawn Info section that you can assign the Player Prefab, determine if the **NetworkManager** can **Auto Create Player** and the **Player Spawn Method**.

There is also a section for Registered Spawnable Prefabs. We need to register all of the GameObjects that will be spawned by the NetworkServer. For instance, the Canon Ball prefab will need to be registered here so that we can spawn it across the network on different clients.

Select the Network Manager GameObject in the scene, and in the Inspector Window assign the appropriate prefabs as needed.

Here is a screenshot of how the *NetworkManager* should look like at this point:

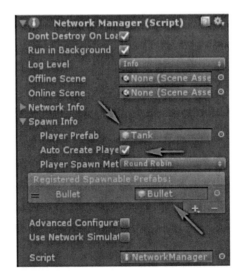

At this point, you are ready to test out what we have built so far. Go ahead and create a standalone version of your game using the **Build Settings** window. Once you have your build ready, launch two instances of the application. We are going to use one instance to host the game and the other to connect as a client.

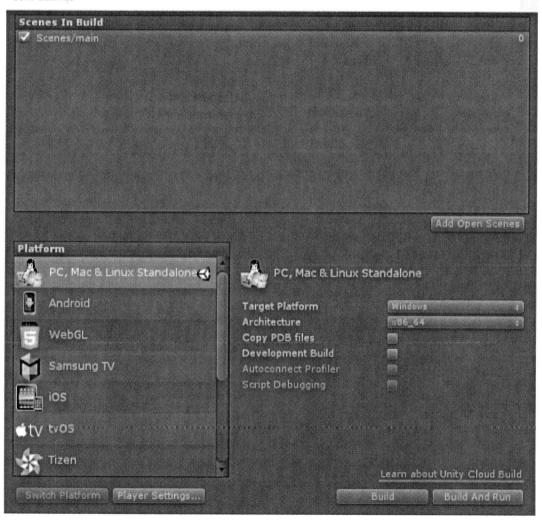

Multiplayer Setup

The following figure illustrates how your game instance will look like when you run it.

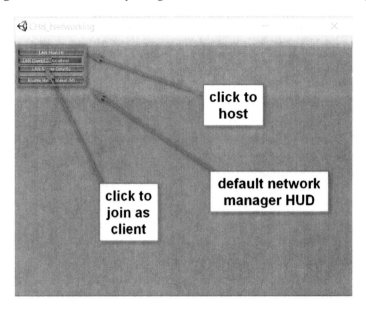

The following figure will illustrate how your screen will look after you click on the **LAN Host (H)** button. I moved the Tank (player character around).

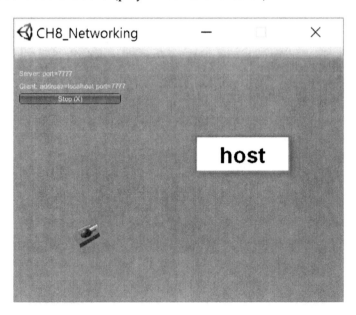

The following figure illustrates host/client with three clients:

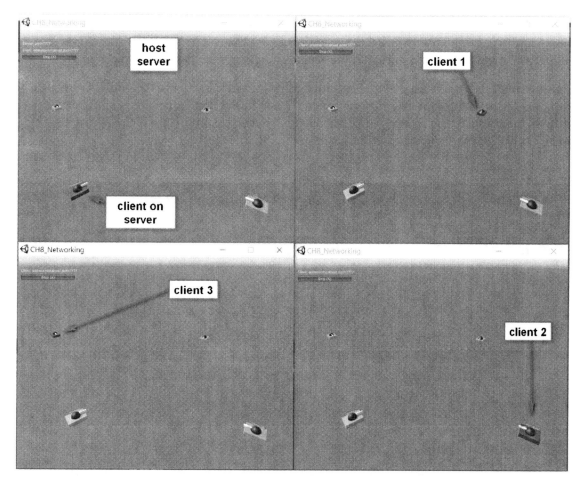

Notice in the preceding figure, each client has highlighted the player character it controls, that is, the Tank it controls. It is going to be difficult to capture the fire command, but you can go ahead and use the Space Bar to fire the Canon and it will be triggered accordingly on all active clients.

You will also notice that the health of each Tank will be reflected accurately if they do get a hit. Now, we are ready to create an enemy to illustrate the non-player character in the game.

Adding the Enemy Tank

Now it is time to add some of the non-player characters to our multiplayer demo. Adding the Enemy Tank is going to be simple as we are going to use our Tank prefab as a base. Go ahead and drop the Tank prefab into the scene and change the name to TankEnemy.

Remove the `PlayerCharacter.cs` script from the `GameObject`. We are going to create a separate script as the controller for the Enemy Tank. I have also gone ahead and applied different material to the Enemy Tank, so visually we can distinguish which tanks are going to be controlled by players and which ones are going to be non-player.

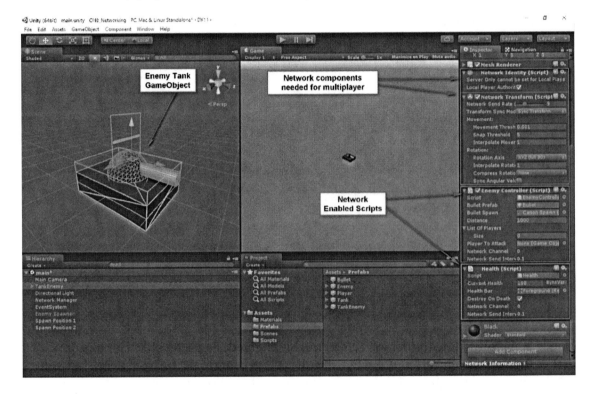

The preceding figure illustrates how your Tank and TankEnemy prefabs should look like. The main difference between the two is the controller script. Tank has the `PlayerController.cs` script and TankEnemy has `EnemyController.cs` script.

Here is a listing of the `EnemyController.cs` script:

```
using UnityEngine;
using UnityEngine.Networking;
```

```
public class EnemyController : NetworkBehaviour
{

  public GameObject bulletPrefab;
  public Transform bulletSpawn;
  public float distance = 1000;

  public GameObject[] listOfPlayers;

  [SyncVar(hook = "OnChangePlayerToAttack")]
  public GameObject playerToAttack;

  float coolOffTime = 0.0f;

  void Update()
  {
    // only execute the following code if local player ...
    if (!isServer)
      return;

    listOfPlayers = GameObject.FindGameObjectsWithTag("Player");
    if (listOfPlayers.Length > 0)
    {

      float distance = 100f;
      foreach (var player in listOfPlayers)
      {
        float d = Vector3.Distance(transform.position,
player.transform.position);
        if (d < distance)
        {
          distance - d;
          this.playerToAttack = player;
        }
      }


      if (this.playerToAttack != null)
      {
        Vector3 direction = playerToAttack.transform.position -
transform.position;

        this.transform.rotation =
          Quaternion.Slerp(this.transform.rotation,
          Quaternion.LookRotation(direction), 0.1f);

        float d = Vector3.Distance(transform.position,
playerToAttack.transform.position);
```

Multiplayer Setup

```csharp
        if (d < 15.0f)
        {
          if(this.coolOffTime<Time.time)
          {
            CmdFire();
            this.coolOffTime = Time.time + 1.0f;
          }
        }
      }
    }
  }

  void OnChangePlayerToAttack(GameObject player)
  {
    this.playerToAttack = player;
  }

  [Command]
  void CmdFire()
  {
    // Create the Bullet from the Bullet Prefab
    var bullet = (GameObject)Instantiate(
        bulletPrefab,
        bulletSpawn.position,
        bulletSpawn.rotation);

    // Add velocity to the bullet
    bullet.GetComponent<Rigidbody>().velocity = bullet.transform.forward *
6;

    // Spawn the bullet on the Clients
    NetworkServer.Spawn(bullet);

    // Destroy the bullet after 2 seconds
    Destroy(bullet, 2.0f);
  }

}
```

The script does the following. It continuously searches for all players that are active in the scene and makes a list of them. Then, it finds the closest one to itself. Once it determines which player is closest, it rotates to face the player.

Then, it calculates the distance between itself and the selected player, if the distance is shorter than the acceptable threshold, then it starts firing at the player. Each time the Enemy Tank fires, it actually calls a *[Command]* named `CmdFire()`.

Chapter 8

This function is run on the server, it instantiates a Canon Ball prefab and spawns it on the network.

The `EnemyController.cs` script also has a `SyncVar` for the `playertoAttack` variable, with a `hook` attached as `OnChangePlayerToAttack()` function. This in turn makes sure that all clients get updated with the latest data on each Enemy Tank GameObject.

The `Health.cs` script works the same as it does on the Tank GameObject.

There is one more item we need to cover, the spawning of the Enemy Tanks by the server. We can do this easily by creating another Empty GameObject, and naming it `Enemy Spawner`. We need to attach a *NetworkIdentity* component and make sure we set the `Server Only` property, to `True`. This will make sure that only the server can instantiate the enemy objects.

The next step is to create the `EnemySpawner.cs` scripts. Here is the listing:

```
using UnityEngine;
using UnityEngine.Networking;

public class EnemySpawner : NetworkBehaviour {

  public GameObject enemyPrefab;
  public int numberOfEnemies;

  public override void OnStartServer()
  {
    for (int i = 0; i < numberOfEnemies; i++)
    {
      var spawnPosition = new Vector3(
          Random.Range(-8.0f, 8.0f),
          0.0f,
          Random.Range(-8.0f, 8.0f));

      var spawnRotation = Quaternion.Euler(
          0.0f,
          Random.Range(0, 180),
          0.0f);

      var enemy = (GameObject)Instantiate(enemyPrefab, spawnPosition,
  spawnRotation);
      NetworkServer.Spawn(enemy);
    }
  }
}
```

[327]

Multiplayer Setup

This code technically takes the prefab provided as the Enemy Tank and randomly spawns each enemy tank within a range over the network.

Make sure all of your prefabs have been assigned in the Inspector Window for both the `Enemy Spawner` GameObject and the `TankEnemy` GameObject. Create a Prefab of your `TankEnemy` if you have not done so already and delete it from the scene. Do not delete the `Enemy Spawner`.

We need to register the `TankEnemy` prefab with the NetworkManager. Go ahead and select the **Network Manager** GameObject and from the *Inspector Window*, add a new Prefab to the **Registered Spawnable Prefabs option**.

Your Network Manager should look like the following now:

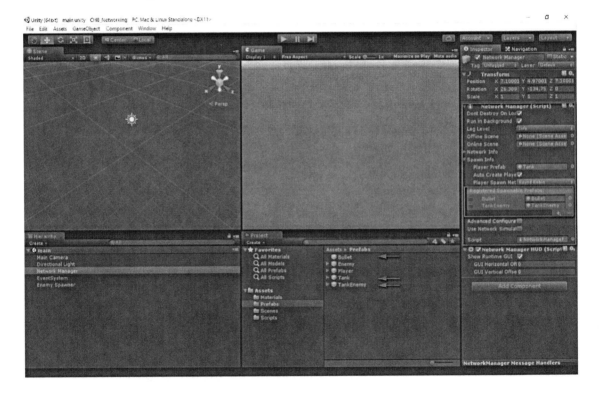

Building and Testing

We are ready to do our final test. Go ahead and build the standalone version of the project and launch a new instance of the game. Click on the **LAN Host (H)** button to start hosting a game.

In the new implementation, you will note that not only the player character tank gets spawned, but also the non-player character enemy tanks.

You will also note that right after initialization, all of the enemy tanks are going to rotate toward the player character tank and if within range, they are going to start firing at it.

The following figure illustrates the initial scene:

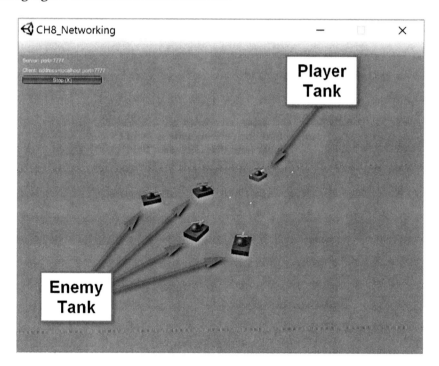

Note that while I was trying to capture the screen, the enemy tank were merciless and fired at my tank continuously. You can see that my health bar has reduced drastically. You can also note that one of the enemy tank has also received some damage.

Multiplayer Setup

I assure you that I had nothing to do with the damage taken by the enemy tank, it was actually caused by friendly fire. Yes, at the moment, the enemy tanks are not smart enough to hold fire if another team member is in the line of fire!

I will let you handle the implementation of that on your own. It shouldn't be too complex.

 Use Raycasting to make sure there is no object between the enemy tank and the player prior to firing.

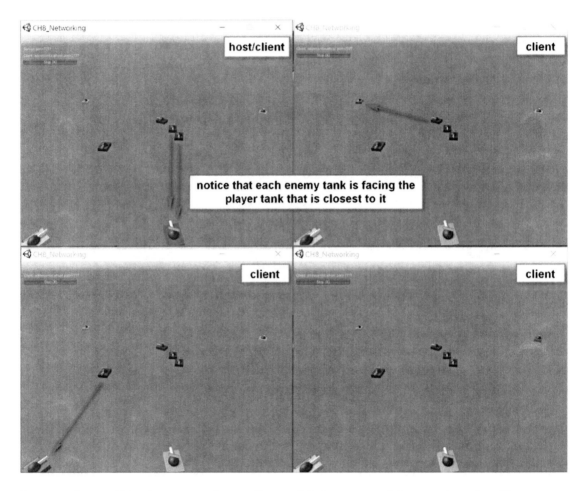

Congratulations! You just created your first multiplayer game! As mentioned earlier, creating, maintaining, and hosting a multiplayer game is no small task, and covering every single aspect on how to do it is simply impossible in a few pages.

Chapter 8

The idea here is to give you the foundation and the fundamentals that you can take and expand upon. I would encourage you to take some time and study what we have just covered and do some more reading on the material, even though, not much exists. The truth is that you will need to do a lot of experimentation and trial and error on your own.

Now that we know the basics, let's go ahead and apply what you learned to our RPG assets.

Network Enabling RPG Characters

In order to make life easier, I decided to create a new scene that will be used to test and implement our network-enabled characters. This example will show you how to network enable the player character and also how to synchronize the player character data such as inventory item across the network and also the ability to network enable the non-player character and make it synchronize its data across the clients.

Creating a Scene for RPG

Create a new scene and save it as *CH8_Networking*. Place a *Terrain* in the scene; modify it so that it has a TerrainWidth and Terrain Length of 30. Modify the Position Transform so that it is at <-15,0,-15>; this will make the center of the terrain at the origin.

Next, we are going to create an Empty GameObject and name it NetworkManager. We are also going to create another Empty GameObject and name is SpawnEnemy.

Select the **NetworkManager** GameObject and attach the following components to it: **NetworkManager** and **NetworkManager HUD** using the *Inspector Windows*, select **Add Component | Network | NetworkManager** and **Add Component | Network | NetworkManagerHUD**.

We will come back to these GameObjects later. We need to make our Player Character network enabled.

Networked Player Character

Go ahead and drag the player prefab you created into the scene. We are going to use it as a base to create a new prefab that will be used for the networked version of the game.

[331]

Multiplayer Setup

Go ahead and remove the existing `CharacterController.cs` and *CharacterCustomization.cs* components from the instance. We are going to create new scripts that are networked enabled and use them. Rename the PC GameObject instance to *PC-CC-Network*. Now, make a prefab of the instance. You should now have a new prefab named *PC-CC-Network*.

Go ahead and attach the following components to the prefab: **NetworkIdentiy**, **NetworkTransform**, and **NetworkAnimator** using the *Inspector Window* and navigating to **Add Components** | **Network** | *<component name>*.

On **NetworkIdentity** component, set the **Local Player Authority** to *True*. On **NetworkTransform** component change the *Transform Sync Mode* to *Sync Transform*. On the **NetworkAnimator** component, you will need to drag the *Animator* components attached to the GameObject into the *Animator* slot.

> You will need to select the *Animator* component and drag it right down into the *Animator* slot on the *NetworkAnimator* components.

Next, we need to create a new character controller so that it is network compatible.

Create a new C# script and call it `CharacterController_Network.cs`. Attach the script to the *PC-CC-Network* prefab. The new character controller is a stripped down version of the original character controller.

Here is the listing for it:

```
using System;

using UnityEngine;
using UnityEngine.Networking;
using System.Collections;

public class CharacterController_Network : NetworkBehaviour {

  public Animator animator;

  public float speed = 6.0f;
  public float h = 0.0f;
  public float v = 0.0f;

  public bool attack1 = false; // used for attack mode 1
  public bool attack2 = false; // used for attack mode 2
  public bool attack3 = false; // used for attack mode 3
```

[332]

```
public bool jump = false;      // used for jumping
public bool die = false;       // are we alive?

public bool DEBUG = false;

// Reference to the sphere collider trigger component.
private SphereCollider col;

// where is the player character in relation to NPC
public Vector3 direction;

// how far away is the player character from NPC
public float distance = 0.0f;

// what is the angle between the PC and NPC
public float angle = 0.0f;

// is the PC in sight?
public bool enemyInSight;

// what is the field of view for our NPC?
// currently set to 110 degrees
public float fieldOfViewAngle = 110.0f;

// calculate the angle between PC and NPC
public float calculatedAngle;

[SyncVar(hook ="OnChangeEnemyToAttack")]
public GameObject enemyToAttack;

[SyncVar(hook = "OnChangePlayerHealth")]
public float Health = 100.0f;

[SyncVar]
public string Shield="";
[SyncVar]
public string Helmet="";

public override void OnStartClient()
{
  if(!String.IsNullOrEmpty(Shield))
    PlayerSetShield(Shield);

  if(!String.IsNullOrEmpty(Helmet))
    PlayerSetHelmet(Helmet);
}

// Use this for initialization
```

Multiplayer Setup

```
  void Start()
  {
    this.animator = GetComponent<Animator>() as Animator;

    // we don't see the player by default
    this.enemyInSight = false;
  }

  // Update is called once per frame
  private Vector3 moveDirection = Vector3.zero;

  Quaternion startingAttackAngle = Quaternion.AngleAxis(-25, Vector3.up);
  Quaternion stepAttackAngle = Quaternion.AngleAxis(5, Vector3.up);
  Vector3 attackDistance = new Vector3(0, 0, 2);

  void Update()
  {
    if (!isLocalPlayer)
      return;

    if (enemyInSight)
    {
      // Create a vector from the enemy to the player and store the angle
between it and forward.
      direction = enemyToAttack.transform.position - transform.position;

      this.transform.rotation =
          Quaternion.Slerp(this.transform.rotation,
          Quaternion.LookRotation(direction), 0.1f);
    }

    if (this.attack1 || this.attack2 || this.attack3)
    {
      #region used for attack range
      RaycastHit hitAttack;
      var angleAttack = transform.rotation * startingAttackAngle;
      var directionAttack = angleAttack * attackDistance;
      var posAttack = transform.position + Vector3.up;
      for (var i = 0; i < 10; i++)
      {
        Debug.DrawRay(posAttack, directionAttack, Color.yellow);
        if (Physics.Raycast(posAttack, directionAttack, out hitAttack,
1.0f))
        {
          if (hitAttack.collider.gameObject.tag.Equals("ENEMY"))
          {
            enemyInSight = true;
            enemyToAttack = hitAttack.collider.gameObject;
```

```
          CmdEnemyToAttack(hitAttack.collider.gameObject);
        }
      }
      directionAttack = stepAttackAngle * directionAttack;
    }
    #endregion

    if (enemyInSight && !die)
    {
      if (animator.GetFloat("Attack1C") == 1.0f)
      {
        CmdEnemyTakeDamage(1.0f);
      }
    }

    if(this.enemyToAttack!=null)
    {
      if (this.enemyToAttack.GetComponent<NPC_Movement_Network>().Health
<= 0.0f)
      {
        enemyInSight = false;
        enemyToAttack = null;
      }
    }

  }

  if (Input.GetKeyDown(KeyCode.C))
  {
    attack1 = true;
    GetComponent<IKHandle>().enabled = false;
  }
  if (Input.GetKeyUp(KeyCode.C))
  {
    attack1 = false;
    GetComponent<IKHandle>().enabled = true;
  }
  animator.SetBool("Attack1", attack1);

  if (Input.GetKeyDown(KeyCode.Z))
  {
    attack2 = true;
    GetComponent<IKHandle>().enabled = false;
  }
  if (Input.GetKeyUp(KeyCode.Z))
  {
    attack2 = false;
    GetComponent<IKHandle>().enabled = true;
```

```
  }
  animator.SetBool("Attack2", attack2);

  if (Input.GetKeyDown(KeyCode.X))
  {
    attack3 = true;
    GetComponent<IKHandle>().enabled = false;
  }
  if (Input.GetKeyUp(KeyCode.X))
  {
    attack3 = false;
    GetComponent<IKHandle>().enabled = true;
  }
  animator.SetBool("Attack3", attack3);

  if (Input.GetKeyDown(KeyCode.Space))
  {
    jump = true;
    GetComponent<IKHandle>().enabled = false;
  }
  if (Input.GetKeyUp(KeyCode.Space))
  {
    jump = false;
    GetComponent<IKHandle>().enabled = true;
  }
  animator.SetBool("Jump", jump);

  if (Input.GetKeyDown(KeyCode.I))
  {
    die = true;
    SendMessage("Died");
  }
  animator.SetBool("Die", die);

  if(this.Health<=0)
  {
    die = true;
    CmdPlayerCharacterIsDead();
  }

}

[Command]
void CmdEnemyToAttack(GameObject go)
{
  enemyInSight = true;
  enemyToAttack = go;
}
```

[336]

```
[Command]
void CmdPlayerCharacterIsDead()
{
  RpcPlayerCharacterIsDead();
}

[ClientRpc]
void RpcPlayerCharacterIsDead()
{
  this.die = true;
  Destroy(this.gameObject, 2.0f);
}

[Command]
void CmdEnemyTakeDamage(float value)
{
  RpcEnemyTakeDamage(value);
}

[ClientRpc]
void RpcEnemyTakeDamage(float value)
{
  if(this.enemyToAttack != null)
this.enemyToAttack.GetComponent<NPC_Movement_Network>().Damage(value);
}

void FixedUpdate()
{
  if (!isLocalPlayer)
    return;

  // The Inputs are defined in the Input Manager
  h = Input.GetAxis("Horizontal");
  v = Input.GetAxis("Vertical");

  speed = new Vector2(h, v).sqrMagnitude;

  if (DEBUG)
    Debug.Log(string.Format("H:{0} - V:{1} - Speed:{2}", h, v, speed));

  animator.SetFloat("Speed", speed);
  animator.SetFloat("Horizontal", h);
  animator.SetFloat("Vertical", v);

}

// Var Sync hook function ...
void OnChangePlayerHealth(float health)
```

[337]

```csharp
  {
    this.Health = health;
  }

  // Var Sync hook function
  void OnChangeEnemyToAttack(GameObject enemy)
  {
    this.enemyToAttack = enemy;
  }

  public void PlayerArmourChanged(InventoryItem item)
  {
    switch (item.TYPE.ToString())
    {
      case "HELMET":
        {
          this.Helmet = item.NAME;
this.GetComponent<CharacterCustomization_Network>().SetHelmetType((PC.HELME
T_TYPE)Enum.Parse(typeof(PC.HELMET_TYPE), item.NAME));
          break;
        }
      case "SHIELD":
        {
          this.Shield = item.NAME;
this.GetComponent<CharacterCustomization_Network>().SetShieldType((PC.SHIEL
D_TYPE)Enum.Parse(typeof(PC.SHIELD_TYPE), item.NAME));
          break;
        }
      case "SHOULDER_PAD":
        {
this.GetComponent<CharacterCustomization_Network>().SetShoulderPad((PC.SHOU
LDER_PAD)Enum.Parse(typeof(PC.SHOULDER_PAD), item.NAME));
          break;
        }
      case "KNEE_PAD":
        {
          break;
        }
      case "BOOTS":
        {
          break;
        }
    }
  }

  private void PlayerSetHelmet(string item)
  {
    Debug.Log("Helmet: " + item);
```

Chapter 8

```
        this.GetComponent<CharacterCustomization_Network>().SetHelmetType((PC.HELME
    T_TYPE)Enum.Parse(typeof(PC.HELMET_TYPE), item));
      }

      private void PlayerSetShield(string item)
      {
        this.GetComponent<CharacterCustomization_Network>().SetShieldType((PC.SHIEL
    D_TYPE)Enum.Parse(typeof(PC.SHIELD_TYPE), item));
      }

    }
```

The first thing you should notice is that we are inheriting from `NetworkBehaviour` instead of `MonoBehaviour`. This is needed if we want to enable certain network behaviors on the GameObject.

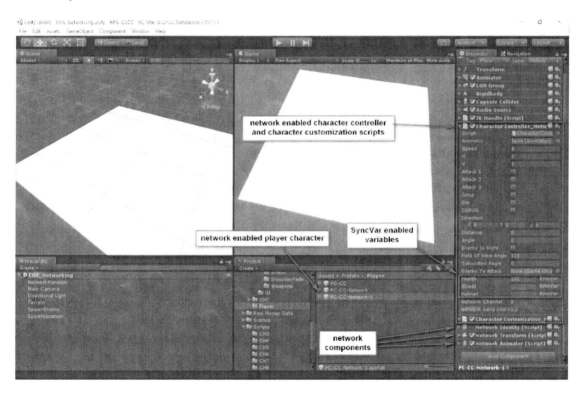

Next, let's look at some of the variables that need to be synchronized across the network for each player character that is connected. These variables are: `enemyToAttack` and `Health`. There are two more variables, `Shield` and `Helmet`, which we will discuss later.

[339]

Multiplayer Setup

In the `Update()` function, we need a way to check and make sure that it is the local player before giving the controller the chance to execute the player. This is done by having the following code check to see if the current client is the local player:

```
if (!isLocalPlayer)
    return;
```

This will make sure that the code runs only for the current client (player). The rest of the code in the `Update()` function check to see if the enemy is in sight and make sure the player charter is facing the enemy to attack.

If the player is in attack mode, and the enemy is in our view, we set the `enemyInSight` to `True` and `enemyToAttack` to the enemy GameObject which is stored in the `hitAttack` variable of type `RacastHit`. The important element here is the `CmdEnemyToAttack()` function. The client needs to send a command to the server telling the server who the target of attack is.

```
[Command]
void CmdEnemyToAttack(GameObject go)
{
    this.enemyInSight = true;
    this.enemyToAttack = go;
}
```

This will make sure that the data is registered correctly on the server, and it is synchronized to other clients. We also have another function called `CmdEnemyTakeDamage()` that is used to reduce the health of the enemy character on the server. The server then calls the `RpcEnemyTakeDamage()` function to synchronize across all clients the health value of the enemy.

```
[Command]
void CmdEnemyTakeDamage(float value)
{
    RpcEnemyTakeDamage(value);
}

[ClientRpc]
void RpcEnemyTakeDamage(float value)
{
    if(this.enemyToAttack != null)
this.enemyToAttack.GetComponent<NPC_Movement_Network>().Damage(value);
}
```

This idea is a bit confusing at first, but it will be clearer as you start to study it more carefully.

Chapter 8

We also have the following function to send commands to the server when the player dies:

```
[Command]
void CmdPlayerCharacterIsDead()
{
  RpcPlayerCharacterIsDead();
}

[ClientRpc]
void RpcPlayerCharacterIsDead()
{
  this.die = true;
  Destroy(this.gameObject, 2.0f);
}
```

The preceding functions make sure that the player character is dead and destroyed on all connected clients at the moment of the game.

And finally, the following hook functions that are used by the SyncVar on Health and enemyToAttack variables:

```
// Var Sync hook function ...
void OnChangePlayerHealth(float health)
{
  this.Health = health;
}

// Var Sync hook function
void OnChangeEnemyToAttack(GameObject enemy)
{
  this.enemyToAttack = enemy;
}
```

This idea is a bit confusing at first, but it will be clearer as you start to study it more carefully.

If you have not done so already, apply and save all of your changes to your *PC-CC-Network* prefab.

At this stage, your character is ready to be integrated with the *NetworkManager,* you can drag and drop the prefab into the Player Prefab slot and build a standalone version to test out your character movement and synchronization.

[341]

Multiplayer Setup

Networked Non-Player Character

Just like the player character network-enabled prefab, we will use the non-player character prefab as our base to get started. Go ahead and create an instance of your NPC in the scene.

Go ahead and remove the existing *NPC_Movement.cs* component from the prefab. Rename the Prefab to *B1-Network* and attach the following components to it: *NetworkIdentity*, *NetworkTransform*, and *NetworkAnimator* by navigating to **Add Component** | **Network** | *<component name>* from the **Inspector Window**.

On the *NetworkIdentity* component, set the *Local Player Authority* to *True*; in the *NetworkTransform* component, set the *Transform Sync Mode* to *Sync Transform*; and for the *NetworkAnimator* component, set the *Animator* slot to the *Animator* controller attached to the prefab, by dragging it and dropping into the slot.

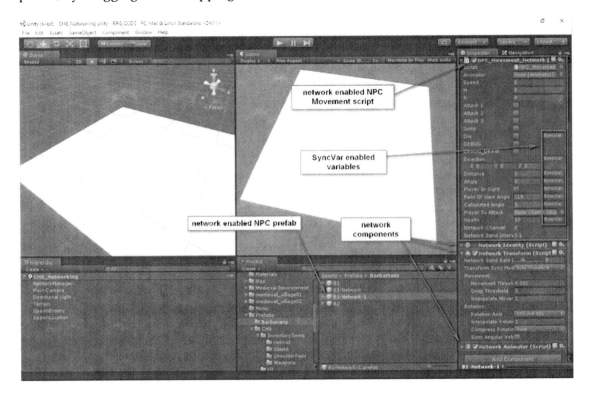

Chapter 8

We not need to create a new script for out NPC movement that is network enabled. Go ahead and create a new C# script and name it `NPC_Movement_Network.cs`. Here is a listing of the scripts:

```
using UnityEngine;
using UnityEngine.Networking;
using System.Collections;
public class NPC_Movement_Network : NetworkBehaviour {

    // reference to the animator
    public Animator animator;
    // these variables are used for the speed
    // horizontal and vertical movement of the NPC
    public float speed = 0.0f;
    public float h = 0.0f;
    public float v = 0.0f;

    public bool attack1 = false; // used for attack mode 1
    public bool attack2 = false; // used for attack mode 2
    public bool attack3 = false; // used for attack mode 3
    public bool jump = false;    // used for jumping
    [SyncVar(hook ="OnNPCIsDead")]
    public bool die = false;     // are we alive?
    // used for debugging
    public bool DEBUG = false;
    public bool DEBUG_DRAW = false;
    // Reference to the NavMeshAgent component.
    private NavMeshAgent nav;
    // Reference to the sphere collider trigger component.
    private SphereCollider col;
    // where is the player character in relation to NPC
    [SyncVar]
    public Vector3 direction;
    // how far away is the player character from NPC
    [SyncVar]
    public float distance = 0.0f;
    // what is the angle between the PC and NPC
    [SyncVar]
    public float angle = 0.0f;

    // is the PC in sight?
    [SyncVar(hook = "OnChangePlayerPlayerInSight")]
    public bool playerInSight;
    // what is the field of view for our NPC?
    // currently set to 110 degrees
    [SyncVar]
    public float fieldOfViewAngle = 110.0f;
    // calculate the angle between PC and NPC
```

[343]

Multiplayer Setup

```
[SyncVar]
public float calculatedAngle;
[SyncVar(hook = "OnChangePlayerToAttackInNPC")]
public GameObject playerToAttack;
[SyncVar(hook = "OnChangeNPCHealth")]
public float Health = 100.0f;

void Awake()
{
  // get reference to the animator component
  this.animator = GetComponent<Animator>() as Animator;
  // get reference to nav mesh agent
  this.nav = GetComponent<NavMeshAgent>() as NavMeshAgent;
  // get reference to the sphere collider
  this.col = GetComponent<SphereCollider>() as SphereCollider;
  // we don't see the player by default
  this.playerInSight = false;
}

void Update()
{
  // only execute the following code if local player ...
  if (!isServer)
    return;
  this.CmdUpdateNetwork();
}
[Command]
void CmdUpdateNetwork()
{
  this.RpcUpdateNetwork();
}

[ClientRpc]
void RpcUpdateNetwork()
{
  // if player is in sight let's slerp towards the player
  if(this.playerToAttack!=null)
  {
    if (playerInSight)
    {
      this.transform.rotation =
          Quaternion.Slerp(this.transform.rotation,
          Quaternion.LookRotation(direction), 0.1f);
      if (this.playerToAttack.transform.GetComponent
      <CharacterController_Network>().die)
      {
        animator.SetBool("Attack", false);
        animator.SetFloat("Speed", 0.0f);
```

```
          animator.SetFloat("AngularSpeed", 0.0f);
          this.playerInSight = false;
          this.playerToAttack = null;
      }
    }
  }
  if(this.Health<=0.0f)
  {
    this.die = true;
    this.Health = 0.0f;
    animator.SetBool("Attack", false);
    animator.SetFloat("Speed", 0.0f);
    animator.SetFloat("AngularSpeed", 0.0f);
    this.playerInSight = false;
    this.playerToAttack = null;
  }
  animator.SetBool("Die", die);
}
// let's update our scene using fixed update
void FixedUpdate()
{
  // only execute the following code if local player ...
  if (!isServer)
    return;
  this.RpcFixedUpdateNetwork();
}

[ClientRpc]
void RpcFixedUpdateNetwork()
{
  if (playerInSight)
  {
    h = angle;          // assign horizontal axis
    v = distance;       // assign vertical axis
    // calculate speed based on distance and delta time
    speed = distance / Time.deltaTime;
    if (DEBUG)
      Debug.Log(string.Format("H:{0} - V:{1} - Speed:{2}",
      h, v, speed));
    // set the parameters defined in the animator controller
    animator.SetFloat("Speed", speed);
    animator.SetFloat("AngularSpeed", v);
    animator.SetBool("Attack", attack1);
    animator.SetBool("Attack1", attack1);
    if (animator.GetFloat("Attack1C") == 1.0f)
    {
      this.playerToAttack.GetComponent
      <CharacterController_Network>().Health -= 1.0f;
```

```csharp
      if(this.playerToAttack.GetComponent
      <CharacterController_Network>().Health<=0)
      {
        this.playerInSight = false;
        this.playerToAttack = null;
      }
    }
  }
  else
  {
    animator.SetBool("Attack", false);
    animator.SetFloat("Speed", 0.0f);
    animator.SetFloat("AngularSpeed", 0.0f);
  }
}

public void OnChangePlayerPlayerInSight(bool value)
{
  this.playerInSight = value;
}

// Var Sync hook function ...
void OnChangeNPCHealth(float health)
{
  this.Health = health;
}
void OnNPCIsDead(bool value)
{
  die = true;
}
public void Damage(float value)
{
  this.Health -= value;
}
void OnTriggerStay(Collider other)
{
  if (die)
    return;
  if (other.transform.tag.Equals("Player"))
  {
    // Create a vector from the enemy to the player
    //and store the angle between it and forward.
    direction = other.transform.position - transform.position;
    distance = Vector3.Distance(other.transform.position,
    transform.position) - 1.0f;
    float DotResult = Vector3.Dot(transform.forward,
    other.transform.position); //player.transform.position);
    angle = DotResult;
```

```
if (DEBUG_DRAW)
{
  Debug.DrawLine(transform.position + Vector3.up,
 direction * 50, Color.gray);
  Debug.DrawLine(other.transform.position, transform.position,
  Color.cyan);
}
this.playerInSight = false;
this.calculatedAngle = Vector3.Angle(direction,
transform.forward);
if (calculatedAngle < fieldOfViewAngle * 0.5f)
{
  RaycastHit hit;
  if (DEBUG_DRAW)
    Debug.DrawRay(transform.position + transform.up,
    direction.normalized, Color.magenta);
  // ... and if a raycast towards the player hits something...
  if (Physics.Raycast(transform.position + transform.up,
  direction.normalized, out hit, col.radius))
  {
    // ... and if the raycast hits the player...
    if (hit.collider.gameObject == other.gameObject) //player
    {
      if(other.gameObject.GetComponent
      <CharacterController_Network>().Health>0)
      {
        // ... the player is in sight.
        this.playerInSight = true;
        this.playerToAttack = hit.collider.gameObject;
        if (DEBUG)
          Debug.Log("PlayerInSight: " + playerInSight);
      }
    }
  }
}
if (this.playerInSight)
{
  this.nav.SetDestination(other.transform.position);
  this.CalculatePathLength(other.transform.position);
  if (distance < 1.1f)
  {
    this.attack1 = true;
  }
  else
  {
    this.attack1 = false;
  }
}
```

```
      else
      {
        this.nav.SetDestination(this.transform.position);
        if (distance < 1.1f)
        {
          this.attack1 = true;
        }
        else
        {
          this.attack1 = false;
        }
      }
    }
  }
}

void OnChangePlayerToAttackInNPC(GameObject player)
{
  this.playerToAttack = player;
}
void OnTriggerExit(Collider other)
{
  if (other.transform.tag.Equals("Player"))
  {
    distance = 0.0f;
    angle = 0.0f;
    this.attack1 = false;
    this.playerInSight = false;
    this.playerToAttack = null;
  }
}
// this is a helper function at this point
// in the future we will use it to calculate distance
// around the corners
// it currently is also used to draw the path of the
//  nav mesh agent in the editor
float CalculatePathLength(Vector3 targetPosition)
{
  // Create a path and set it based on a target position.
  NavMeshPath path = new NavMeshPath();
  if (nav.enabled)
    nav.CalculatePath(targetPosition, path);
  // Create an array of points which is the length of the
  number of corners in the path + 2.
  Vector3[] allWayPoints = new Vector3[path.corners.Length + 2];
  // The first point is the enemy's position.
  allWayPoints[0] = transform.position;
  // The last point is the target position.
  allWayPoints[allWayPoints.Length - 1] = targetPosition;
```

```csharp
// The points inbetween are the corners of the path.
for (int i = 0; i < path.corners.Length; i++)
{
  allWayPoints[i + 1] = path.corners[i];
}
// Create a float to store the path length that is
// by default 0.
float pathLength = 0;

// Increment the path length by an amount equal to the
// distance between each waypoint and the next.
for (int i = 0; i < allWayPoints.Length - 1; i++)
{
  pathLength += Vector3.Distance(allWayPoints[i],
  allWayPoints[i + 1]);
  if (DEBUG_DRAW)
    Debug.DrawLine(allWayPoints[i], allWayPoints[i + 1],
    Color.red);
}
return pathLength;
    }
}
```

There are a few variables that have been indicated as `SyncVars`, these are: `die`, `distance`, `direction`, `angle`, `playerInSight`, `fieldOfViewAngle`, `calculatedAngle`, `playerToAttack`, and `Health`.

Some of the `SyncVars` have a `hook`, these are `Health`, `playerToAttack`, `playerInSight`, and `die`.

In the `Update()` function, we check to make sure we are the server by the following line:

```csharp
// only execute the following code if server ...
if (!isServer)
  return;
```

Multiplayer Setup

If we are the server, we use `CmdUpdateNetwork()` and `RpcUpdateNetwork()` functions to perform our duties. These are just for the movement and action for the NPC. The key here are the `SyncVars` and `hook` functions that are used to synchronize the NPC data to all clients.

```
public void OnChangePlayerPlayerInSight(bool value)
{
  this.playerInSight = value;
}

// Var Sync hook function ...
void OnChangeNPCHealth(float health)
{
  this.Health = health;
}

void OnNPCIsDead(bool value)
{
  die = true;
}
void OnChangePlayerToAttackInNPC(GameObject player)
{
  this.playerToAttack = player;
}
```

That is all we need for the NPC. Go ahead and add the script to the prefab and apply the changes. Save it!

Your new NPC prefab should have the following components attached:

Synchronizing Player Customization and Items

In order for this to work, we need to perform several other configuration and creation of new inventory item prefabs. I am going to use two inventory items to demonstrate this particular point.

[350]

I am going to use one of the Helmet prefabs from my inventory items, duplicate it, and remove the *InventoryItemAgent.cs* component. We are going to create a new script that is network enabled as we did for our PC and NPC.

Attach the following components to the instance: **NetworkIdentity** and **NetworkTransform** using **Add Component** | **Network** | *<component name>* from the **Inspector Window**.

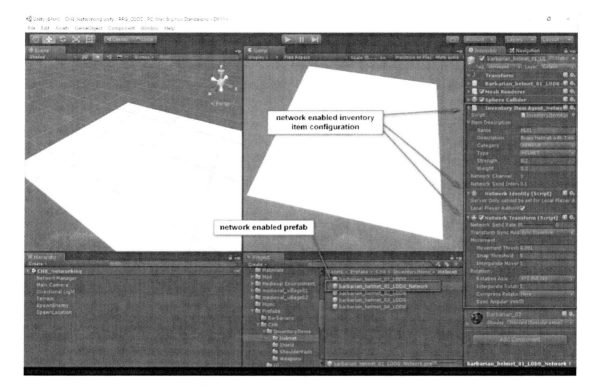

Multiplayer Setup

Create a new script named `InventoryItemAgent_Network.cs`. Here is the listing:

```
using UnityEngine;
using UnityEngine.Networking;
using System.Collections;

public class InventoryItemAgent_Network : NetworkBehaviour {

  public InventoryItem ItemDescription;

  public void OnTriggerEnter(Collider c)
  {
    // make sure we are colliding with the player
    if (c.gameObject.tag.Equals("Player"))
    {
      // Make a copy of the Inventory Item Object
      InventoryItem myItem = new InventoryItem();
      myItem.CopyInventoryItem(this.ItemDescription);

c.gameObject.GetComponent<CharacterController_Network>().PlayerArmourChange
d(myItem);
    }
  }
}
```

All this script is doing is assigning the inventory item to the player character using the `PlayerArmourChanged()` function in the `CharacterController_Network.cs` script.

The `PlayerArmourChanged()` function uses another script we need to create that is network enabled, and that is the *CharacterCustomization_Network.cs* script. I will not list the script here as it is very long. You can look at the script in the code supplied by the book.

Spawning NPC and Other Items

We need a way to spawn our NPC and also the inventory items we are going to be using for the next demonstration.

In the **Hierarchy Window**, right-click on and select **Create Empty**. This will create an Empty GameObject. Rename it to *SpawnEnemy* and add a **NetworkIdentity** component to it by navigating to **Add Component | Network | NetworkIdentity** from the **Inspector Window**.

Chapter 8

We are going to create a new script called `EnemySpawn_Network.cs`. Here is the listing:

```
using UnityEngine;
using UnityEngine.Networking; // used for chapter 8

using System.Collections;

public class EnemySpawn_Network : NetworkBehaviour
{
  public GameObject enemyPrefab;
  public Transform spawnLocation;

  public GameObject inventoryItemPrefab;
  public GameObject inventoryItemShield;

  public override void OnStartServer()
  {
    GameObject go = GameObject.Instantiate(enemyPrefab,
spawnLocation.position, Quaternion.identity) as GameObject;
    NetworkServer.Spawn(go);


    GameObject goInventoryItem1 =
GameObject.Instantiate(inventoryItemPrefab, new Vector3(2, 1, 2),
Quaternion.identity) as GameObject;
    NetworkServer.Spawn(goInventoryItem1);

    GameObject goInventoryItem2 =
GameObject.Instantiate(inventoryItemShield, new Vector3(3, 1, 2),
Quaternion.identity) as GameObject;
    NetworkServer.Spawn(goInventoryItem2);

  }
}
```

The script is very simple as you can see. We are just referencing the GameObjects that are representing the prefabs for the NPC and also inventory items prefab.

Attach the new script to the **SpawnEnemy** prefab in the **Hierarchy Window**.

Testing Our Network-Enabled PC and NPC

At this point, we have all of the assets needed to test out our network-enabled PRG characters. There is one final step that you need to perform, if you have not done so already.

[353]

Multiplayer Setup

Select the **NetworkManager** GameObject in the **Hierarchy Window**, and from the **Inspector** Window, you will need to make sure the following have been assigned in the *Spawn Info* section:

Player Prefab should be assigned to your player character prefab, mine is named *PC-CC-Network-1*. Make sure **Auto Create Player** is set **True**.

You will also register your NPC prefabs and other network-enabled non-character prefabs in the *Registered Spawnable Prefabs*. I have the barbarian prefab named *B1-Network-1* assigned, *barbarian_helmet_01_LOD0_Network* and *shield_01_LOD0_Network*.

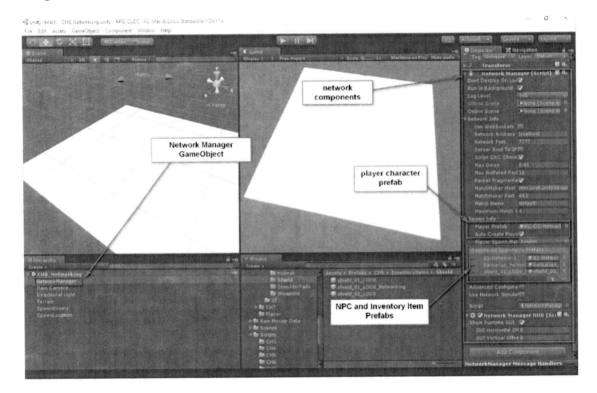

Alright, at last we can do a build. Let's go ahead and make a standalone build of our game. Make sure that the current scene is in the build configuration.

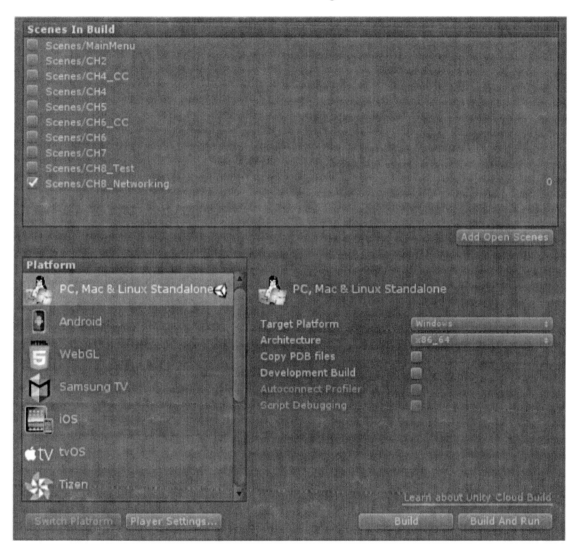

Go ahead and launch two instances of the build. Make one of them the host and the other the client.

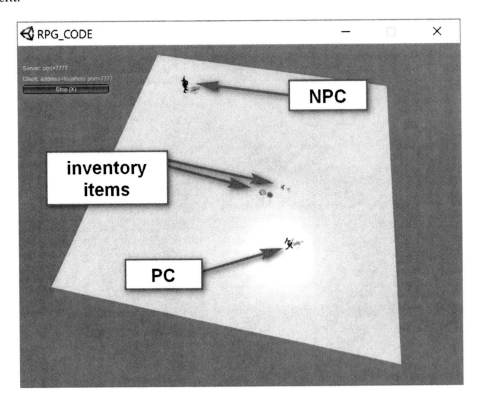

In the preceding figure, we have started a client as a server and the player character has picked up one of the inventory items, a shield. When we connect the second client, it should correctly take into consideration the current state of all PC and NPC active in the game.

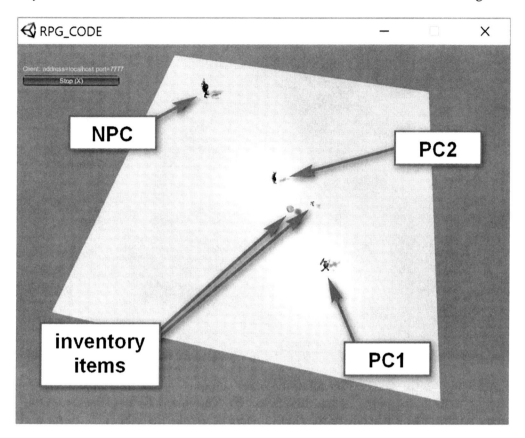

Multiplayer Setup

Keeping both of the instances running, use the Unity IDE to connect the third client. You can use the client to perform debugging on the client end and also seeing what is going on.

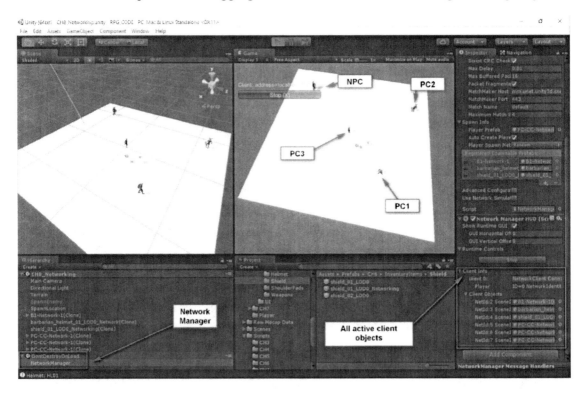

In the preceding figure, you can see all of the player characters and how they have been accurately synchronized with one another. Select **B1-Network-1** GameObject from the Hierarchy Window, and use one of the client instances to take the player character and attack the NPC.

We are going to pause the editor and inspect the variables and how they have been properly synchronized.

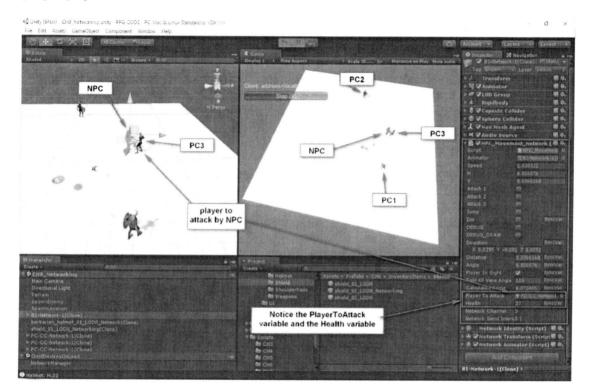

What's Next

As you witnessed, network programming is simple but at the same time, it can be difficult. The difficulty is going to be on managing and understanding the synchronization of the data between all players in an efficient and meaningful way.

It can actually get a bit more involved if you are truly considering creating a game with large numbers of clients. Unity networking will not be able to handle that; you will need to create your own backend server managers and messaging systems.

What we have covered in this chapter will give you a good understanding to take it to the next level. Keep coding until we meet again!

Multiplayer Setup

Summary

In *Chapter 8*, we looked at network programming using the Unity networking components. The main objective of the chapter was to introduce you to the fundamental of networking in Unity by implementing two samples.

We start the chapter by giving some of the challenges that you will face as a game designer and developer for a multiplayer game. One of the main questions raised is whether you really need to invest the time and energy to create a multiplayer mode for your game. Assuming you really do want or need to create a multiplayer game, we start looking at the different types of multiplayer games popular today.

We start with our first example of a simplified multiplayer game. The multiplayer game we develop are real time, that is, all clients are synchronized with one another based on the activity on each active player's state. That is, the position, rotation, movement, and other important data needs to be synchronized with all clients connected to the game session.

We look at the fundamentals of Unity's networking components such as the Network Manager, Network Manager HUD, Network Identity, and Network Transform. These are the base components that are used to illustrate multiplayer programming in Unity. Once we understand what these components are used for, we start with a simple sample.

We create a simple tank game that demonstrating how to put together all of the essential components for a multiplayer game. We create the necessary player character prefab with the appropriate network enabled scripts and components. We also create the non-player character prefab with its own network-enabled scripts. The game demonstrates how to spawn, synchronize between the player characters and non-player characters.

During the construction of the tank game, we cover how to synchronize variables and use network callbacks that are crucial for the development of a multiplayer game. We also cover what *Commands* and *ClientRPC* calls are and how to use them properly.

Next, we apply what you have learned to the RPG characters we developed in previous chapters. We used the existing prefabs as a base and extended them to include the networking components and create new network-enabled scripts to handle the character movement, character customization, and NPC movement scripts.

One of the crucial elements that is covered is the synchronization of each player character's inventory items visually with the rest of the players. We close the chapter by the testing and discussing how to debug your code on the client and the server while developing your multiplayer game.

Index

3

3rd Person Controller (3rdPC) 58

A

Animator Controller
  about 74, 75
  animation states 76, 77, 78, 79, 80
  creating 123, 124
  creating, for NPC 122
asset inventory
  about 39
  character assets 40, 41
  environment assets 39
Asset Store 51

B

Base character class
  attributes 66, 67
Blend Tree 78

C

character controller
  about 81, 84, 86
  animations, modifying 86, 87, 88
character model 70, 72
  about 69
  rigging 72, 73
character motion
  about 74
  Animator Controller 74, 75
character
  defining 65
  states 68
combat system 19
Computer RPG (cRPG) 8, 10
Contest Tree 31

D

Dark Souls 3 24
Divinity with Original Sin 26
Dungeons & Dragons (D&D) 8
Dynamic Item Viewer
  designing 209
  elements, adding to PanelItem 211
  elements, adding to Scroll View 211
  Scroll View, adding 209
  txtItemElement, adding dynamically 213

E

enemy stats
  in HUD 290
  NPC canvas, creating 290, 292, 293
  NPC health, defining 294, 295, 298
  NPC stats, user interface 290
Escalating Conflict 31

F

Fallout 4 25
fbx 197

G

Game Master (GM)
  about 8, 148, 149
  Audio Controller, handling 161
  audio, managing 149, 153
  Game Settings, managing 149, 153
  improving 158
  Level Controller, handling 158, 161
  scenes, managing 153
  testing 183, 184
  UI Controller, modifying 182

H

Heads Up Display (HUD)
  about 21, 256
  code, integrating 270, 272, 285, 286, 287, 288
  designing 256, 257
  enemy stats 290
  framework 258
Horizontal parameter 79
HUD design
  completing 259
  panel active inventory item, creating 265, 266, 267
  panel character 259, 262, 263, 264
  special items panel, designing 268, 269
Hydraulic Erosion 46

I

Inventory Interface
  about 204, 206
  Dynamic Item Viewer, designing 209
  final Inventory Item UI, building 215
  Inventory UI Framework, creating 206
Inventory Item
  Agent, adding 199
  applying 231
  creating 197
  defining, as Prefabs 203
  Prefabs, creating 198, 199
  using, with player character 230
inventory system
  about 12, 188
  item types, determining 189, 194, 196
  testing 227
  UI, integrating with 217
  Weighted Inventory 188, 189
Inverse Kinematics (IK) 88, 89, 92, 93

L

Last Man Standing 32
level design, Zazar Dynasty
  about 41, 42
  awakening 47, 48, 49, 50, 51, 52, 53, 54, 55, 56, 57, 58
  stage, setting 42, 43, 44, 45

Live Action Role Playing (LARP) 8

M

Mecanim Animation System 69
multiplayer game
  about 309
  building 329
  challenges 308
  networking components 309
  player character (PC), adding 311
  project, networking 310
  testing 329

N

Negotiated Contest
  about 33
  using 33
network-enabled NPC
  testing 353
network-enabled PC
  testing 353
networking components, multiplayer game
  Network Identity 309
  Network Manager 309
  Network Manager HUD 309
  Network Transform 309
non-player characters
  about 115, 116
  Animator Controller 122, 123, 124
  basics 116
  code, enhancing 298, 302, 303, 304
  NPC AI 127, 133, 134, 135, 136
  NPC_Attack, creating 124, 125, 126, 127
  player-character (PC), interaction 136, 137, 139, 141, 144, 145
  setting up 116, 118, 119, 120

P

patterns, RPG
  about 28
  contest tree 31, 32
  Last Man Standing 32
  Negotiated Contest 33
  terminology 29, 31
player character (PC)

[362]

about 58
adding 311
Canon Ball, creating for Tank 318
character state, preserving 113
client RPC calls 316
code, customization 101, 113
commands, sending 316
customizing 96, 98
Enemy Tank, adding 324
network callbacks 315
NetworkManager, configuring 320
non-player characters, interaction 136, 137,
  139, 141, 144, 145
summarizing 114
Tank Prefab, creating 320
user interface 98, 99, 100
using, with Inventory Items 230, 249
variable, synchronizing 315
player data management
about 164
character customization class, updating 166
PC class, enhancements 164, 166

R

Root motion 74
RPG games
  Dark Souls 3 24
  Divinity with Original Sin 26
  Fallout 4 25
RPG
  Base character class, attributes 66, 67
  building 36
  character definitions 65
  character model 69, 70, 72
  character states 68
  character, developing 15
  characteristics 9
  characters, network-enabling 331
  combat system 19
  existing games 23
  experience 17
  exploration 10
  graphics 20
  history 7
  inventory items, spawning 352

inventory system 12
items, synchronizing 350
levelling 17
networked non-player character 342
networked player character 331
NPC, spawning 352
player customization, synchronizing 350
quests 11
scene, creating 331
setting 10
story 9
upcoming games 23
user interface 20

T

Tank Prefab
  creating 320
terminology list, RPG
  attribute 29
  character 29
  characteristics 29
  common characteristic 29
  conflict 29
  contest 29
  derived attribute 29
  drama 29
  flaw 29
  fortune 29
  Game Master (CM) 29
  gauge 29
  gift 29
  karma 30
  non-player character (NPC) 30
  optional characteristics 30
  player 30
  player character (PC) 30
  primary attribute 30
  rank 30
  ranked trait 30
  selected characteristic 30
  shared gauge 30
  skill 30
  trait 30
terrain toolkit
  creating 46

filters 46
Fractal 46
Hydraulic Erosion 46
Perlin 46
Thermal Erosion 46
Tidal Erosion 47
URL 43
voronoi 46
The Commonwealth 26

U

UI and Inventory System integration
about 217
Category Buttons, hooking 217
data, displaying 217
UI Controller

modifying 182

Z

Zazar Dynasty
about 36
asset inventory 39
character motion 74
exploration 37
game master, creating 60, 62
horizon 38
Kingdom 39
level, testing 58
Main Menu, creating 59, 60
objectives 37
plot 36
quests 37
village 37

CPSIA information can be obtained
at www.ICGtesting.com
Printed in the USA
LVOW09s2241311016
511079LV00010B/31/P